THE

War

FOR THE

Heart
& Soul

OF A

Highland
Maya
Town

D0796826

THE
War
FOR THE
Heart
& Soul
OF A
Highland
Maya
Town

REVISED EDITION
BY

ROBERT S.
CARLSEN

❀

WITH A NEW
PREFACE AND A NEW
FINAL CHAPTER
AND WITH A
CONTRIBUTION BY

MARTÍN
PRECHTEL

FOREWORD BY
DAVÍD
CARRASCO

UNIVERSITY OF TEXAS PRESS ◆ *Austin*

Fourth paperback printing, 2004
Revised edition, 2011

Requests for permission to reproduce material from this work
should be sent to: Permissions, University of Texas Press
P.O. Box 7819, Austin, TX 78713-7819
www.utexas.edu /utpress/about /bpermission.html

♾ The paper used in this book meets the minimum requirements
of ANSI /NISO Z39.48-1992 (R1997) (Permanence of Paper).

Portions of Chapter 2 appeared in *Crafts in the World Market*,
ed. June Nash (Albany: State University of New York Press,
1993). An earlier version of Chapter 3 appeared in *Man* 26,
no. 1 (1991). Portions of Chapter 7 appeared in *Report on
Guatemala* 15, no. 1 (1994). All are reprinted by permission of
the previous publishers.

The Library of Congress catalogued the first edition as follows:

Carlsen, Robert S. (Robert Stanley), 1950 –
The war for the heart and soul of a highland Maya town / by Robert
S. Carlsen; with a contribution by Martín Prechtel; foreword by Davíd Carrasco. — 1st ed.
p.   cm.
Includes bibliographical references and index.
ISBN 0-292-71194-8 (pbk.: alk. paper)
1. Tzutuhil Indians—Social conditions.   2. Tzutuhil philosophy.   3. Tzutuhil Indians—
Religion.   4. Social change—Guatemala—Santiago Atitlán.   5. Santiago Atitlán (Guatemala)—
Folklore.   6. Santiago Atitlán (Guatemala)—Politics and government.   7. Santiago Atitlán
(Guatemala)—Social life and customs.   1. Title.
F1465.2.T9C37   1997
972.81'64 — dc20   96-35613

ISBN for the revised edition: 978-0-292-72398-6 (pbk.: alk. paper)

To Nathaniel Tarn, whose pioneering anthropological work in Santiago Atitlán established the standard that still exists, and whose support and continued sharing of his time mean so much to me.

To my dear friend and mentor, the martyr Pascual Mendoza.

To Vincent Stanzione—described as "the Sahagún of our time" by the late, great archaeologist Henry Nicholson—whose knowledge of and compassion for the people of Santiago Atitlán is without precedent.

❀

Contents

Figures

Foreword:
Complex Performance
in Santiago Atitlán

By Davíd Carrasco

I FIRST HEARD OF ROBERT S. CARLSEN after giving a lecture on shamanism in Mesoamerican religions at the University of Colorado in Boulder. A colleague came up to me and said, "You need to meet Robert Carlsen. The guy knows a lot about shamanism. He's been working and living in Guatemala with Maya peoples." When I met the soft-spoken Carlsen, I was immediately impressed with how carefully he seemed to listen and his easy way of getting to the point. He had been living and working in Santiago Atitlán, becoming familiar with the cofradía community, and he felt that he was discovering how the Atiteco Mayas survived the shower of changes, pressures, and violations to their cultural practices and beliefs. He wanted to deepen his understanding of social change, religious resistance, and creative adaptation. He had seen that the Atiteco Mayas had "successfully resisted their spiritual conquest" by Europeans. Carlsen had learned this, in part, from Luch Chavajay, a former alcalde of the Cofradía Santiago. He taught Carlsen the truth: "The Old Ways of Santiago Atitlán are so vital that if they are not performed, the town itself must literally die." Performance, it seemed was the key. It was Carlsen who introduced me to the opaque genius of Martín Prechtel (whose contribution to the present book is found in Chapter 3) and to Dennis Tedlock's remarkable translation of the *Popol Vuh*, the ancient K'iche' Mayan "Book of Council." Through him I met the "Sovereign Plumed Serpent," the "sowing and dawning," "Hunahpu Coyote," and the "overjoyed . . . True Jaguar" who animated the religious imagination of the Maya. Carlsen pointed out a passage in the *Popol Vuh* which could serve as a key theme to *The War for the Heart and Soul of a Highland Maya Town*, which is a wonderful, complex, and challenging book. In the *Popul Vuh* we learn that the world was created and continues to be created through ritual actions. In the words of the text, "It takes a long performance and account to complete the emergence of all the sky-earth." Carlsen's account of the struggles and complex creativity of the Atitecos contributes to those vital performances which help to repair the world.

There are at least three things to keep in mind as you work your way through this innovative study. First, Robert Carlsen is uniquely situated to write about the ongoing evolutionary process of Atiteco existence. In other words, he is an anthropologist *on the edge and in the edge.* Like many anthropologists who have been in the field working with the local community that is the object of their study, he established the crucial rapport with the Atitecos. But Carlsen was not just in the field. As anyone who spends time with him learns, and as you will see in reading this book, the Atiteco "fields" of history, maize, pain, imagination, religious commitments, and symbols are *in* him and do not get dissolved under the work of his pen. The point is that Carlsen employs his *on/in the edge* perspective—an understanding that overlaps the Maya world view and anthropological theory—as a place to write *from* and not just a place to write *about.* It enables him to see both Maya and anthropological theory from new angles and to tell us about processes of creation and interpretation (by Mayas and anthropologists) previously unseen.

Second, Carlsen is not claiming that he has achieved a kind of "deep play" analysis of the Atiteco, though he is doing a historically layered interpretation of the social archaeology of the culture. Rather, he is consistent in showing a *complex* web of dualities, contradictions, juxtapositions, foot-dragging evasions, and subverting syncretisms, which give as much weight to the view that "some things remain the same" as to the view that "everything has changed." A number of anthropologists have been slinging ideas, theories, and even mud at each other trying to give one of these approaches the status of truth. Others, such as Marshall Sahlins and Gananth Obeyesekere, have jumped beyond the fail-safe zone by launching culture wars about what one can actually know about the "native point of view." Carlsen listens and learns (some things) from these wars, but he is of the opinion that while much has changed in the world views, ritual practices, and daily lives of the Mayas, a great deal of what is crucial to their lives has remained constant. As he writes, "I am prepared to argue that perspectives which stress similarity within a society, like those which stress difference, are useful, just as they both have their limitations. Accordingly, the present study pays considerable attention to difference in contemporary Santiago Atitlán, particularly as it concerns religious factionalism. At the same time, however, it makes use of the valuable information available in similarity."

Third, Carlsen believes that with the help of the Atiteco Mayas and his work in libraries, in particular through an exposure to the history of religions, he has been introduced to one of the central conceptions in Maya religiosity which has enabled the Mayas to adapt while celebrating continuity. But this "central conception" called "Jaloj-K'exoj" by the Atitecos, is also complex, made up of "Flowering Mountain Earth" and Maximón (The Lord of Looking Good), the umbilicus of the world, "faces coming out" and faces going away (certainly including the thousands of Mayas murdered in contemporary political violence), cofradía love, Mayan saints and Catholic idols, and much more! Carlsen says it best:

> Moreover, the entire Jaloj-K'exoj–centered nexus has in turn provided a mechanism to integrate intrusive elements into Atiteco culture, converting them to a form acceptable to the local Mayan population. We submit that when revealed in their obvious contrast to highland Mayan culture, Hispanic cultural intrusions have triggered indigenous responses which have ultimately resulted in the modification and normalization of the original practices and beliefs.

Robert Carlsen's labor of understanding about the creative survival of the Atiteco Maya is done with profound concern for the future performances of the community. Their world (and ours which is becoming linked with theirs!) is changing as *never* before, and the crisis of the immediate future is grave. This alters the question of Carlsen's first chapter from "What in the world is going on in Santiago Atitlán?" to "What in the world will happen to this community at the end of the millennium?" Carlsen has written an outstanding and complex book that helps prepare us for that performance.

Princeton, N.J.

June 1996

Preface to the Revised Edition

On October 2, 2005, as the remnants of Hurricane Stan reached Santiago Atitlán, a gentle rain began to fall on the town. Although Stan had moved steadily westward since it began to form off the coast of Africa in mid-September, once it arrived at Lake Atitlán it seemed to stop dead in its tracks. Within hours of Stan's arrival, the gentle rain had become a deluge that converted the streets of Santiago Atitlán into cascading rivers. Two days later the downpour only intensified. That day, October 4, is the annual celebration of Saint Francis of Assisi and, although the deluge had considerably slowed the pace of life in town, in Atitlán the Saint Francis celebration went on in the religious sodality of the same name, Cofradía San Francisco. While significantly more will be said about cofradías in due course, for the present suffice it to say that in Atitlán, they are superficially Catholic and substantially Mayan religious organizations based on *costumbre*, the "Old Ways." Cofradía members conceive of their town as the "Umbilicus of the World," which is to say the center of all existence. They associate each of the town's ten cofradías with different aspects of human existence, from food to water to life itself. It is significant that Cofradía San Francisco, often simply called Animas (souls), pertains specifically to death.

As is the custom, the members of Cofradía San Francisco spent the night of October 4 drinking "canyon water" (moonshine) and dancing to marimba music. A few months later the head of the cofradía, the *alcalde*, and his son told me that, late that night, the ancestors who inhabit the surrounding mountains began singing songs to the celebrants in the form of lightning. The *alcalde* and his son recounted that the songs warned of impending death. The ritual drinking, the dancing, the lightning, and the rain continued into the early morning hours of October 5, long after most of the town was sound asleep. Suddenly the noise of the marimba and the storm outside was drowned out by a deafening roar that lasted for several minutes, followed again by the sound of the rain. Everyone in town would soon learn that the saturated side of the Toliman Volcano, which towers above Santiago Atitlán, had given way, sending a half-mile-wide and ten-to-twenty-foot-deep avalanche of mud, car-sized boulders, and shredded trees down into the outlying part of the town known as Panabaj. Although many hundreds of people were killed the morning of October 5, the exact number will never be known. Following a couple of days of recovery efforts, the sheer volume of rubble and the threat of disease finally forced authorities to decide to leave most victims where they lay. The entire area has officially been declared a cemetery.

Soon after the October 5 mudslide, government experts descended on the town to study the tragedy. Why did the side of the mountain give way, and what could be done to prevent it from happening again? An initial suspect was deforestation. As the population of Atitlán has grown, slash-and-burn horticulturalists have pushed steadily up the sides of the surrounding volcanoes. Government geologists quickly dismissed this theory, as the mudslide had begun well above the deforestation line. Nonetheless, overpopulation was certainly a contributing factor in the tragedy. Explosive local population growth has led to dense inhabitation throughout the immediate area. As a result, a mudslide just about anywhere in the region is certain to take a significant toll on human life. The geologists concluded that the independent variable in the tragedy was the torrential rain unleashed by Hurricane Stan.

But many people in town begged to differ. In stark contrast to the scientists' ecological explanations for the event, several competing religious explanations soon emerged. In Cofradía San Francisco, the *alcalde* told me that the slide was a result of the local Mayas' abandonment of the Old Ways in favor of Protestantism. In turn, many Protestants quickly pointed fingers at the town's cofradía members. I heard various accusations of witchcraft. While these explanations may seem to be at odds, it is ironic that they might not be. In Chapter 8, the new chapter in this edition, I explain that some Working People believe that slain *aj'kuna* (shamans) have joined the rain gods on their mountain thrones surrounding the town. From there they create the rain and lightning which can either water the fields or smite enemies, even their own killers. It is precisely those slain shamans that the Protestants consider to be witches. These explanations are indicative of a town that is out of balance. Accusations of witchcraft, particularly when those accusations lead to actual witch "cleansings" as in contemporary Atitlán, often occur when there is significant social disharmony. Clearly, the war for the heart and soul of Santiago Atitlán rages on.

This book looks at the efforts and mechanisms employed by local Mayas, known as Atitecos, to adapt to their post-European contact existence. In the first edition (Chapters 1 through 7 in the present volume) I show that, by employing a varying strategy of resistance and accommodation, Atitecos were for centuries remarkably successful in refusing their own conquest, spiritual and otherwise. Where the initial challenge presented by the Spanish Conquest was staged by Europeans, any clear demarcation of Mayas versus outsiders soon blurred. An example is the cofradía. That institution was originally brought by the Spanish and was unquestionably Catholic. Over time the local population in Atitlán, as elsewhere in Guatemala, southern Mexico, and Yucatán, refabricated it into a distinctly indigenous institution. Throughout the region, local indigenous populations subsequently utilized the superficially Catholic but now largely indigenous cofradías as weapons in their struggles against outside interests. This model no longer applies. In the new chapter of this book, "Season of the Witch: The New Millennium in Santiago Atitlán," I demonstrate that the war for the heart and soul of Santiago Atitlán is no longer a struggle of the town versus the outside. Rather, Atitlán has turned in on itself. I show that, even among followers of the Old Ways, the infighting is vicious and sometimes fatal. I also look at the remarkable ascendance of one of the chief protagonists, the local Protestant megachurch Iglesia Palabra MIEL. At first glance it may seem that, as a Protestant church, MIEL must represent outside intervention in the form of missionization from the United States. This is true only in a historical sense (Garrard-Burnett 1998:117). While MIEL's roots ultimately wind back more than a hundred years to the United States, it is now what is termed in Protestant studies a "native church." In other words, it is entirely weaned from any foreign mother church. In fact, I show that, in a most remarkable turn of events, MIEL in Santiago Atitlán is now the mother church to nearly a hundred congregations of the same name in the United States, as well as to many more throughout Latin America and even Europe.

Although the religious conflict being played out in Santiago Atitlán today may be a local affair, it certainly does not exist in isolation from the world outside. On the contrary, contact with the outside is a primary cause. The first edition of this book argues that, historically, the town's—and indeed the region's—capacity to resist acculturation was largely a function of the relative disinterest of global economic powers in Guatemala's economic potential. The resulting environment allowed Mayan towns like Atitlán to employ religious beliefs and cofradía-based civil-religious structures to maximize autonomy. The first edition also shows how, beginning in the middle of the nineteenth century, the world economic system began increasingly to intervene in Guatemala. The rise of Guatemala's coffee economy and the subsequent consolidation of the Guatemalan state gradually overwhelmed the adaptive capacity of towns like Santiago Atitlán. In terms of religion, the changed social landscape eroded cofradía hegemony while opening the door to Roman Catholicism and Protestantism. The new chapter of this book picks up these themes. I argue that the momentum for change has only accelerated with the ascendance of that multifaceted dynamic known as "globalization." While I look at how various secular aspects of globalization have affected Atitlán—including the effect on local weaving traditions of thrift-store donations in the United States, international crime and the rise of Atiteco gang culture, and the introduction of the Internet—I give particular attention to the religious implications.

For the revised edition of *The War for the Heart and Soul of a Highland Maya Town* I have added this preface, a revised acknowledgments section, and a new concluding chapter. I have resisted the temptation to make any changes to the original chapters of the first edition.

Acknowledgments

MY TIME IN SANTIAGO ATITLÁN has benefited from the contributions of numerous town residents, both indigenous and foreign. They know who they are. I can only hope that fortunes in Guatemala improve enough that someday I may be able to thank them openly and fully.

This book has been greatly influenced and improved by the direct and indirect contributions of colleagues elsewhere in Guatemala and in the United States. Although I do not assume that all will agree with what I have to say on the subject, my thanks are extended to the following who, in conversations, broadened my understanding of aspects of Mayan "tenacity": Betsy Alexander, Sheldon Annis, Linda Asturias de Barrios, Jorge Luis Arriola, Peter Canby, Duncan Earle, Ricardo Falla, Olga Arriola de Geng, Tracy Ehlers, James Loucky, James Mondloch, Rosario Miralbes de Polanco, Victor Perrera, Martin Prechtel, Gwen Ritz, Margot Schevill, and Vincent Stanzione.

My work has benefited greatly from the writings of Sandra Orellana and Robert Carmack. While I have challenged these two scholars on a few points, my respect for both should not be doubted.

Thanks also to June Nash, Ben Paul, and Nathaniel Tarn, whose enduring interest in things Mayan, like their sharing of their scarce time and considerable knowledge, has been greatly appreciated. Marilyn Moors' extensive contributions to the community of Guatemala scholars has been an inspiration. I remember Sol Tax and am grateful for his kind words and encouragement. I also am grateful to those scholars who have critiqued various aspects of this volume, especially David Stoll for clarifying fine points of Guatemalan mission history, and John Early, Barbara Tedlock, and Evon Vogt for their comments and suggestions about the "Flowering of the Dead" chapter. At the University of Colorado I would like to thank Kitty Corbett, Fred

Lange, Russ McGoodwin, Charley Plot, Paul Shankman, and Payson Sheets.

Finally, thanks to my colleagues at the Mesoamerican Archives— Anthony Aveni, Robert Bye, Ed Calnek, Larry Desmond, Jane Day, Doris Heyden, Lindsay Jones, Charles Long, Alfredo Lopez Austin, Eduardo Matos Moctezuma, Henry Nicholson, Scott Sessions, and Peter van der Loo—whose camaraderie and inspiration have been invaluable. Particular gratitude is extended to Davíd Carrasco, whose continued support of my work has meant so much.

For the new edition of this book I would like to thank David Stuart and Bill Fash for their encouraging words. To Linda Brown, Rob Scott, and especially Violeta Luz Foregger Velasquez, I offer thanks for their very helpful comments and suggestions on the new preface and chapter. Finally, thank you to David and Susie at the Posada de Santiago for all that they do.

Despite my debt to so many, the pages and chapters that follow are my own. I alone am responsible for any failings.

THE

War

FOR THE

Heart
& Soul

OF A

Highland
Maya
Town

Introduction

ON NEW YEAR'S DAY 1994 the world awoke to the surprising news of a massive Mayan revolt in Chiapas, Mexico. As stunning as the "Zapatista" uprising itself was its coincidence, to the day, with the implementation of NAFTA, the North American Free Trade Agreement. In hindsight, the uprising perhaps should have come as no surprise whatsoever. Amid incessant heralding of the widespread benefits that free trade must inevitably bring, even proponents of NAFTA confessed that its implementation would entail certain "adjustments" for some of those involved. Simply put, the Mayas who took to arms in the mountains and jungles of Chiapas believed that they themselves were in danger of being adjusted, and that confessions such as these constituted little more than euphemism for the sacrifice of their already marginalized way of life and of any right to self-determination. As the uprising demonstrated, they refused to cooperate.

The history and very culture of the Mayas might also have forewarned of the Chiapas uprising. In fact, in the eighteenth century one of the more notable Mayan revolts took place in the same area as the 1994 Chiapas uprising and involved the same group of Mayas. That incident, the Tzeltal Rebellion of 1712–1715, was itself an extension of Mayan rebellions in the Yucatán Peninsula. Over a century later in Guatemala, Mayan rebels were instrumental in the War of the Montañeses, which put peasant leader Rafael Carrera into power as Guatemala's head of state. A primary rebel target was free trade–oriented laissez faire economics which threatened their way of life. Resonating with the 1 January 1994 Mayan "counter-adjustment," Carrera's *montañeses* underscored the potential consequences of failing to reconcile economic theory with social reality (see McCreery 1990:100). Supplementing the historical record, a legacy of resistance and rebellion remains apparent in contemporary Mayan religious, social, and artistic expressions. This is, for instance, given graphic display in an unmistakably anti-Catholic dimension of certain Mayan religious images, as discussed in the pages and chapters which follow.

In short, like scores of uprisings, layers of Mayan cultural behavior corroborate what over two centuries ago Guatemalan Archbishop Cortés y Larraz identified as the Mayas' "invincible tenacity" (in García Añoveros 1987:72). Commenting on the Archbishop's view, Spanish historian Jesús María García Añoveros writes that while the Mayas did not accept Christianity, "they accepted and submitted to the colonial order even less" (1987:157). Intrigued by such characterizations, and with a primary focus on the Tz'utujil Mayan town of Santiago Atitlán, Guatemala, in this book I look into the complexities of Mayan "tenacity."

Although I am quite aware of the limitations of any single community to exemplify the vast population of Mayas—contemporary Santiago Atitlán alone is remarkable for the scope of its own internal diversity—I am nonetheless prepared to argue that data from Atitlán illuminate general cultural mechanisms utilized by otherwise disparate groups of Mayas to address the demands of their post-(European) contact existence. It is clear that the Mayas of Atitlán, hereafter called Atitecos, have been neither passive witnesses to their own existence nor powerless in determining the nature of their relations with external sociopolitical interests. While the range of strategies has included outright confrontation, more commonly the Atitecos have turned to less vulnerable mechanisms, such as those offered by what James Scott (1985) identifies as "weapons of the weak." Scott explains that "individual acts of foot dragging and evasion, reinforced by a venerable popular culture of resistance and multiplied many thousand-fold, may, in the end, make utter shambles of the policies dreamed by their [the rural poor] would-be superiors in the capital" (1985:xvii). As *The War for the Heart and Soul of a Highland Maya Town* explains, even the Atitecos' utilization of syncretistic religiosity has demonstrated significant potency in subverting the agendas of would-be superiors.

Underlying much of the following discussion, however, is recognition that the capacity of Mayas to successfully adapt to their sociocultural environment has limits and cannot be accepted as a mere given. Quite simply, Mayan tenacity has proven less invincible than Cortés y Larraz once thought. In the case of Atitlán, outside intervention into the town's affairs has fueled economic instability and severe ecological imbalance and has triggered destabilizing factionalism within the local populace, particularly along religious lines. Yet even under those conditions, recent events in Atitlán, as described in some detail in this volume, demonstrate the error in dismissing the local populace's capacity to adapt, to resist, and to subvert.

The primary goal of this book is the explanation of sociocultural realities in contemporary Santiago Atitlán. That requires situating the present in a larger historical context. Only this type of historical perspective can realistically be expected to provide the points of reference needed to accurately evaluate change. Equally important for the task at hand, taking the long view provides a context in which to develop this book's discussion of conquest. At first glance, it may seem peculiar to situate a critique of Mayan conquest in a study designed primarily to explain contemporary dynamics in a highland Guatemalan town. After all, the Conquest of Mesoamerica, that "most astonishing encounter of our history" (Todorov 1982:4), occurred nearly five centuries ago. In this volume, however, the Conquest as a historical *event*, so remarkable that convention has it spelled with a capital *C*, is contrasted with conquest as a *process*, the subduing and the controlling of a given population. To confuse the two is to risk both mistaken finality and artificial neatness. As the Mayas' post-Columbian history demonstrates, the process of conquest may demand hundreds of years. Moreover, to be successful conquest must be implemented on multiple levels.

In a remarkably candid statement, Bernal Díaz del Castillo, a soldier in the Conquest and the primary chronicler of that event, writes, we came to the New World "to bring light to those in darkness, and also to get rich" ([1568] 1968 2:366). As this appraisal implies, aside from a military component, conquest entails an economic dimension. Moreover, at least in the case of Mesoamerica, it attaches what Robert Ricard identified as "spiritual conquest" in his classic 1933 study *Conquête spirituelle du Mexique*. Although this book pays considerable attention to multiple aspects of conquest, past and ongoing, consideration of spiritual conquest in particular provides a backdrop to much of the ensuing discussion.

Adding to the complexities of conquest is that the process of subduing and controlling a given population is subject to regional variation. As Ricard argues, conquest, spiritual and otherwise, may have been nearly total in core areas of central Mexico, though even that contention is debatable. (Incidentally, Ricard, a Catholic, endorsed the spiritual conquest of Mexico.) In the Mayan region, however, a culture area which, according to Ricard, has its own history and personality and has been particularly prone to rebellion, the reality has been quite different. Yet dynamics which earlier accounted for the disintegration of indigenous societies in areas of central Mexico, and their eventual reintegration into an identifiably European political, economic, and religious order, are now highly evident throughout the Mayan region. It is useful to recall the earlier assessment of Spanish political and spiritual control of the Mayas, defining aspects of conquest: "While the Mayas did not accept Christianity they accepted and submitted to the colonial order even less." In light of that assessment, it is revealing that at present much of the Mayan region, particularly in Guatemala, is fully militarized, and that over the past couple of decades millions of Mayas have fully embraced fundamentalist Protestantism or orthodox Catholicism. The implications for assessing conquest are abundant.

In its critique, this book analyzes the wide-ranging expression of Mayan attempts at adaptation, and includes substantial consideration of economic and political concerns. However, lest the reader anticipate a political economy, I should note that in the attempt to situate the Mayas as meaningful participants in their own existence, past and present, the volume presents a rigorous exploration of indigenous cultural ideas and the causal interplay of those ideas in adaptive behavior. Yet, as "so much of Mayan activity and thought was intentionally hidden from the eyes and ears of Spanish writers," such an approach must inevitably have certain methodological limitations (Jones 1989:93). If based purely on historical accounts, which even under the best of circumstances have been quite biased against the indigenous population, it is difficult to escape the conclusion that post-Columbian Mayan cultural ideas and behavior expose "the most complete ignorance."

To overcome such limitations, this book exploits certain nontraditional approaches. As is demonstrated, the past can be recorded in ways other than conventional written history. While I have certainly used conventional historical data, I have added epigraphic data, myths, standardized prayers, indigenous conceptions of kinship and lineage, and other such types of data to cast light on the considered populace and on the diverse and sometimes ingenious expressions of Mayan philosophy and resistance. Similarly, I have used both conventional and novel stylistic approaches. In particular, the opening and closing chapters frame the volume's larger discussion within a narrative context. That is, I have narrated incidents which I contend stand out from daily existence in Atitlán not because they so differ from that day-to-day context, but because they have the capacity to illuminate it. A narrative approach also serves my goal of making the book accessible to a diverse readership.

Chapter 1 is primarily designed to orient the reader to the sociocultural climate defining current and recent Santiago Atitlán. I explain that much of the day-to-day existence has, in one way or another, been influenced by military occupation and political violence. Certainly not unrelated has been the fragmentation of the local population into mutually incompatible religious factions. Particular attention is given to the emergence of local fundamentalist Protestantism. Adding to the local social mix is a still potent "traditional" cultural background to the town, as best exemplified by members of the religious organizations known as *cofradías*. The chapter also raises certain theoretical concerns, particularly about the causality of cultural ideas. That theoretical section may prove formidable for some. However, the nonprofessional reader should be able to give it only a superficial reading without losing sight of the chapter's larger arguments. Building on the discussion of the local social climate, Chapter 2 analyzes defining physical characteristics of the town, including geographical setting and the town layout. Salient characteristics of the local population, such as linguistic and dress patterns, are also discussed.

The book continues by arguing in Chapter 3 that a defining characteristic of post-Columbian Santiago Atitlán is a distinct and identifiable continuity with the pre-Columbian past. In terms of an earlier point, the Atitecos, including many today, have successfully resisted their spiritual conquest. Reflecting collaborative efforts with Martín Prechtel, the chapter identifies an ancient Mayan core paradigm, called Jaloj-K'exoj by the Atitecos, that helped to shape the "reconstituted" Mayan culture, and which continues to have relevance. I argue that Jaloj-K'exoj proved to be a mechanism which integrated intrusive foreign elements into Atiteco culture, converting them to a form acceptable to the local Mayan population. However, I do not believe that culture in Santiago Atitlán in any way represents a pristine form of some ancient Mayan culture. Over time virtually no aspect of Atiteco culture was to be left untouched by European contact. Nonetheless, reflecting cultural resilience and transformative capacity, most aspects could be traced to the pre-Conquest past.

Following arguments that post-Columbian culture in Santiago Atitlán is continuous with the pre-Columbian past, it falls largely on Chapter 4 to reconstruct the historical environment which explains how that continuity was possible. Although this book is largely based on my own field research in Santiago Atitlán, in the historical reconstruction of the town, represented in Chapters 4 and 5, I draw frequently on published primary historical documents and on the research of other specialists. Where they shed light on earlier existence in Atitlán, I include examples of contemporary Atiteco cultural behavior. In part to provide a baseline against which post-Columbian change can be measured, the chapter commences by considering aspects of local pre-Columbian society. Shifting the focus, first to the Conquest in 1524, and then to the culture which was to emerge from that event, I argue that fundamental changes *of* the local sociocultural configuration were neither necessitated nor did they occur. Rather the changes tended to be *within* that configuration, as best explained by Atiteco adaptive behavior.

Inspired by the core and periphery arguments formulated by Christopher Lutz and George Lovell (1990), and drawing on recent work by Ralph Lee Woodward (1993) and David McCreery (1994), Chapter 5 posits that beginning approximately 125 years ago, a series of events was unleashed which has ultimately led to fundamental sociocultural change in Santiago Atitlán and elsewhere in highland Guatemala. Triggered by a heightened foreign interest in Guatemala's economic potential, and the related consolidation of the Guatemalan nation-state, this change has resulted in a steady deflation of the Atiteco capacity to mediate intrusive and generally exploitative interests. Consequently, Atitlán is now engaged in a transformation which in many ways eclipses even that which followed the Conquest.

The final two chapters return to direct consideration of this book's primary concern, explaining and analyzing the sociocultural climate in contemporary Santiago Atitlán. In Chapter 6, I devote considerable effort to measuring the changes which have occurred, as well as to isolating any adaptive advantage that may be related to that change. (As with parts of Chapter 1, some readers may want to detour around the more technical parts of this chapter.) Based on quantitative data which pertain to economic and religious behavior over the past quarter century, I am forced to conclude that economic disarray, made worse by the destabilizing effect of the town's military occupation, has not been selective in the community's deterioration. In short, the local population has yet to establish an economic and cultural base to successfully answer the demands of its contemporary existence. This accounting leads directly to consideration in Chapter 7 of Guatemalan political realities. Interweaving elements of traditional religiosity, of local Protestantism, and of civil violence, this concluding analysis employs a narrative approach. I explain in detail how in December 1990 the Atitecos were able to put aside their differences and force the Guatemalan Army to permanently and entirely vacate their town, in that way engineering a remarkable state of peace in a land of war.

The pages and chapters which follow reflect my work in Santiago Atitlán, which spanned more than fifteen years, including seventeen individual trips to the town and residence for approximately two and one-half years. Aside from political violence, which provided a nearly constant backdrop to all activities in Atitlán, perhaps the most unusual aspect of this tenure has been my direct participation for a year (1989–1990) in the town's cofradía system. I was informed by town elders (*principales*) that because of my extensive study of local cofradías I would become the fifth *cofrade* (*r'uu'*) in Cofradía San Juan. The "invitation" was meant to be an honor and, along with the characteristic identifying headcloth (*x'kajkoj zut*), was received as such. Declining was not a viable option, and I dutifully fulfilled the position's obligations. To my knowledge, only two other non-Guatemalans have ever had this kind of formal relationship with any of the country's Mayan cofradías.

My participation in this regard, of course, raises questions. In particular, might not this experience have compromised my objectivity as an anthropologist? To be sure, the experience did influence my thinking. (But is not having one's thinking influenced a central point of doing fieldwork?) Moreover, the experience contributed to my respect for the local cofradía system, particularly as a cultural response to a specific set of ecological and socioeconomic conditions. That said, in no way do I believe that this participation has undercut my capacity to be an objective observer, or somehow rendered me a propagandist for the institution. This assessment is supported by my conclusion in this volume that as the local ecological and socioeconomic environment of Santiago Atitlán has changed, the cofradía system has become socially irrelevant, if not even dysfunctional. Anthropology's earlier faith in fieldworker neutrality and invisibility notwithstanding, over the course of extensive fieldwork, virtually any anthropologist will be confronted by multiple exceptional situations and experiences, any number of which may alter his or her thinking or behavior. Some such experiences may prompt the anthropologist's direct involvement, at times even virtually demanding concerted activist participation. In my own case, more relevant than the cofradía experience in this regard was the political violence in Santiago Atitlán, including the murders of several friends and neighbors, which ultimately triggered my active participation in human-rights efforts (Carlsen 1990, 1994; Loucky and Carlsen 1991). Yet, as I believe the chapters which follow bear out, when combined with critical thinking, the information gained from such intense and participatory experiences tends to enhance the anthropologist's capacity to arrive at accurate conclusions, not detract from it.

This leads to another concern. In light of the deconstructionist reverberations at the center of contemporary anthropological discourse, including a postmodern angst about the very concept of culture, could my time spent in the cofradía have been all that useful for ethnographic representation? A primary focus in cultural anthropology today is on internal disorder, difference, and inconsistency in any given society, to the point of arguing that anthropological claims about understanding another society or culture constitute little more than comforting illusion (e.g., see Crapanzano 1980; Rosaldo 1993).

Conspicuously absent in such discussions (not to dismiss their usefulness) is the simple fact that while internal disorder and inconsistency certainly exist, so do significant similarity and consistency. To be sure, from the outset this book makes abundantly clear that contemporary Santiago Atitlán resonates with the "nervousness" of an increasingly postmodern world, in fact that the Guatemalan Army has even engineered local disorder for strategic purposes. Yet even within such disorder, consistency abounds. For instance, to those sitting inside a cofradía (foreign anthropologists included) knowing that heavily armed soldiers are on the street directly in front severely beating passersby, a unifying characteristic is shared fear. To argue that such fear is experienced differently by those involved is to belabor a too-evident point of scarce value. Further demonstrating consistency, the Mayas sitting inside that cofradía, like those elsewhere in the town, are unified by characteristic and identifiable culturally determined conceptions of time and by understandings of their natural environment.

I am prepared to argue that perspectives which stress similarity within a society, like those which stress difference, are useful, just as they both have limitations. Accordingly, the present study pays considerable attention to difference in contemporary Santiago Atitlán, particularly as it concerns religious factionalism. At the same time, however, it makes use of the valuable information available in similarity. I have chosen to pursue the potential of these perspectives to enhance understanding of Atiteco culture rather than to be preoccupied by their limitations. As Clifford Geertz (1973:20) reminds us, "it is not necessary to know everything in order to know something."

My embrace of a concept of culture challenges certain prevailing orthodoxies about that concept and requires brief comment. Rather than interpreting Atiteco culture as a remnant of an exploitative past, as part and parcel of an ecology of repression, I have been impressed that across the centuries local Mayas have commonly utilized their own culture to help mediate exploitation. In this sense, I have turned to the origins of the concept of culture. In *How "Natives" Think*, an unabashedly titled polemic on postmodern/postcolonial ethnographic representation, Marshall Sahlins explains that the concept originated as a defense to eighteenth-century English and French rationalizations of their own imperialist exploits. Those rationalizations were embedded in the Enlightenment concept of "civilization," which, in contrast to the "barbarism" and "savagery" of those yet to be civilized, constituted a general and nonpluralizable ideal order of human society. In uncivilized neighboring Germany, at that time bereft of power and political unity, defense of the national *Kultur* became essential. In short, culture, the pluralizable "way of life of a people," originated in defiance of, and hence constituted a potential tool against, external hegemony.

Returning to the question posed above, my time spent in the cofradía was particularly useful for gaining insight into both similarity and difference in Santiago Atitlán as well as diverse aspects of Atiteco culture. Quite simply, not only did the camaraderie and trust born of the experience allow valuable access to information, but it also provided unusual opportunities for cross-checking. By variously checking information in cofradía and non-cofradía settings, I was able to gain a sense of sociocultural similarities and differences within and across Atitlán's faction lines. Within the cofradías, I found the information related to points of religious philosophy and cultural ideas to be particularly helpful.

Exemplifying the scope of the experience and of the information gained, and to bring closure to this brief introduction to Mayan resistance, an example of a "weapon of the weak" comes to mind. I am thinking of a particular Sunday morning visit to Cofradía Santiago, one of Atitlán's most important individual cofradías. Upon being informed that he had missed an Army-organized meeting of military representatives with local cofradía leaders earlier that morning, the leader (*alcalde*) of the cofradía became visibly shaken and let out an anguished groan; actions which were matched by other members of the cofradía. Immediately, however, exaggerated despair gave way to uproarious laughter, upon which the alcalde turned and said aloud, "Sometimes it's better to forget." The meeting, incidentally, was canceled by the Army when only two cofradía representatives showed up.

PART ONE

Establishing Place and
Imagining Community

1

What in the World Is Going On
in Santiago Atitlán?

"Hallelujah! And there's nothing that Satan can do about it."

AMERICAN MISSIONARY JOHN FRANKLIN

IN THE DARKNESS OF A MORNING early in 1990, a municipal ambulance departed down the rutted dirt road from Santiago Atitlán, bounced past my house (where my family and I were sleeping soundly), and continued on its two-hour trip around Lake Atitlán to the regional hospital in Sololá. Inside the ambulance was my gravely wounded friend and contributor to the present volume, Jerónimo Quieju Pop.[1] It was not until some hours later that I was told Jerónimo had been shot fourteen times the night before.

Throughout the 1980s and into the 1990s, incidents of violence had been particularly common in Atitlán. Yet the buzz of conversation in town that morning left no doubt that this shooting somehow differed from the rest. After all, Jerónimo was the town's leading shaman (*aj'kun*).[2] Even more important, at the time of his shooting Jerónimo was *telinel*, the shaman in charge of the notorious "idol" Maximón. Eclipsing any other single element, Maximón casts into high relief the gaping social rift that divides the Atitecos, and as telinel, Jerónimo personified that rift. According to his most vociferous critics, largely Protestant Mayas categorically opposed to the Maximón cult, Jerónimo's shooting reflected divine intervention triggered by his association with the vile object. However, according to his supporters, members of the traditional indigenous religion known as the cofradía system, the fact that he had been shot fourteen times and had not died instantly was testimony to

13

the efficacy of the "Old Ways," the *costumbres*. Seemingly desperate for hope, some even dared to suggest a miracle.

Upon hearing the news about Jerónimo, I caught the first boat across Lake Atitlán to Panajachel, and from there I drove to the hospital in Sololá. Throughout the trip, I was preoccupied with thoughts about Jerónimo. I remembered when I met him in 1983, shortly after arriving for my first extended stay in Santiago Atitlán. The purpose of that meeting was to ask his permission to attend a certain private religious ceremony in his house the following evening. Through a Tz'utujil Mayan translator, Jerónimo apologized for not being able to speak Spanish, and after voicing various customary niceties, he granted my request. One of my most gratifying experiences in Guatemala occurred in the wee hours the next night when, following the ceremony, Jerónimo came and sat next to me. He then began to elaborate on aspects of the ritual that I had just witnessed—all spoken in quite good Spanish. Most of my trip across the lake, however, was given to contemplating Jerónimo's inevitable death. Among my concerns, I knew that his family would be pressed to come up with the money needed to have his body transported back to Atitlán for burial. And then there was the problem of time. According to Guatemalan law, interment must take place within twenty-four hours of death. As such, I prepared myself for the ugly task of transporting his body back home.

It was with such thoughts that I passed through the door of the hospital, where at the front desk I asked dutifully whether they had an Atiteco patient who had been shot. To my surprise, the receptionist replied that they did. He then asked me which one. Minutes later, the receptionist, a Kaqchikel Maya from Sololá, showed me to the trauma-patient room. Various of the patients in the room had been shot, and most were from Atitlán. The receptionist pointed to a corner bed surrounded by visiting Atitecos in their characteristic white and purple hand-woven garb. Looking in that direction, I saw Jerónimo dressed in a hospital gown and lying still. Right then, however, Jerónimo glanced over at me, and in a surprisingly strong voice said, "Roberto, what are you doing here?" In fact, Jerónimo had been shot but once, the bullet entering his midsection and exiting cleanly through his back. Those Atitecos gathered about were marveling among themselves that Jerónimo had been shot at fourteen times but that only one bullet had found its mark. Few doubted a miracle.

During the short time I visited, Jerónimo told me that he was not sure who had attempted his murder, but that there were three gunmen, all masked. He added that he had already had a dream about the inci-

1. For most of the past decade, Santiago Atitlán has been occupied by the Guatemalan Army. During that time, the town has suffered tremendous violence, much of it at the hands of the soldiers. It is telling that the people often refer to the soldiers as kiks, a Hispanicized Tz'utujil term which means "the bloody ones." This photograph is of an elite Army unit in Santiago Atitlán. (Photograph by Paul Harbaugh, 1988.)

dent, and that in due course further dreams would reveal the identities of the would-be assassins. Soon thereafter, the Kaqchikel Mayan receptionist returned and warned the visitors that a member of the National Police was making his rounds of the hospital. Leaning toward me, he confided that one must be very careful around the Police, and added that because I was a foreigner my presence might be construed as suspect. The receptionist quietly remarked that the Police collaborate with the Army and politely suggested that it would be best if I left. After scanning the room of shot and battered Atitecos he confided, "You know, I don't believe that the guerrillas are doing this." As he and I turned to leave, this man whose job forced him daily to confront the mangled and moaning remains of a confusing civil war looked at me and asked, "What in the world is going on in Santiago Atitlán?"

I had heard that same question another time. It was during a period when I was living close to Santiago Atitlán's largest Protestant church, ELIM.[3] That Pentecostalist church often broadcasts its goings-on through loudspeakers aimed outward to the town. A disconcerting hum caused by up to a thousand Atitecos simultaneously possessed by the Holy Ghost commonly flows through the streets and alleys of Atitlán. That hum, interrupted only by the amplified shouts of "Hallelujah" that intermittently bounce off the walls of the houses and stores, was particularly annoying considering how close to the loudspeakers I lived. Sitting there in my room listening to the hum and the chorus of Hallelujahs, I eventually realized that this was in fact a kind of war cry directed not only at other Atitecos, but also at Atiteco culture itself. I could not help recalling F. E. Williams' *The Vailala Madness* (1977), a 1923 study of New Guinea which describes the railings against their own traditional culture by such characters as the "Head-he-go-round Men" and the "Jesus Christ Men." The commotion emanating from the Head-he-go-round Men of ELIM often reached such intolerable levels on the weekends, when it started as early as five in the morning and lasted well into the evening, that I spent my weekends across the lake in Panajachel.

Ironically, during my escapes I periodically visited the director of Panajachel's Pentecostalist seminary, American missionary Don Jenkins. Those visits—which typically included chats about the town that both Don and my mother were from, Hanford, California—provided me with a wealth of information on Protestantism in Guatemala. The incident that I am concerned about here, however, involves Jenkins' predecessor, the legendary missionary John Franklin.

According to the *Historia de la iglesia evangélica en Guatemala* (Zapata 1982), in which Franklin merits his own section, he arrived in Guatemala from Springfield, Missouri, in 1937. In Guatemala, he was given to riding his mule, Esterlina, to remote Mayan villages to "bring comfort to the souls tortured by sin." Eventually Franklin settled in Panajachel, where he founded the Assemblies of God seminary which bears his name. That seminary now turns out more than a hundred newly ordained Indian pastors per year. Given Franklin's stature in Guatemalan Protestant circles, I was most pleased when Don Jenkins asked me if I wanted to meet the venerable old missionary, who happened to be down visiting from the States.

In introducing me to Franklin, Don Jenkins noted that I was an anthropologist and that I was working in Atitlán. John Franklin responded, "Good. We need boys to spread God's word in that town." Before I had time to ponder the meaning of that statement, Franklin posed the question, "What's going on in Santiago Atitlán?" Guessing that he wanted information about the political violence, I began to tell him and Don Jenkins, who was standing with us, about the latest such incidents in the south lake region. Interrupting, John Franklin said forcefully, "No, I mean what's happening with God!" Not having the slightest idea what to say, I submitted weakly that there were eighteen Protestant missions in

2. *At present, just over one-third of the population of Santiago Atitlán is Protestant, with the great majority belonging to one of the town's approximately eighteen Pentecostalist missions and churches. Shown above are Atiteco Pentecostalists in various stages of spiritual ecstasy. (Photograph by the author, 1991.)*

Atitlán, a figure which has since grown considerably. Franklin's gaze at that point seemed almost to bore through me. Perhaps in his mind's eye he was seeing somewhere out there the hordes of Atitecos still mired in devilish paganism, not all that different from the Indians that he and Esterlina used to encounter. In any case, the thought of so much evil exposed to the light of so many missions apparently lit the wellspring of Franklin's soul, for inches from my face he yelled "Hallelujah!" followed by a considerably quieter yet equally intense, "And there's nothing that Satan can do about it."

Taken aback, I glanced over to Don Jenkins for support. By that time, however, Franklin had already launched into a minisermon that was to touch on the witch doctor, the Catholic priest, and the tavern keeper. Countering that "diabolical trinity" (Stoll 1982:33) was what Franklin called the "spontaneous expansion of the church." Particularly note-worthy was the miraculous expansion of his own Assemblies of God denomination. He pointed out that this Protestant denomination was now Guatemala's largest, and that for nearly a decade its growth rate in that country had approached 10 percent annually.[4] In comparison, Franklin noted, the Catholics had enjoyed five hundred years during which to bring their brand of religiosity to the Indians and had failed. Franklin, who by this time was quite carried away with the potency of his own message, then turned toward Don Jenkins, and after a pause said longingly, "If only we could get into China."

COSMIC EVENTS AND HISTORICAL PROCESSES

So what is going on in Santiago Atitlán? Several aspects of that question have already been touched upon. First, even in Guatemalan terms, the level of political violence in the community over the past ten years and more has been extraordinary (e.g., see Carlsen 1990; Americas Watch 1991; Perera 1993). According to the Committee of Campesino Unity (CUC), as many as 1,700 Atitecos out of a total population approaching 20,000 have been killed since 1980 (Cockrell 1991:4).[5] Although local guerrillas have by no means been innocent, the great majority of the violence has been at the hands of the Guatemalan Army. In addition, as is underscored by the amplified goings-on of ELIM, the community is now severely factionalized according to religious affiliation. The primary actors in that factionalization are Atitlán's Protestant population, with some of the most vicious factionalization occurring among Protestant sects (ELIM is invariably a party); Catholic Action, a group which, by and large, conforms to standard Roman Catholicism; and the members of the cofradía, the followers of the Old Ways. This last group is often categorized in the anthropological literature under the dubious rubric "folk Catholic," but I shall refer to them using their autonym "Working People" (Asamaj Acha).[6] Underlying all of this is a situation which, given the technological resources available to the Atitecos, severely strains the carrying capacity of the immediate environment. The problems inherent in this climate of strain and factionalism are compounded by a local population which is doubling approximately every twenty years.

In short, on ecological, sociopolitical, and socioreligious grounds, recent existence in Santiago Atitlán has been, if not chaotic, certainly dysfunctional. This raises a most important point, one that frames the primary inquiry of this volume. As is evident in the response of the Protestant Atitecos to Jerónimo Quieju's attempted murder (it should be recalled that some Protestants suggested a religious cause for that shooting), in the minds of many, these ecological, religious, and political dynamics are interwoven by divine hands. According to the world view of many Protestant Atitecos, like that of many Protestant Guatemalans in general, what is transpiring in their country is symptomatic of *the* immanent and defining moment of human existence. Quite simply, those Protestants argue that unfolding right before their eyes are the very spasms which prefigure Christ's return.[7] (See Stoll 1982, 1990; R.C.B. 1987, 1988.) Apart from reflecting millennia of accumulated sin, this great cosmic event, as with all miraculous occurrences, is not believed to be the outcome of explicable historical processes. To the faithful, the explosive growth of Guatemalan Protestantism adds a level of proof to this interpretation. The miraculous potency demonstrated by this "spontaneous" growth is characterized by the absence of the spatial and temporal constraints which define normal historical processes. As is embedded in the words of John Franklin, it is believed that the power guiding this event is such that the efficacy of evangelical mission would have been just as potent had it been unleashed five hundred years ago upon the Conquest-period Mayan population. Moreover, it is held that if evangelical missionaries had access even to China, the sorts of miracles transpiring in Guatemala would be replicated in that distant land.

In the chapters which follow, a quite different interpretation is offered. I argue that the circumstances which characterize contemporary Atiteco existence are consistent with an ongoing and evolutionary process, one that is solidly grounded in both time and space. In order to understand what is going on in contemporary Atitlán, it is essential to consider the community's historical past. Two primary characteristics stand out as particularly significant. First, while the Conquest period undoubtedly ended the previous *isolation* of the European and the Mayan sociocultural systems, the essential *autonomy* of those systems was not quickly extinguished. In other words, while the collision of the Old and New Worlds clearly led to many changes within highland Mayan culture, in locales such as Santiago Atitlán those changes tended to be engineered according to identifiably Mayan sociocultural dynamics.[8] Second, the erosion of Mayan autonomy over the past century, and hence the loss of adaptive capacity, goes far in explaining the turmoil in Santiago Atitlán today.

The theoretical approach taken is inspired by world system analysis, although in considering the adaptive role of cultural ideas, I take considerable liberty with that paradigm. A cornerstone of world system theory is its evolutionary approach, which addresses the relationship over time between economic environment and sociocultural change. While early applications of the theory often focused on the sixteenth-century integration of formerly autonomous global regions into the emerging "European world-economy" (Wallerstein 1974), more recent studies have challenged the all too hasty acceptance by scholars of "global views of peasant communities without consideration of the interplay between local and global processes" (C. Smith 1984:193). Earlier world system studies of colonial Spanish America, for instance, concentrated on the absorption into the European economic colossus of the "internally-colonized" Latin American hinterland (e.g., Stavenhagen 1968). Exemplifying the vicissitudes of the theory, world system analysis of Guatemala has increasingly stressed an enduring regional socioeconomic peripherality, commensurate with retarded encroachment from the outside (e.g., Lutz and Lovell 1990). It now seems that Guatemala's high degree of integration into the world system is relatively recent and was triggered by an external thrust into Guatemala's economy in the mid to late nineteenth century (C. Smith, ed. 1990; Woodward 1993), a subject to which I shall return shortly.

ISOLATION, AUTONOMY, AND CULTURAL IDEAS

While conventional world system analysis is particularly suited to the consideration of global economic consolidation, data raised below suggest that, despite previous modifications, it remains unsatisfactory for the explanation of social autonomy. Those data show Mayan indigenous cultural ideas to have exhibited considerable potency in the capacity to mediate the advances of the world system.[9] Yet, when cognitive aspects of culture enter world system analysis, they are typically employed to illustrate the causal supremacy of material conditions and the extent of foreign hegemony. For instance, in a world system study explicitly designed to demonstrate material causality in sociocultural dynamics, Waldemar Smith argues that the relevance of post-Columbian Mayan "folk Catholic" beliefs and practices becomes clear when viewed against the backdrop of Guatemala's exploitative colonial economy, that they are in fact but "part of an ecology of colonial repression" (1975:238).

That raises an underlying premise of this study. Much of Western analytical thinking, materialist approaches to the social sciences certainly included, has since the Renaissance been informed by a mind-and-matter dualism. As just described, that dualism undoubtedly colors the literature's portrayal of the post-Columbian Mayas. However, data presented in this book demonstrate that, at least so far as earlier highland Mayan autonomy is concerned, by isolating and/or prioritizing material (or mental for that matter) components of social processes we have achieved what Gregory Bateson (in Yowell 1986:14) calls the "false neatness of abstract intellectualism." The consequences have been profound.

As Davíd Carrasco (1993:112) notes, not only did the Mayas endure being "discovered" and "invaded," but they have even had to suffer being "invented" according to Eurocentric cultural and theoretical conceptions.

In raising this consideration I am purposefully confronting the debate between the "symbolic" and "materialist" approaches to the social sciences, as perhaps best delineated by Marx's ([1859] 1970:21) famous polemic that "it is not the consciousness of men that determines their social existence, but on the contrary, their social existence determines their consciousness." To be sure, the materialist determinism conveyed by Marx resonates with Atiteco understandings of the political violence in Atitlán, as exemplified in the accounts of the attempt on Jerónimo Quieju's life. Granting that political violence in Santiago Atitlán stems largely from social factors (e.g., see Carmack, ed. 1988; Manz 1988; Jonas 1991), the Atitecos' symbolically oriented explanations must then be epiphenomenal, and hence the applicability of Marx's argument seems evident. In fact, attempts by the Guatemalan Army to control Atiteco religiosity in order to manipulate Atiteco behavior have been somewhat common. The motivation underlying those efforts is really quite evident, conforming with an Army strategy to advance local factionalism and thereby weaken potential opposition. Moreover, not only has the Army throughout Guatemala sought to counter socially active religiosity (e.g., see Berryman 1984), but it has also nurtured the belief promoted by many Guatemalan Protestant leaders that the country's social problems stem from religious causes (e.g., see Stoll 1982:42–58).[10] Such beliefs are perhaps best exemplified by El Shaddahai, a leading Guatemalan Protestant sect, which has issued statements that the country's woes stem in part from a pre-Columbian Mayan curse. Accordingly, it has sought to have 50,000 "prayer warriors" transform that curse into a blessing (Stoll n.d.).

Though at first glance these sorts of situations seem to lend credibility to materialist determinism, at the same time they expose problematic levels of complexity. For example, while the subordinate social position of the Atitecos vis-à-vis the Army has certainly been exploited by the latter group in order to influence Atiteco consciousness, it is equally evident that by functioning to maintain the sociopolitical status quo, that consciousness in turn affects Atiteco social existence. Another example from the cofradía system goes right to my larger point. Until a few decades ago, when its civil component was made illegal by national decree, the cofradía system was structured around a joint civil and religious hierarchy of ascending positions (DeWalt 1975). Simply stated, the cofradía system was (and to a degree remains) theocratic. Community religious leaders directed the local civil government, managed the town's communal lands, and even delegated labor. As I shall discuss in some detail, due to the social status of the cofradía leaders, a status sanctioned in part by their exclusive power to perform vital rituals, those leaders have received the community's authority to negotiate with outside cultural and economic interests.[11] It is important that, through the system, potential exploitation directed from without was often minimized (also see MacLeod 1973, 1983; Farriss 1984). In a word, it is difficult to escape the conclusion that religious ritual and ideas have traditionally strengthened the delicate walls of Atiteco social existence, even that indigenous political leadership has been in part a consequence of esoteric Mayan knowledge.

All of this raises two fundamental problems with orthodox materialist theoretical models. First, on a methodological level, in order to quantify the causal value of material and mental inputs in social relations, it is necessary to separate the two. Yet, given their complex interrelationship, as exemplified in the cases just cited, the reduction of these two factors into discrete units of study can be virtually impossible. The more important consideration, however, is purely epistemological. Even if reduction in this manner were possible, of what value is it to argue that some material input A exercises more causal value than some other mental input B when $both$ play mutually dependent and vital roles in social operations? To use an organic metaphor, this seems rather like debating whether one's aorta is more important than one's gizzard. Clearly, both are vital.

Several implications arise from this line of analysis. As is demonstrated by the Atitecos' overlay of religious rationalizations on the political violence that has ravaged their existence, there are certainly cases in which a materialist interpretive focus is of value. Yet, as is exemplified in situations where the performance of religious ritual exhibits a mutually dependent relationship with other socioeconomic activities, it is equally evident that there are limitations to the application of such analysis. All told, given that materialist approaches may be justified in some cases, and not in others, it might seem that any "struggle for a science of culture" must in the end satisfy itself with a "strategy of eclecticism" (Harris 1980:x), what Price (1982:712) calls a "nonstrategy." Although I am not convinced that such eclecticism must in all cases be avoided, an alternative is to turn to more holistic theory, toward explanations which account for what might otherwise appear as eclectic. I return to consideration of Mayan sociocultural autonomy to illustrate my position.

It was stated above that Guatemala's high degree of integration into the world economic system is fairly recent. Yet to view previous Mayan autonomy as being merely a consequence of external lack of interest in southern Mesoamerica would be overly simplistic and mechanical, if not also unacceptably ethnocentric. This is certainly not to deny that such a lack of interest—punctuated by spasms of economic activity—provided a backdrop to Guatemala's colonial history (e.g., MacLeod 1973). Such a view, however, entirely discounts the role of the huge Mayan population in shaping the history of the region in which they remain the majority. In so doing, it utterly ignores the Mayas' capacity to resist, to subvert, to adapt; in short, to think. Yet, based on the historical data presented in this volume, what to the outside observer may appear simply as peripher-ality included a very significant component of Mayan self-determination. The fact is that the Mayas actually buttressed the region's marginal status and thereby maximized their own sociocultural autonomy. In the chap-ters which follow, I shall demonstrate that Mayan cultural ideas were vital in this adaptive process.

All of this leads to a crucial point. Simply stated, even the most suc-cessful adaptive strategies may eventually be rendered obsolete. In par-ticular, when materially based parameters vital for group survival are breached, the functional role of ideas will be challenged and may be-come irrelevant. For instance, when variables related to loss of land, ex-plosive population growth, and/or access to resources are irreparably violated, a given culture's adaptive capacity will be undermined. Clearly, at that point, when there is no stability to be maintained, cultural ideas cannot be expected to maintain any kind of stability. It is precisely this situation which underlies current existence in Santiago Atitlán. As David McCreery (1986:113) notes, changes in Guatemala since the late nine-teenth century have undercut the "self-reproductive capacity of the in-digenous peasantry at both the level of simple economics and at the sociopolitical and ideological levels as well." In such an environment, certain and profound cultural transformation must follow.

MAYAN SAINTS, CATHOLIC IDOLS, AND THE WORLD SYSTEM

The data and arguments presented in this book add to a growing under-standing that post-Columbian Mayas were not successfully drafted to serve as "accomplices in their own oppression," as one anthropologist writes about a neighboring group of Indians (Friedlander 1981:139). As exploitative as the interaction of the Mayas and their Hispanic over-seers has been, the included data expose the error of dismissing post-Columbian Mayan culture as being part and parcel of an ecology of colonial repression (e.g., see Hawkins 1984). Quite to the contrary: The

Mayas have utilized disparate sources of available power, at times ingeniously, to optimize their social existence vis-à-vis exploitative interests (see Farriss 1984; Jones 1989; C. Smith, ed. 1990; Watanabe 1992). Even the power of the "saints" of "folk Catholicism" has been tapped. Contrasting with a theological brand of anthropology which views the presence of a few saints and/or a Catholic rite or two as constituting "Catholicism," data from Santiago Atitlán demonstrate those same religious elements to have instead been integral in a process which has historically mediated the very intrusions of which actual Catholicism was but a part. I turn to Rilaj Mam, the "Venerable Grandchild," to illustrate my case.

The name Venerable Grandchild is clearly misleading. First, it is obviously not a real name but some sort of a title. In fact, the Grandchild represents but one point in the conflation into a complex whole of a mass of personalities, concepts, and heteronyms, a topic to which I shall return momentarily. The name also misleads in that it resonates with a degree of acceptability, perhaps even gentle kindness, that withers in the face of the Grandchild's actual persona, an outrageous entity introduced earlier as Maximón.[12] While detailed discussion of this complex figure must wait, even a quick survey of some of its more prominent aspects throws into high relief the audacity to which I allude. On the one hand there is the explicit sexuality, as perhaps most easily exemplified by Maximón's female dimension, Yamch'or, the "Virgin-Whore." And then there is the San Judas/San Simón component. To be sure, this component incorporates Judas Tadeo (a.k.a. Saint Thaddeus), the "good" Judas of the New Testament. Yet Tadeo is conflated with and clearly subsumed by his infamous namesake, Iscariot. In short, the pairing with San Simón (a.k.a. Simon Peter), elevates the two betrayers of Christ to a prominent status.

It is hardly surprising that both Catholic and Protestant detractors of the Old Ways have equated Maximón with Satan (e.g., Molina 1983). Yet such an interpretation grossly misunderstands not only Maximón but more important, the Old Ways in general. While it is perhaps beyond argument that Judas worship incorporates a certain anti-Catholic dimension, it would be incorrect to conclude that Maximón exists in some variety of inverse or dialectical relationship with Roman Catholicism, as would be the case if Maximón worship represented a Satan cult. In fact, Maximón demonstrates that the Atitecos adapted to their post-Columbian environment in such a way that, while significant change *within* their cultural configuration certainly occurred, change *of* that configuration was avoided. On this point, Yamch'or is illustrative.

Indicative of the overwhelmingly indigenous character of the cult,

3. Included among Maximón's multitude of names and attributes are Masiik (Lord Tobacco), as reflected in his ever-present cigar or cigarette, and Matzajtel (Lord Tzajtel Tree), indicative of the type of wood (Erythrina corallodendron) from which he is constructed. (Photograph by the author, 1991.)

Yamch'or is but one of the many dozens of heteronyms that are Tz'utujil Mayan, as opposed to the mere five or six names which are of Old World derivation. Even those few names have virtually nothing to do with their Old World namesakes, mere foreign actors in a distinctly local production. On a related note, the designation Virgin Whore is reflective of the binary opposition which informs the Old Ways and which has under-written Mesoamerican cosmology since long before the Conquest (e.g., see Coe 1984:152). Other such names include Ancient Boy, and Man of Mountain Man of Plain.[13] In fact, the designation Venerable Grandchild falls into this category. Finally, Maximón's sexual promiscuity, as implied by Yamch'or, is most important and requires introductory comment. A primary characteristic of Maximón is the capacity to transform, even into a bee, a flower, or "a piece of garbage tossed about in the wind" (O'Brien 1975:246). Similarly, Maximón is capable of assuming the form of the ideal sexual partner of any man or any woman. However, should one succumb to Maximón's sexual temptations, the price is death. Importantly, in this way the cult functions to protect community norms. That function, however, is not limited to sexual fidelity, but has an impact on ancient rituals and community solidarity as well. As is explained in some detail in this volume, the Atiteco Working People vow allegiance to the ancient traditions of the community and pledge to fulfill ritual obligations to those traditions. Failure to complete that vow is to risk the very considerable wrath of Maximón, his friend San Gregorio, or even the notorious "Bad Man" (Itzelwinuk).

While these and other arguments expressed in this book challenge the value of "folk Catholicism" as a direct indicator of an ecology of colonial repression, the implications are certainly not limited to Atitlán's historical past. The recent inroads Protestantism has made into Atitlán are a case in point. Throughout highland Guatemala the initial significant challenge to the Old Ways occurred in the 1940s and was spearheaded by the international lay Catholic movement Catholic Action (see Ebel 1964; Mendelson 1965; Falla 1980). Only in recent years has the greater intensity shifted to the Protestant camp (see Stoll 1988, 1990; Burnett 1989). Importantly, underlying virtually all scholarly interpretations of recent religious change among the Mayas has been an acceptance of the former hegemony not of the Old Ways, but of Catholicism. As such, the interpretive focus of scholars has centered on the explosive growth of Protestantism, at the expense of Catholicism.

Building on points introduced above, the following chapters offer a far different argument. Specifically, utilizing historical documentation and analysis of religious behavior to challenge assumptions of former Catholic hegemony, and employing quantitative data to assess religious change over the past twenty-five years in Santiago Atitlán, I show that the growth of orthodox Catholicism has easily outstripped the otherwise impressive Protestant gains. The growth of both of these competing religious factions has come at the expense of the Old Ways and of the Working People. It is certainly relevant to note that the stakes involved are not limited to spiritual conquest but have important global economic implications. David Stoll (1990:181), for instance, quotes an elder in former dictator General Efraín Ríos Montt's (California-based) Guatemalan evangelical church who claims that fundamentalist gospel is a way to transform Guatemala into a "spiritual stronghold" that will keep the country and its rich oil and titanium reserves from falling into Marxist hands. As is evident in the following pages, while Atitlán is indeed a child of its immediate environment, this Mayan community is now linked with a modern world whose economic, political, intellectual, and spiritual centers exist well beyond the bounds of the Lake Atitlán basin.

ADDENDUM

I have recently received word that Pastor John Franklin has passed on. The amplified railings against Atiteco culture which continue to flow through the streets and alleys of Santiago Atitlán testify to his enduring legacy. And while I shall have considerably more to say about Jerónimo Quieju Pop in due course, suffice it to say here that he remains solidly among the living. In fact, he is now well established in the realm of Atiteco legend. Shortly after Jerónimo's attempted murder, a neighbor who had witnessed the incident announced that just as the would-be assassins began fire, a veil descended from the sky, enveloped Jerónimo, and deflected all but the one shot.[14] A miracle is now certain. And demand for his shamanic services has soared.

2

The Atiteco Mayas at the End
of the Twentieth Century

*"Santiago Atitlán . . . is the most colorful, the most charming, and the
most frightening place that I've ever lived in."*

ELEANOR LOTHROP, *THROW ME A BONE* (1948)

SOME FIFTY YEARS AGO, the cultural geographer Felix McBryde observed
that there is probably "no region in the New World that surpasses western Guatemala for illustrating the relationship between culture and nature. Here is one of the largest concentrations of individualistic Indian
populations, preserving much of its Maya background" (1947:2). Mc-
Bryde proceeds to explain this individuality and cultural conservatism
in terms of the high degree of micro-geographic diversity, including formidable natural obstacles to the interaction between communities. Significantly, he cites the Lake Atitlán basin as displaying the highest degree
of such geographic diversity anywhere in Guatemala, even in the world,
noting that "many of the villages may be separated from their neighbors
by two miles or less, and yet being isolated by physical barriers such as
precipitous headlands, cliff shores, and a dangerous lake surface, they
may have distinct economies, dress, and even vocabularies."

REGIONAL GEOGRAPHY AND ECOLOGY

Lying at the juncture of three volcanoes and the crystalline water of Lake
Atitlán, Santiago Atitlán is a place of rare beauty. With Guatemala's (Pa-
cific) coastal piedmont region situated to the south and Lake Atitlán and
the mountain highlands to the north, Santiago Atitlán assumes an integral position in the regional geography. The town occupies a border

zone between tropical and mesothermal winter-dry climatic environments. Rains are monsoonal, with the wet season lasting from May to November. Soils in the area are mostly of a rich basaltic type resulting from regional volcanism (Madigan 1976:25). The benefits of the rich soil, however, are counterbalanced by an overabundance of basaltic andesite lava. In fact, only those areas which have been laboriously cleared are free of expansive jumbles of this rock. As is evident from the ubiquitous local archaeological remains, this stone has been used by the area's residents as a primary construction material since long before the Conquest.

The town is located at an elevation of 5,125 feet above sea level and sits on a gently sloping shelf about one and one-half miles wide which forms the border between a bay of Lake Atitlán to the north and the basal ridges of the Tolimán (10,282 feet) and Atitlán (11,590 feet) volcanoes to the southeast. To the northwest, the opposing shoreline across the bay gives immediate way to the steep slopes of the San Pedro volcano (9,908 feet). At the base of that volcano, toward the mouth of the bay, a mound some five hundred feet high (what appears to be a parasitic volcanic cone) contains the poorly preserved remains of Chiyá, the most important site of the pre-Conquest Tz'utujil Mayas (S. Lothrop 1933; Fox 1987).

Not to diminish the dominating presence of the volcanoes, it is Lake Atitlán that must be considered the region's primary geographical feature. The lake was formed over forty thousand years ago when, after having expelled their magma, subterranean chambers underlying the volcanoes gave way in a violent collapse. As the destination of several rivers, and with no major outlets, this "volcanic collapse basin" formed the receptacle for the ninety-two-square-mile lake (Williams 1960). Praised by John Lloyd Stephens as being "the most magnificent spectacle we ever saw" ([1841] 1969 2:158), and by Aldous Huxley as being like Italy's Lake Como with the "additional embellishment of several immense volcanoes" (1934:128), Lake Atitlán's clear blue water reaches a depth of more than a thousand feet. For unknown reasons, the level of the lake fluctuates greatly over approximately fifty-year cycles (McBryde 1947:132). Since the mid-1970s, the lake has been in its retractive phase. As the water level has been dropping about one foot per year, lakeshore property owners are receiving a windfall in the form of expanding land holdings.

Lake Atitlán is home to various types of fish. The native species include several types of small fish, regionally called simply *pescaditos*.

4. Santiago Atitlán is located on the south shore of Lake Atitlán in Guatemala's central highland region and sits approximately one hundred miles to the west of the country's capital, Guatemala City. (Adapted from Loucky and Carlsen 1991.)

Around 1575, Franciscan priests introduced another type of fish, the *mojarra* (Betancor and Arboleda [1585] 1964:102). And toward the beginning of the present century, the government introduced black crappies into the lake (S. Lothrop 1933:4). Both of these types of introduced fish seem to have fit with the existent lake ecology. Then, in 1958, due largely to the efforts of the now defunct Pan American Airlines, largemouth bass were introduced into the lake to promote sport fishing and as Douglas Madigan (1976:96) notes, "an entirely new ecological balance was created." He writes that the largemouth bass, which he describes as an "ecological dysfunction," quickly "vacuumed the lake of its native forage fishes." Gradually, the average size for bass, which had become quite robust from gorging on pescaditos, began to decline. As a result, not only did the sport-fishing industry fail to develop, but the ancient industry of trapping pescaditos became obsolete. Only through the adoption of a new technology, hook-and-line fishing for the crappies, has commercial fishing made something of a recovery. In addition, in 1993 a small cooperative of Atitecos began fish-farming tilapia in cages in the Santiago Atitlán bay. It should be noted that the introduction of the bass, besides its devastating effects on the native species of fish, has been equally damaging for the native freshwater crab and bird populations. In fact, one type of flightless grebe (*Podilymbus gigas*) found only on Lake Atitlán has become extinct, due in large part to the bass' predilection for the grebe chicks (LaBastille 1990a, 1990b).

In its natural state the area which surrounds the lake is vegetated with chaparral and oak-pine forests. In decades past, resplendent quetzals, deer, jaguarundis, wild pigs, and many other types of animals were abundant. Elderly Atitecos speak of the days when even jaguars roamed the forested hills, accounts which are supported by a couple of now nearly hairless jaguar hides used in the sacred Deer/Jaguar dance of Cofradía San Juan, and another such hide in Cofradía San Antonio. This past ecological state, however, stands in marked contrast to the area's current condition. The terrain around Atitlán has been converted into a vast agricultural complex. A checkerboard of maize fields now extends from the lake's edge to near the tops of the surrounding peaks. Only there do the fields give way to islands of dense cloud forest. While there has been a trend over the past few decades to plant coffee, maize is still far and away the primary agricultural crop. Other local crops include avocados, beans, chickpeas, citrus, patayas, tomatoes, and chiles. Except in certain small garden plots (*tablones*) situated along the immediate lakeshore, Atitecos use no irrigation. Garden-plot irrigation is a primitive process in which hand-carried containers of water are dumped directly on the crops. This labor-intensive activity is typically the work of children. In general, Atitecos rely exclusively on the seasonal rains to irrigate their crops.

Importantly, explosive growth of the local population has led to the expansion of the maize field (*milpa*) gridwork in all directions. As a result, some Atitecos must walk several hours to get to their mountaintop milpas. While some Atitecos continue to utilize swidden (slash-and-burn) farming techniques, because of population pressure few Atitecos possess the land needed to rotate their fields. Virtually all Atitecos now utilize large amounts of costly chemical fertilization. Many claim that overuse of fertilizers is "burning" the soil. Underscoring the crisis of local population growth is that despite the expansion of land under cultivation, as well as increased yields due to the chemical fertilizers, Santiago Atitlán has for some years been an importer of maize. This is in marked contrast to the situation a few decades ago, when Atitlán was the primary maize-exporting center in the region (McBryde 1947:75).

It might then seem strange that in the late 1980s vast sections of the volcanoes to the south of the town could be seen to be reforesting, the still discernible checkerboard pattern of the milpas giving way to scrub vegetation. Moreover, because of a resultant expanded habitat, types of wild animals not seen for years now occasionally wander right into town. While the casual observer might surmise some program countering the region's catastrophic deforestation, the reality is far more sinister. Several years ago guerrillas of the Organization of People in Arms (ORPA) mined the hillside. Although the intended targets were soldiers of the Guatemalan Army, some Atitecos have stepped on mines. But more than the ORPA mines, it is the presence of the Army that explains the reforesting hillsides. Throughout the 1980s the consequence of an Atiteco's being caught on the mountain by the soldiers, even if there just to plant maize, tended to be torture followed by execution.

Because of this situation, not only have numerous Atitecos been denied access to their milpas, hence to what may be their primary means of livelihood, but the townspeople's access to certain mountain products has been affected as well. The effects have ranged from escalating prices for firewood and dugout canoes to increased pressure to abandon the traditional use of thatched roofs. Even the ancient road over the pass to the Tz'utujil-speaking town of Chicacao in the coastal piedmont zone was rendered useless because of this martial activity. As this previously busy road goes through the conflict area, throughout most of the past decade it was abandoned by all but the Army and the occasional ORPA guerrilla.

COMMUNITY INFRASTRUCTURE

The Atitecos' land-based access to the outside is by and large limited to the road which passes through the east lake town of San Lucas Tolimán. Although rumors (fueled predominantly by would-be local politicians) that this road is to be paved have flourished for years, more than forty years after its 1951 opening it remains graveled. The road is traveled daily by eight buses to Guatemala City, four to Mazatenango, and one to Quezaltenango. In marked contrast, William Douglas (1969:26) reports that in 1966 one locally owned bus company provided service every other day to the capital and to Mazatenango, and that companies from San Pedro and San Lucas provided additional weekly service with those two Tz'utujil-speaking communities.

Yet even these attempts to improve municipal transportation have been undermined by the ever-present political violence. All too frequent incidents of soldiers, guerrillas, or common thieves holding up buses, at times burning them, and even murdering drivers and/or passengers, have put a severe strain on the system. In fact, from early 1990 until mid-1993 such incidents led the Rebulli line to discontinue its service to Atitlán altogether. Moreover, there is strong evidence that, for reasons to be discussed later, bus passengers traveling outside the community have been singled out for violence by elements of the Guatemalan armed forces (Carlsen and Kik Ixbalam 1992). Consistent with this allegation, in a May 1992 attack on a bus from Atitlán, two Atitecos were shot and several Atitecas were raped. During one of the rapes, the *cedula* (national identification document) of the attacker fell from his pocket. Demonstrating remarkable presence of mind, the victim (who happened to be in a late stage of pregnancy) quietly grabbed and hid the cedula. That document identified the rapist as a soldier. Despite the quality of the evidence, including the accounts of more than twenty eyewitnesses, the authorities refused to prosecute the case.

The danger of bus travel has provided a windfall for the owners of the several boat transport companies which service the lake communities. By taking a boat to the north lake tourist town of Panajachel and continuing on land from there travelers can avoid the often dangerous south lake road. Although this alternative constitutes an additional expense for the already impoverished Atitecos, many have been forced to take it. Typically, following incidents of violence on the south lake road, the buses may be nearly empty, while the boats are overloaded. Commercial boat service between Panajachel and Atitlán dates from the last century, when multimasted sailing ships would make the crossing. Mirroring the growth of Atitlán's bus service, this boat service has expanded greatly. By 1932, one or two boats per week ventured across the lake (E. Lothrop 1948:81), a rate which was little changed in 1952 (Tarn, pers. comm. 1989). By 1966, however, there was daily boat service between the two lake communities (Douglas 1969:26). In 1990, three companies provided between six and ten daily crossings to Panajachel, depending on passenger traffic. One company is owned by a Kaqchikel from Panajachel, one by a Kaqchikel from Santa Catarina Palopó, and one by a Ladino consortium from Guatemala City. In addition to boat service with Panajachel, there are six boats daily to San Pedro la Laguna, a virtually landlocked Tz'utujil-speaking town which engages in much of its commerce via Atitlán. Once again, none of the boats which service San Pedro are owned by Atitecos.[1]

PUEBLO AND MUNICIPIO

Approaching Atitlán by boat, a traveler arrives at one of several crude log-piling and wooden plank docks. To one side of the docks are dozens of beached dugout canoes. Atiteco craftsmen have long supplied canoes constructed from wild avocado trees harvested high up the volcanic slopes, to the other Lake Atitlán communities (S. Lothrop 1929). To the other side of the docks, women and girls stand knee-deep in the water washing clothes on rocks polished from centuries of use. An opaque stream of detergent-saturated water flows from the wash area well out into the bay. As the women wash their clothes, others come to the shoreline and scoop the polluted water into jugs for domestic use. At present, nearly half of local households get their water in this manner, a figure that jumps considerably during the common interruptions in municipal water service (P.C.I. 1987:46). The women, dressed in colorful hand-loomed costumes, heading back into town with the water jugs gracefully balanced atop their heads are a constant source of delight to tourist shutterbugs as they debark from the boats.

Just down the shore from where the women and girls wash their clothes, and in stark contrast, sits an ultramodern stone and mirrored glass structure. This building is part of an architectural complex that, utilizing the age-old talents of the master stone carvers from Atitlán, has been under construction for over a decade. A focal element of the complex is a towering natural rock formation, which the Atitecos call Tiox Abaj, or "God Rock." This formation is sacred to many Atitecos and figured into the rituals of the Working People until a few years ago, when the complex's guards began harassing would-be worshippers. Queries about this construction project invariably bring the response, "Oh, that's

Don Pepe's 'tourist center.'" In fact, Pepe operates one of Guatemala City's most profitable brothels. Rumors abound that when completed this intrusive establishment is to be some kind of an exclusive sex resort for select clients from the capital.

From the lakeshore, a dirt path quickly gives way to Atitlán's main street into the town center. The area alongside this street has been transformed into Atitlán's primary tourist shopping district by town merchants, a group about which Sol Tax (1953) coined the term "penny capitalism." Appropriately, this street is sometimes called Gringo Street (Calle Gringo). With convenient boat service from the popular Lake Atitlán resort of Panajachel, Atitlán is commonly included in the travel itinerary of foreign tourists.[2] A primary draw is Atitlán's reputation for indigenous traditionality, including the use of native costumes. The typical tourist stint in the town is a short one, with most visitors staying only the hour and fifteen minutes until the boat returns to Panajachel. During the time in which the foreigners are present, Gringo Street is transformed into a money extraction machine. Although hand-woven textiles are the primary commodity of trade, peanuts, bananas, and locally braided "friendship bracelets" (pulseras) are for sale everywhere.

As the gringos begin to arrive, Atiteco merchants elbow each other for position. Shouts of compre ("buy") and regaleme ("give me") soon fill the air. Driven by the vendors, the tourists quickly wind their way up Gringo Street. Their harried stroll carries the visitors past the Four Square Gospel mission and the video theater with its incessant fare of Bruce Lee and Chuck Norris features. At the side of the road just before the Assemblies of God mission, an aged and serene Tz'utujil woman who daily spins cotton using a drop-spindle invariably draws the tourists' attention. At last, here is what they came for: a "real Indian." Soon enough, however, the visitors learn that photos even of this category of Indian do not come cheap. After a peek into the sixteenth-century Catholic church where if they are lucky they may see shamans performing ancient rituals—"peekcher-meester, one dollar"—the tourists typically seek refuge from their rude confrontation with penny capitalism behind a Coke in one of the town's grungy restaurants.

Such Atiteco/tourist relations on Gringo Street are hardly novel. In 1970, Douglas Madigan (1976:99) observed that "the first contact that the tourist has with the Indian is with a horde of dirty, barefoot, runny-nosed children who approach the tourists either selling clay whistles, or with hands outstretched screaming, 'Take peetch' ('Take a picture')." And over forty years before Madigan took exception to his Atiteco hosts, Eleanor Lothrop ([1932] 1948:81) observed tourists in Atitlán "stumbling along the stony street to the plaza," children running alongside "with hands extended, whining 'pennylady, pennylady.'"

Past the missions and video arcades Gringo Street reaches the town center. That area is set on two levels. The lower level is dominated by municipal buildings and the market, while the upper level is the exclusive domain of the sixteenth-century Catholic church. In 1964, after being without a priest for centuries, the parish was adopted by the archdiocese of Oklahoma City and staffed with its priests. That relationship continues to the present. Underscoring the violence of the past decade, one of the Oklahoma priests, Stanley Rother, was murdered in the church compound in July 1981 by elements of the Army (see *Time* 10 August 1981). Rother's fate may have been sealed when, after he gave a talk in Edmond, Oklahoma, someone wrote a letter to the Guatemalan Embassy in Washington, D.C., falsely claiming that Rother was advocating the overthrow of the Guatemalan government. In an act resonating with ancient ritual, the Mayan parishioners refused to surrender Rother's body to his family in Oklahoma until his heart had been removed for enshrinement in the Atitlán church. Rother's heart, reportedly in a peanut butter jar, remains sealed in a marble monument at the back of the church (see Figure 34). That monument is inscribed in Spanish with the words:

STANLEY FRANCISCO ROTHER
Martyred Priest
Born March 27 1937 Okarchee Oklahoma
Ordained May 25 1963
Arrived in Diocese June 17 1968
Remained in this parish of Santiago Apostle 13 years
Assassinated July 28 1981
"There is no greater love than this:
To Give One's Life for One's Friends"
John 15:13

In front of the church, a large dirt plaza is bounded on the far side by a new building which houses the church's school for orphans—the continuing political violence has left hundreds of orphans in Atitlán—as well as the church-operated public library, which includes several Arthur Miller volumes. On another side of the plaza a structure built by the parish in 1990 serves as a locale for widows—also numbering in the hundreds—to market their weavings. Literally reflecting attempts to integrate the Working People into the Church, that structure butts against a formerly free-standing and aged building used during Holy Week by followers of the Maximón cult. Demonstrating their independence, not only do the Working People retain sole use of Maximón chapel, but they agreed to the entire project only after the current priest, Oklahoman Tom McSherry, consented to build a session hall for their exclusive use. In fact, McSherry has made considerable efforts to accommodate the Working People, even going so far as to attend an important Maximón ritual in 1992. McSherry, however, was quickly reminded of the prevailing social realities of the town when shortly thereafter he received death threats. Although the threats were anonymous, he is convinced that they were sent by lay Atiteco Catholic leaders (pers. comm. 1992).

At the north edge of the plaza, an ancient, perhaps pre-Columbian, stone stairway drops steeply to the lower level of the town center. There, a remodeled park is faced by a recently constructed and impressive municipal building as well as by a town hall dedicated only in 1990. At the time of this writing, while a new indoor market is being rebuilt at the northeast corner of the plaza, the streets of the lower plaza are serving as an outdoor market. In 1988, a building behind the town hall became the center for Santiago Atitlán's first-ever telephone system. It certainly bears mention that 1988 also marked another milestone in Atitlán's electronic integration with the outside world. That year American entrepreneur "Chuck-the-Gringo" began his local cable-television operation. Although Chuck's enterprise has been slow in conquering the town, he remains hopeful of duplicating the success of his cable operation in Sololá. One of his more notable marketing ploys in that nearby Kaqchikel Mayan town was the broadcasting on Friday nights of XXX-rated pornographic videos imported from the United States (pers. comm., 1990). Under extreme pressure from both that town's mayor and from the bishop of the Catholic diocese of Sololá, Chuck was forced to curtail that exercise in capitalism. When I last talked with him, he remained angry about the lost revenues.

While the recent spurt of municipal construction in Santiago Atitlán would seem to indicate vital and healthy local and regional governments, the truth is quite different. First, the municipal building had to be rebuilt after ORPA guerrillas bombed it in 1984. Moreover, political graft has been a primary factor underlying this construction. Virtually all recent town mayors have profited handsomely from their tenures in office. And work on the new market has been at a standstill for several years because so much of the construction money has disappeared. It is no secret among Atitecos that overcharging by as much as 50 percent for labor on municipal construction projects has been the primary source of the mayors' ill-gotten gains. Some Atitecos even claim that following his term, former mayor Atun Ixbalam was able to invest in Pepe's "tourist center." Even the Catholic parish's construction projects in the upper plaza have not been entirely altruistic and underscore an ongoing historical drama. In 1879, reflecting the anticlerical mood of the era, then-President Justo Rufino Barrios outlawed Church ownership of property. That restriction held until 1955, when it was overturned. Yet, as with numerous such properties in Guatemala, the legal status of the upper plaza in Atitlán remains a point of contention. By developing this property, the Church thus strengthens its claim.

Fanning out from the town center are Santiago Atitlán's five *cantones*, or neighborhoods. In alphabetical order, these are Pachichá, Panaj, Panul, Tzanjuyú, and Xechivoy. The various cantones maintain distinct and sometimes endogamous autonomy in some other contemporary highland Mayan towns (e.g., C. Smith 1984; Lovell 1985; Hill and Monaghan 1987), but not in contemporary Atitlán. (I do suggest later in this volume that in centuries past, cantón autonomy may have existed in Atitlán.) In fact, cantón identifications in Atitlán now serve for little more than designating location. In Atitlán, each cantón comprises a number of blocks, or *cuadras*. These in turn are composed of extended family compounds called *sitios*. Finally, the sitio is made up of individual family units, or *viviendas*, though it is common for several viviendas to share a kitchen.[3] An aerial photo taken of the town in 1935 and published in McBryde (1947) establishes that the boundaries of Santiago Atitlán have expanded little over the past fifty years. To accommodate the growing population, Atitlán is building up, not out.

The town of Santiago Atitlán is the seat of the *municipio* of the same name. In Guatemala, a municipio is a unit of social organization that consists of an administrative town (*pueblo*), varying numbers of dependent satellite residential units (*aldeas* and *caserios*), and the land which this entire configuration occupies. In his classic 1937 study, Tax shows that the municipio rather than the "tribe" is the basic ethnic unit in highland Guatemala. He notes that the cultures of any two K'iche'-speaking communities (for example) may have no more in common than a K'iche' and a Kaqchikel community. Tax adds that neither is it clear that such linguistic terms as K'iche', Kaqchikel, or Tz'utujil represented political or cultural groups that existed at the time of the Conquest (1937:424), a point relevant to later discussion in this book. Tax defines two types of contemporary Guatemalan municipios, the "vacant center" type, in which the pueblo is by and large empty, except during special occasions, and the "town nucleus" type, in which the majority of the population lives full-time in the municipio seat. He cites (1937:431) Santiago Atitlán as being perhaps the "purest representative" of the latter type.[4]

In 1994, Santiago Atitlán contained just under 20,000 inhabitants (based on P.C.I. [1987:34] figure adjusted for 3 percent annual growth). This compares with a 1966 population of 9,393 (Douglas 1969:24). At present, less than 5 percent of the population is Ladino (ethnic mestizo). Moreover, some 25 foreigners reside permanently in the town. In 1994, the municipio of Santiago Atitlán, including aldeas Chacaya and Cerro de Oro, plus caserios Panabaj and Tzanchaj, had a population of just over 27,500.

THE ATITECOS TODAY

The Atitecos are often considered to display the most "traditional" behavior of any of Lake Atitlán's indigenous communities. This reputation is emphasized in the Guatemala tourist literature and explains the hordes of tourists that descend on the town daily. Of course, neither have such aspects of Atiteco existence been lost on anthropologists, as elements of local cultural conservatism have been the focus of various anthropological studies (e.g. Mendelson 1965; O'Brien 1975; Carlsen and Prechtel 1991). Yet the blanket categorization of Atitlán as traditional clearly ignores such features of contemporary Atiteco existence as Pepe's purported pleasure palace.[5] To raise the level of analysis of contemporary Atiteco culture beyond questions of traditionality, a description of empirical aspects of that culture follows. I begin by considering Atiteco architectural patterns.

ATITECO ARCHITECTURE

McBryde described households in 1936 Santiago Atitlán as a "compact mass of stone-and-cane walled, grass-thatched houses, many of them of the primitive, square type with pyramidal roof, . . . built along a network of narrow zigzag, stone walled alleys that seldom approach a straight line" (1947:85). Thirty years later, William Douglas observed that the town still conformed to McBryde's description (1969:23). At present, though the winding stone walled alleys described above remain largely unchanged, domestic architectural styles have changed dramatically. In 1990, fewer than 5 percent of the houses were of the traditional cane and thatch type. Instead, most Atiteco houses are now constructed with full-height stone or cement block walls and tin (lámina) roofs. While several factors have contributed to this change, including increasing scarcity of some traditional building materials such as thatch and cane or the introduction of construction techniques which allow full-height stone walls to be earthquake resistant, a driving force has been explosive population growth. This factor underlies Douglas' 1966 observation of shrinking distances between houses in Atitlán and the disappearance of open areas under cultivation within the town. Reflecting continued population pressure, the process of change noted by Douglas continues to the present. Not only are open cultivated areas within the town now virtually absent and the spaces between houses nearly gone, but the houses are increasingly being stacked one on top of the other in multistoried fashion. In a few displays of daring construction prowess, basement-level habitats have even been dug under existing multistoried dwellings. Given the engineering limitations, it is evident that the thatched hut no longer represents a viable construction type in Santiago Atitlán.

In addition to architecture, other significant data demonstrate change in Atiteco household patterns. For instance, Douglas reported that in 1966 a community-owned power plant provided electricity to 100 sitios. However, by 1987 the town was integrated into the (Army-controlled) national electrical grid, and 1,671 sitios, roughly 48 percent of the total, were receiving power (P.C.I. 1987:44). In addition, while in 1966 there were 91 water spigots in Atitlán, in 1987 this figure had risen to 981 (P.C.I. 1987:46). Clearly, these figures on domestic existence demonstrate an area of significant cultural change. But other elements of Atiteco culture have not been affected so dramatically. One such area pertains to the use of the Tz'utujil language, an aspect of the local culture to which Atiteco commitment is unwavering.

INDIGENOUS LANGUAGE

The name Tz'utujil at one time referred to a leading regional pre-Conquest polity and literally means "Flower of the Maize Plant." It is a language of the Greater K'ichean branch of the Eastern division of Mayan languages (Kaufman 1976). According to Kaufman, Tz'utujil and its linguistic relatives Kaqchikel, Sakapultek, Sipakapa, and K'iche' began to diverge into separate languages around A.D. 900. Even among Tz'utujil speakers there is lexical, phonological, morphological, and syntactic variation in their use of the language (Dayley 1985:3).[6] This variation depends on which of the seven Tz'utujil municipios or satellite hamlets one comes from. I might add that this linguistic variation extends to even more of a micro level. Within Atitlán itself there is some linguistic variation according to cantón. This micro variation aside, Atitecos consider their own form of Tz'utujil to be the most correct. In fact, differing from Tz'utujil, which Atitecos almost invariably refer to as Ktz'oj'bal,

"The Language," they often state that the people of San Pedro la Laguna speak Pedrano, those of San Juan speak Juanero, and so on.

Douglas (1969:29) reports that for 1964, some 40 percent of Atiteco males and less than 10 percent of Atiteco females had speaking knowledge of Spanish. At present, perhaps half of all local residents can converse in Spanish. Importantly, however, this change has entailed a rise in bilingualism, and not a loss of Tz'utujil. Among Atitecos, Tz'utujil remains by far the more widely spoken language. In fact, at present it is most uncommon that an Atiteco, regardless of sex, age, or religious affiliation, will speak Spanish to another Atiteco. Even most local Ladinos are at least conversant in Tz'utujil. Having stated this, it should be noted that the Tz'utujil spoken by Atitecos is undergoing change. For instance, where just a few decades ago, Tz'utujil numbers were used almost exclusively, most Atitecos can no longer even count past twenty in their native tongue. Moreover, knowledge of the sacred and esoteric aspects of the language is increasingly restricted to the elderly Working People.

PATTERNS OF DRESS

The highland region of Chiapas and Guatemala has long been recognized as an important center of indigenous textile production. An often noted characteristic of the highland Mayan textile art is the tendency for each community to weave its own unique style of costume (e.g., O'Neale 1945:249). In a 1989 study, however, Margot Schevill raises questions about unqualified assumptions of this pattern. Basing her observations on a collection of late-nineteenth-century Guatemalan textiles housed in the Hearst Museum of the University of California at Berkeley, the author is able to demonstrate that costume styles were shared between some communities even at that early date. She adds that in those communities where it ever did exist, by the 1980s "the one-costume one-village syndrome had broken down" (1989:72).

Santiago Atitlán is an exception to Schevill's observations. Not only have Atitecos woven and worn a distinctive style of costume (*traje*), but by and large, they continue tenaciously to embrace that tradition. Most commonly, Atiteco weavings are elaborately embroidered with birds, a trait that may extend to the pre-Columbian past, when the leading Tz'utujil-speaking polity was the Ajtz'iquinajay, the "Bird House." At present, virtually all Atitecas (female members of the community) wear one of several varieties of village-specific traje. Moreover, Atitlán is one of the increasingly rare Guatemalan towns in which a significant percentage of males habitually use traje. In 1988, I conducted a survey which showed that approximately 70 percent of males aged 1 to 10, 55 percent

5. The typical daily dress of women from Santiago Atitlán includes a backstrap loom woven blouse (pot) embroidered with birds, a skirt (uq) woven by men on a treadle loom, and sometimes a tightly wound hair ribbon (xk'ap), called a "halo" in English. Although the use of such hair ribbons among the town's women was the norm until a couple of decades ago, that usage is increasingly restricted to elderly women. Children typically wear the local style of dress. (Photograph by Paul Harbaugh, 1990.)

of the 10- to 25-year-olds, and 95 percent of males over 25 conformed to this traditional pattern (see Carlsen 1993). All told, in 1988 almost 75 percent of males in Atitlán habitually wore traje. While these data may seem to support a case for Atiteco conservatism, when compared to figures for 1966, a somewhat different picture emerges. For that year,

6. Daily dress for men from Santiago Atitlán typically includes a backstrap loom woven belt (pas) and pants (skav). Most men now wear industrially manufactured shirts, although a few still wear local backstrap loom woven shirts (ktuon). Although local dress for men can be elaborately woven and heavily embellished with embroidery, the rather plain attire shown here is typical of a poor Atiteco. (Photograph by the author, 1992.)

Douglas (1969:30) established that more than 95 percent of Atitecas wore traje, a figure that has changed little. For males, however, the situation is quite different. Douglas reported that about 91 percent of Atitecos habitually wore traje in 1964, a figure that when compared to the 1988 figure of 75 percent establishes a relatively rapid change away from use of the local costume.

This trend is even more pronounced when one considers that the criteria for what constitutes traje-use have changed since Douglas made his observations. At that time all but a few men wore locally woven shirts. Now, however, more than 90 percent of males wear industrially manufactured shirts. The shirt has been subtracted from the traditional male costume of pants (*skav*), sash (*pas*), and shirt (*k'tuon*). Moreover, in 1964 approximately two-thirds of males did not use footwear, and of those that did, most wore locally made sandals (*x'jab*). By 1988, however, few men went barefoot, and most wore industrially manufactured shoes. (In fact, to own a pair of Nike shoes is a dream of most Atiteco boys.) These trends have not been limited to males. In 1964, according to Douglas, only 2 percent of Atitecas wore any kind of shoes. However, by 1988, fully 55 percent were using them. Certainly a primary reason for this change has been the recent availability of cheap plastic shoes for women (often called "jellies" in the United States), which cost the equivalent of one dollar.

Most important, the trend away from traje use for males in Santiago Atitlán seems to be accelerating. Although I do not have exact figures for current patterns of dress in Atitlán, even a superficial visual survey demonstrates conclusively that considerably fewer than the 75 percent of males who were wearing traje in 1988 now wear local styles of costume. Exemplifying the increasing interconnection of the Atitecos with the outside world, a primary factor in that trend derives from the lifestyle of the good citizens of the United States. Specifically, within recent years the American preoccupation with current fashion, in combination with a national throwaway mind-set, has led to even the most remote Guatemalan towns' becoming inundated with used *ropa americana*. This used clothing costs only the equivalent of a few American cents per piece. To the increasingly impoverished Atitecos, such a deal can be too good to refuse.

In light of all this, it might seem strange that the art of weaving in Santiago Atitlán is in the midst of a renaissance. Until a few decades ago, nonspecific social controls such as gossip and ridicule dictated conservatism in the weaving art. Today, however, weavers in Atitlán are free to experiment with the local costume. Resulting variations include novel weaving techniques and design motifs, an expanded use of the color palette, and new weaving materials. There is, however, an evident irony in this. The creativity apparent in the contemporary weaving art is due to the fact that strict conformity to tightly defined local group behavior no longer explains Atiteco existence. Hence, just as the weaver is now free to experiment with her art, so is the Atiteco ever more likely to exchange his local costume for a pair of slacks, a double-knit shirt, and some tennis shoes. Embedded in those factors leading to the renaissance of weaving in Atitlán are the seeds of the local weaving art's potential demise. The license for the contemporary weaver's flings with creativity also permits the laying down of her loom forever.

INFORMATION-AGE MAYAS

This chapter began with McBryde's observations about the relationship between Lake Atitlán's geographical isolation and the cultural conservatism of its indigenous communities, what he described as the relationship between nature and culture. More than fifty years after his research in the area, many of McBryde's observations about such cultural components as language, costume, and economy remain valid. For instance, not only do most Atitecos continue to wear the local costume masterfully embroidered with birds, but virtually all of them continue to speak the local variant of Tz'utujil, "Flower of the Maize Plant." However, as is exemplified by the town's linkage to the outside world via roads and telecommunications networks, it is equally evident that the cultural ecology of Lake Atitlán is quickly changing. Clearly, even precipitous cliffs and dangerous lake surfaces now present little challenge to the likes of Don Pepe or Chuck-the-Gringo.

3

The Flowering of the Dead

COAUTHORED WITH MARTÍN PRECHTEL

*"A flower was blossoming at the brink of the abyss: the perennial, daz-
zling golden flower of the little tortured tree."*

MARC CHADOURNE, *ANAHUAC* (1954)

A SURVEY OF THE ANTHROPOLOGICAL LITERATURE demonstrates that the
twentieth century highlands of Guatemala and Chiapas, Mexico, are
among the most studied cultural regions in the world. These studies
range from Oliver La Farge's accounts of his investigations in the Cuchumatán Mountains (1931, 1947) in the 1920s, through Sol Tax's work in the
Lake Atitlán area (1937, 1941, 1953, 1990) to the impressive list of publications that grew out of the Harvard Chiapas Project (too numerous to
be cited). Despite Guatemala's ongoing revolution and the difficulty of
working in that country, important studies continue to be published
(e.g., Sexton 1981; B. Tedlock 1982; Ehlers 1990; Watanabe 1992; Wilson
1995). Yet, nearly sixty years since La Farge first stepped into Jacaltenango, a scholarly consensus on certain of the most fundamental aspects
of highland Mayan culture has yet to be forged.

Following Eric Wolf's seminal study of "closed corporate communities" (1957), numerous scholars have argued that during the decades and
centuries which followed the Conquest, the culture of the indigenous
inhabitants of the Mayan highlands was formed into something of an
artifact of the Spanish-dominated colonial society (e.g., W. Smith 1977;
Wasserstrom 1983). According to Wolf, the Mesoamerican closed corporate peasant configuration, which he identified (1957:7) as a "creature
of the Spanish Conquest," represented an indigenous response to Hispanic culture. This interpretation continues to find support among

scholars (e.g., Annis 1987; Warren 1989). Analyzing how the process of post-Columbian culture change may have occurred, John Hawkins (1984:80) states that the Indian world view has become "the inverse, a negative transformation, of the Spanish ideology or world view." Similarly, Severo Martínez Peláez (1971) claims that the Spanish *conquistadores* never even encountered Indians in Mesoamerica. Instead, he writes, they found "aborigines," the category "Indian" resulting from a gradual process of acculturation.

Where Wolf's position recognizes that the huge indigenous population had a role in the determination of post-Columbian Indian culture, other scholars consider the Indians' input to have been virtually nil (e.g., Harris 1964). For example, Hawkins argues that the Spanish "broke down elements of the aboriginal culture and created the Indians from the pieces" (1984:44). According to this position, much as the impact of one billiard ball determines the projection of another ball (the metaphor is Gregory Bateson's [1972:229]), the Mesoamericans were knocked off their pre-Columbian cultural bases by European contact. With the Indians thought to be total victims of the Spanish and utterly powerless to influence their own destinies, elements such as adaptation and subversion are deemed irrelevant, and are therefore ignored.

Theories which posit an abrupt discontinuity between pre- and post-Columbian cultures have, however, been increasingly confronted with significant cultural and historical anomalies (e.g., Mendelson 1965; Vogt 1969; Gossen 1974a; Carmack 1981). Two recent works present arguments which are particularly noteworthy in this respect. First, Barbara Tedlock's *Time and the Highland Maya* (1982) demonstrates remarkable continuities in ancient Mayan calendrics and the Mayan conception of time. And Robert Hill and John Monaghan's *Continuities in Highland Maya Social Organization* (1987) presents a strong case that the "closed corporate community," a cornerstone of most arguments for Mayan cultural discontinuity, was actually a basic unit of pre-Columbian highland Mayan society. In short, the accumulation of anomalies seems to indicate that, despite Spanish efforts, Mayan culture has been far more resilient and self-directed than many scholars have believed. Evidently the conquest of a people requires more than military subjugation. Perhaps aware of this, upon completing their Mesoamerican military campaigns the Spanish commenced to "put an end to everything indigenous, especially in the realm of ideas, even so far as to leave no sign of them" (Garibay K., in Anderson 1960). Clearly, it was their intention that this process should culminate in the spiritual conquest of the Indians. However, studies have shown that this hegemonic ambition was ill-fated (e.g., Gossen 1974b; Colby 1976; Earle and Snow 1985). As Dennis Tedlock (1985:19) notes, the "'spiritual conquest' [of the Mayas] has in fact never taken place."

This observation is of considerable importance for the reconstruction of Mayan post-Columbian history. Quite evidently, the continuity of ideas, religious or otherwise, is essential to cultural stability and continuity. Returning to an earlier metaphor, it is the influence of ideas that makes the path of cultural development quite unlike a mere progression of billiard balls. With billiards, the collision of the first ball determines the course of a second. According to Bateson (in Yowell 1986:52), "in that world, there is not information, there are no metaphors. It's just bump." When living things are involved, however, the process is far more complicated. Contrasting billiard balls to dogs, Bateson notes that a kicked dog may turn and run, but then again, it is just as likely to turn and bite. While the billiard ball cannot stabilize its situation, entities which have the capacity to process information can.

Unlike mindless billiard balls, the newly "conquered" Mayas possessed that element necessary to stabilize the "contact" experience. Just as ideas and information affect social organization, with the Mayas this complex has affected social reorganization, ultimately leading to what has been called "reconstituted Indian culture" (MacLeod 1973:230). Describing this culture for the lowland Mayas, Nancy Farriss states that "it is not the preservation of an unmodified cultural system under a veneer of Spanish customs, but the preservation of a central core of concepts and principles, serving as a framework within which modifications could be made and providing a distinctive shape to the new patterns that emerged" (1984:8). She adds that the cultural configuration which did emerge "remained, for all the transformations, distinctively and identifiably Mayan." The pages which follow demonstrate that Farriss' observations apply equally to numerous highland Mayas.

Based on data from the contemporary Tz'utujil Mayas of Santiago Atitlán, Guatemala, this chapter considers a formalized normative construct called Jaloj-K'exoj, which guided the transformations of the local Mayan culture configuration. We propose that Jaloj-K'exoj, a Mayan conceptualization of observed processes and patterns in the natural environment, particularly of agricultural production, is a central paradigm of the local culture. After defining Jaloj-K'exoj as it exists in contemporary Atitlán, we use data from the ancient text the *Popol Vuh* and from the archaeological site of Palenque, Mexico, dating from the Maya Classic period (c. A.D. 300–900), to argue that some form of this paradigm, including its socially integrative functioning, has been central to Mayan culture since long before the Spanish Conquest. The survival of Jaloj-K'exoj demonstrates an area of significant cultural continuity; moreover, this paradigm helps to explain the cultural patterns which emerged from the Conquest period.

FLOWERING MOUNTAIN EARTH: THE CONTEMPORARY CONTEXT

Despite the inevitable presence of tourists lured to Santiago Atitlán by its beauty, the dogged efforts of missionaries, and the effects of a rapidly changing ecology, a significant number of Atitecos continue to embrace the Old Ways. To the Working People, religion provides a self-evident background to which the world conforms. In fact, until recently most components of Atiteco culture were in some way informed by the underlying principles of this religion. (For instance, see the discussion in Prechtel and Carlsen 1988 of the relation of Atiteco religion to weaving and cosmos.) In this regard, the religion is pervasive: Its meaning is known to some extent by most Atitecos. It would be entirely incorrect, however, to assume that all Atitecos have equal religious knowledge. In recent years, deviation from the traditional religion has been growing. Until a few decades ago it would have been virtually correct to state that to be Atiteco was to be a Working Person, but there are now significant competing claims to religious identity. Even Working People differ in their knowledge of the Old Ways, as each level of initiation in the cofradía system allows increased access to the religion.

Differences among the Working People aside, a unifying concept underlying the Old Ways is contained in the term Jaloj-K'exoj. As will be shown, myth, standardized prayers, and discussion among the Working People assume a didactic role in the transmission of Jaloj-K'exoj. The term itself is derived from two words, *jal* and *k'ex*, both of which denote types of change. Jal is the change manifested by a thing as it evolves through its individual life cycle. Traditionally, Mayas have believed that life arises from death. Consistent with this belief, beginning in death, jal is the change manifested in the transition to life through birth, through youth and old age, and finally back into death. Symbolically, jal is change on the outside, at the "husk." By contrast, k'ex occurs at the "seed" and refers to generational change. While it maintains a distinct concern with ancestral origin, k'ex relates to the transfer, hence the continuity, of life, and may account for anthropological observations of Mayan "ancestor worship" (e.g., Wasserstrom 1983:77). Moreover, it relates to what might best be described as a form of reincarnation, an integral aspect of Mayan religion which has by and large been excluded from scholarly consideration (Ruz 1973; Mondloch 1980; and Coggins 1989 are among the exceptions). K'ex is a process of making the new out of the old. At the same time, just as a single plant produces multiple offspring, k'ex is change from one into many. Together jal and k'ex form a concentric system of change within change, a single system of transformation and renewal.

Although the process of Jaloj-K'exoj has not been discussed in the literature, aspects of k'ex have been. The earliest available reference dates from c. 1710 when the friar Francisco Ximénez, best known for his translation of the *Popol Vuh*, defined *k'ex* (*quex*) as "to change one thing for another," and "to transform" (1985:483). Much more recently, James Mondloch (1980) has written a paper about the relationship of k'ex to K'iche' Mayan naming patterns, particularly as it involves naming a grandchild with his or her grandparent's name. He concludes that k'ex is a "social mechanism for replacing the ancestors" as well as "a way for obtaining personal immortality" (1980:9). Two years before the publication of Mondloch's study, Kay Warren, although she did not use the term, cited various key components of k'ex. For instance, she states ([1978] 1989:57) that the naming of a grandson with his grandfather's name acts as a "form of transmission" to make these two people the same. While Warren focused on the Kaqchikel community of San Andrés Semetebaj, Mondloch's observations were for the K'iche' towns of Nahualá and Santa Catarina Ixtahuacán. In addition, he mentions evidence of k'ex in Momostenango and Jacaltenango. Francesco Pellizzi (pers. comm. 1986) has observed aspects of k'ex among the Mayas of Chiapas, Mexico. Interestingly, citing the similarity between the Mayan k'ex and the Nahua *tocaitl*, Mondloch (1980:21) speculates that at one time k'ex may even have extended beyond the Mayan area.[1]

Perhaps the best way to approach the understanding of Jaloj-K'exoj is as Atitecos themselves often do—through myth. The late historian of religions Mircea Eliade stated that religions have a "center," a "central conception which informs the entire corpus of myths, rituals and beliefs" (1969:10). With Atitecos, Jaloj-K'exoj is this center. However, beyond its conceptual centrality, Jaloj-K'exoj takes form as a symbolic physical center, what Eliade termed the *axis mundi*. Working People call this aspect Kotsej Juyu Ruchiliew, or "Flowering Mountain Earth." Although this element will be approached through agricultural metaphor, the imagery is multidimensional and refers to more than vegetation. Flowering Mountain Earth is a unifying concept, inextricably linking vegetation, the human life cycle, kinship, modes of production, religious and political hierarchy, conceptions of time, and even of celestial movement.

In Atiteco religion Flowering Mountain Earth is a place at the world's center whose primary manifestation is a maize plant or tree. In this, Atiteco belief conforms to a widespread myth among contemporary Mayas. For instance, Miguel León-Portilla (1988) discusses the symbolic centrality of the "World Tree" for the Tzotzil Mayas of Chiapas, Mexico. In Atiteco myth, before there was a world (what we would call the universe), a solitary deified tree was at the center of all that was. As the world's creation approached, this deity became pregnant with potential life; its branches grew one of all things in the form of fruit. Not only did gross physical objects like rocks, maize, and deer hang from the branches, but so did such elements as types of lightning, and even individual segments of time. Eventually this abundance became too much for the tree to support, and the fruit fell. Smashing open, the fruit scattered their seeds; and soon there were numerous seedlings at the foot of the old tree. The great tree provided shelter for the young 'plants,' nurturing them, until finally it was crowded out by the new. Since then, this tree has existed as a stump at the center of the world. This stump is what remains of the original "Father/Mother" (Ti Tie Ti Tixel), the source and endpoint of life.

The focus of Atiteco religion is in one way or another oriented backward, to the Father/Mother, the original tree. This tree, if properly maintained, renews and regenerates the world. E. Michael Mendelson (1956:65) quotes an Atiteco who referred to this regenerative process as *palabra del mundo* and said that "it is the root (*raiz*) of the world, it is ancient. . . . The village cannot go on living without it because it is an original thing: it is tied to the beginning of the world." As Flowering Mountain Earth it is given graphic representation in the main altar of Santiago Atitlán's Catholic church. This altar, constructed when the church was without a resident priest and under full cofradía control, is dominated by a mountain carved in wood. To either side of the mountain are carvings of cofradía members, complete with their staffs of office and shown ascending the mountain. Atop the mountain is a World Tree in the form of a sprouting maize plant.

Atitecos believe that as long as the primal ancestral element, as Flowering Mountain Earth, is "fed" it will continue to provide sustenance. In Atiteco religion, this "feeding" can be literal. For example, some Atitecos will have an actual hole on their land through which offerings are given to the ancestor. In the Tz'utujil dialect, this hole is called *r'muxux* ("umbilicus"). More commonly, "feeding" is accomplished through ritual, the Old Ways. For instance, dancing sacred bundles, burning copal incense, or praying can feed the ancestral form. The following prayer, one of the most common standard prayers in Santiago Atitlán, is appropriate

7. At first glance, the altar in Atitlán's church appears typical for any Catholic parish. Upon closer inspection, however, several unique aspects emerge. Perhaps most notable is that the altar is in the form of a mountain, what the Working People call "Flowering Mountain Earth." This mountain, capped by an emerging corn plant, is said to mark the world's center. Significantly, just a few yards in front of the altar is a hole in the floor (generally capped) referred to as the "umbilicus of the world." The panels at the bottom of the altar depict various cofradía scenes, including the Deer-Jaguar dance and Maximón. Incidentally, the two "saints" in the niches to the lower left of the altar are San Juan Carajo and his concubine Andaloor. (Photograph by the author, 1993.)

for this type of activity. This beautiful poetic text also synthesizes various of the concepts explicated above.

> What was said, lives.
> It has become a jewel,
> and it flowers.
> But it is something now lost,
> Something relegated to death.
> Lost in dust, lost in earth.
>
> It holds us like a baby.
> It guards us like a child.

It trusses the World at the edges, like a house.
It holds up the sky.[2]

Giver of life.
Giver of food.
Giver of water.

You who are the great-grandmothers and great-grandfathers,
We are your flowers, we are your sprouts.
We are the ones who fall off the trees,
We are the ones who fall off the vines.

For many Atitecos, the logic which informs their religion is constantly reified in daily existence. Let us consider the maize field, that fundamental element of Atiteco livelihood that not only validates Jaloj-K'exoj but also replicates the primal myth. The first step in the life cycle of the maize plant is as a seed planted in the ground. Demonstrating how this process originates in death, the Working People often refer to maize seeds which are to be planted as *muk*, meaning "interred ones," or sometimes as *jolooma*, which signifies "little skulls" (Tarn and Prechtel 1981). With proper care the seeds will sprout, eventually to become small plants. These plants are addressed as *tak ai'*, which means "little ones" (children).[3] As the plants mature, flowers form, and eventually ears of maize are produced. Next, the plants with husks still attached dry up and die. The steps in this process represent jal, or transformation on an individual level. It is noteworthy that this last stage of maize, as dried ears with the husk attached, is itself called jal. Finally, the death of the individual maize plant results in numerous seeds. In turn these seeds, the little skulls, are returned to the earth, ultimately resulting in many plants, all in the image of their ancestor. In this process life has sprung from death and the ancestral form has been recycled. Jaloj-K'exoj is demonstrated.

As indicated in the anthropomorphized references to maize seeds and plants cited above, the Working People perceive a likeness between the life cycles of plants and humans. This likeness is founded in a perception of the universality of Jaloj-K'exoj. The Tz'utujil language testifies to the priority of the native conception. When an infant is born it can be said "he (or she) sprouted," or sometimes "he returned" (*x'ula*). It is believed that, as with maize, after death a person's life essence is regenerated in his or her descendants, specifically in grandchildren. This explains the aforementioned custom of naming a grandchild with the grandparent's name. Accordingly, in Santiago Atitlán a grandparent's namesake is referred to as *k'exel* (from *k'ex*), which means "my replace-

54

ment." Importantly, the k'exel, as the grandparent's "replacement," becomes the symbolic parent of the biological parent. Consequently, one's child is sometimes actually addressed as "parent," and males will address their fathers as *nuk'jol*, or "my son." Likewise, a woman will often call her father *wal*, which translates as "child." As "replacements" are necessary for the grandparents' regeneration, the k'ex naming pattern has more than superficial significance. Upon the death of a k'exel, the oldest surviving sibling is sometimes even renamed with the name of the deceased, hence the name of the grandparent. Additionally, because of high infant mortality, until recently it was common in Atitlán for parents to give many of their children the same (grandparent's) name, thus insuring a k'exel to pass on the ancestral life form. For this reason, it is common in Atitlán to encounter a nuclear family with various siblings who all have the same name.

To return to discussion of the link between children and vegetation, the Working People perceive of their children as fruit, flowers, and leaves. *Xoc chie* is a word for "leaves," which to the followers of the Old Ways represent fingers. In Atiteco society only when a person has children is that person considered "complete." Lacking "completion," there is no k'exel through which to maintain the vital ancestral link. To Atitecos, the figure 10, the number of fingers, signifies a "complete" being. The Tz'utujil word for 20 is *winuk*, which also means "person." According to Atiteco symbolism, half of 20 lives in the hands; the other half exists at the roots, the ancestral element from which the living receive their sustenance. When the fruit—the children—eventually drop to the ground, splitting open to form new sprouts, these are the grandchildren. Significantly, grandparents will often call their grandchildren *tzej jutae*, which means "sprout." As the grandparents become older, they symbolically assume the position of the old tree. In fact, old people will sometimes be addressed as Nim Chie Nim Kam, or "Big Tree Big Vine," perhaps the most respectful title that can be given an Atiteco.[4]

To articulate their beliefs, the Working People often rely on symbolically consonant aspects of their language. For instance, in Tz'utujil, the space beneath a person is *r'xie*, "at a person's root." The space in front of a person is *chuech*, or "at its fruit." Behind a person is *tz'rij*, or "at its bark." A person's feet are called *r'kan*, or "trunk." In Tz'utujil the word for "hand" is *r'ka*, which also means "branch." The word for "face" and "fruit" is the same, *uech*, which also means "children."

Incorporating these concepts, a most important aspect of Jaloj-K'exoj in Santiago Atitlán is to be found in the town's cofradía system. More than any other mechanism, cofradía ritual serves to renew and to regenerate the community and the world. Consistent with the logic that permeates the Old Ways, this cofradía function is expressed in vegetational symbolism. This is immediately evident in conversations between Working People or in cofradía prayers. For example, cofradía prayers often begin with the statement "We are the sprouts at your hands and feet. We are the branches at your trunk. We come in front of trees and stones. We are at your bark, at your fruit. We are your flowers. We are your tendrils. We are the ones who need your shade." Underlying these words is a belief that the people of Atitlán are the fruits and flowers of the community; each cofradía is a branch; the trunk is the *principales* (elders); and the roots are the ancestors, the dead. This understanding is commonly expressed in cofradía meetings in which a participant wanting to make an important point might address the leader of the town's cofradía system with the words, "Hey Trunk." In turn, "Trunk," depending on whether the speakers are cofradía members or unaffiliated, might respond "Oh you branches" or "You flowers and sprouts."

Finally, related to the above is a very important temporal consideration. To the Mayas, as to all people, the sun is the primary element in defining time. We have explained elsewhere that basic to Atiteco cofradía ritual is the attempt to help move the sun across the sky, which is understood by the Working People to constitute "sacrifice" (Prechtel and Carlsen 1988). Sacrifice (their word) gives the world its power of movement, thus enabling it to evolve through its endless cycles of birth and death. This movement is effected by a series of solar deaths and births ("dawnings"). Appropriately, Atitlán's individual cofradías are often called "dawn houses." At dawn, Atitecos often say *xlexa kdta*, or "our father was born." The dawning of the sun, the sprouting of a seed, and the birthing of a child are expressed using *xlexa*, from the verb *lexic*, which means "to be derived from." (At times the related term *x'ela*, "it worked," is used to express these same phenomena.) All of these uses of xlexa represent the same process, and all reflect K'exoj, regeneration and renewal in the form of the original.

These various aspects come together in Flowering Mountain Earth, the World Tree. As a dry stump, the tree is associated with death. The time of death takes form both as the night and as the period from the autumnal equinox until the spring equinox. In deified form, the tree during these times is sometimes named "Gourd Head" (Tzimai Awa) and is symbolically represented as a skull. At the spring equinox the world is inseminated. This is a delicate time: the much celebrated five "delicate" days of the Mayan calendar. At this point, if the world has been properly cared for, if the Old Ways have been correctly performed, the world springs into life. Simultaneously the dry stump, as gourd/ skull, flowers into new growth, the maize sprouts, the sun dawns (is born), and time itself is regenerated. It has "worked."

GRINDING BONES UNDER GRANDMOTHER'S HOUSE: THE PRE-COLUMBIAN CONTEXT

Thus far we have been concerned with the definition of Jaloj-K'exoj in its contemporary context. The argument has been made that it constitutes a process of transformation, renewal in an ancestral form, and that it is founded on an empirical understanding of the vegetational cycle. Moreover, it has been shown that Jaloj-K'exoj symbolically permeates the local Mayan culture, informing the operation of multiple phenomena. In this section, data from two texts, the book *Popol Vuh* and carved stone monuments from the archaeological site of Palenque, dating from the Maya Late Classic period (c. A.D. 600–900), are used to demonstrate the salience of the paradigm for the ancient Mayas. It is shown that both texts conform to the principles of Jaloj-K'exoj, as set out above. Data from contemporary Santiago Atitlán will be included where they help explain the significance of the ancient texts. Although many scholars believe that the living Mayas have no recollection of the *Popol Vuh*, Atitecos retain considerable knowledge of that text. In fact, a version of the *Popol Vuh* (what the Atitecos call "Grandmother Sweat-bath" [Prechtel 1990]) is alive and well in Atiteco oral tradition. A primary reason for this is that in the *Popol Vuh* can be found the seeds of the Atitecos' religion.

Our discussion of the ancient Mayan texts begins with the descent of the *Popol Vuh*'s "lead characters," the Hero Twins, into the underworld, where they die.[5] In the state of death one of the twins, in the form of a skull in a tree, impregnates a woman named Blood Woman by spitting into her hand.[6] Upon impregnation, she ventures to the earth's surface and gives birth to twins—namesakes of the ancestral twins.[7] This section is of primary importance in the *Popol Vuh*, as well as for this chapter's arguments about Jaloj-K'exoj, and requires careful examination.

In his translation of the *Popol Vuh*, Munro Edmonson (1971:76) speaks of this section as a "rare excursion into explicit philosophy, which makes it clear that in [K'iche'] theory to participate in the chain of reproduction is to . . . attain immortality." The ancient author (or authors) of this section of the *Popol Vuh*, in the discussion of spittle (which is said to be "like one's essence"), not only talks about K'exoj but also alludes to it by name. Of particular importance is the K'iche' word for "spittle," *k'axaj*. This word (*k'exaj* in Tz'utujil) is derived from the same root as K'exoj; the *Popol Vuh* plays on the meanings inherent in this term. The intent of this section is made absolutely clear in the line in which the twin as skull explains that henceforth, "The father does not disappear, but goes on being fulfilled" (D. Tedlock 1985:114). Moreover, in specifying that this "fulfillment" applies to the "son of a lord or the son of a craftsman, an orator," the text asserts that this immortality applies to all people. To this day, at the time when the little skulls of maize are sown, Atitecos have a ceremony in which a maize drink called *maatz*, which to the Working People represents semen, is drunk from a gourd, representing a skull. This ceremony is carried out in anticipation of the time of the year when death flowers into new life.

The *Popol Vuh's* "rare excursion into explicit philosophy" clearly attests to the importance of what Atitecos call Jaloj-K'exoj to the ancient K'iche' Mayas. The *Popol Vuh* is also clear that this process guides the transformation and renewal of more than just anthropomorphized deities and humans. This is apparent from the beginning of the text when the creator deities ponder, "How should it [the world] be sown, How should it dawn?" (D. Tedlock 1985:73), a question whose implications surface throughout the *Popol Vuh*. Likening the terms "dawning" and "sowing" to a Möbius strip, in his recent translation of this text Dennis Tedlock (1985:251) explains:

> If we start with the literal meaning of sowing in the present context, the reference is to the beginning of plants; but if we trace that idea over to the other side of our strip, the sprouting of those same plants is expressed metaphorically as "dawning." If on the other hand, we start from the literal meaning of "dawning," the present reference is to the first of all dawns; but if we trace the idea back to the other side of the strip, the origin of that dawning is expressed as a "sowing."

Tedlock explains that in K'iche' the sowing/dawning combination can have human connotations. The interpretation offered by Tedlock for sowing, dawning, death and birth is remarkably similar to that given by the Working People. However, according to the Atitecos, sowing/ dying or dawning/birthing might not be viewed simply as singular events. Rather, they can be understood as simultaneous expressions, each driven by the same process, which Atitecos call Jaloj-K'exoj. Further analysis indicates that this was the understanding of the ancient K'iche's as well. This interpretation is given support by the performance of the Hero Twins. While they are primarily deities, they also incorporate such diverse aspects as segments of time (Cohodas 1976:160), celestial bodies (D. Tedlock 1985:159–60), and perhaps most importantly, the maize. These diverse aspects are simultaneously represented in an exemplary episode of the *Popol Vuh*, referred to here as "Grinding Bones under Grandmother's House."[8]

At the end of their stay on the earth, and realizing that they are about to descend back into the underworld, the Hero Twins sow maize in the house of Grandmother, a character who to the Working People is the divine embodiment of the female principle. To Grandmother the twins say, "When the corn dries up this will be a sign of our death: 'Perhaps they died,' you'll say, when it dries up. And when the sprouting comes: 'Perhaps they live,' you'll say" (D. Tedlock 1985:133). (This act of "sowing" by the Hero Twins, as maize deities, is a metaphorical act of self-burial, indicating their own deaths.) At this point the boys descend into the underworld. Imagery of Jaloj-K'exoj is evident again around what the *Popol Vuh* refers to as the "epitaph" of the Hero Twins.

Near the time of their deaths in the underworld, the twins devise a plan by which their bones are to be ground on stone, "just as corn is refined into flour" (D. Tedlock 1985:148). Upon their death, by jumping headfirst into an oven, this plan is carried out. The ground bones of the twins are subsequently cast into a river. On the *fifth* day, after having "germinated" in the water, the twins are regenerated. (This certainly refers to the five-day "delicate" period of the Mayan calendar, which, as noted, to Atitecos prefigures the world's flowering from death.) At this, the corn which had been planted in Grandmother's house sprouts. Coupled with the "sprouting" of the maize in the middle of Grandmother's house is a "dawning." The *Popol Vuh* declares, "the boys ascended this way, here into the middle of the light, and they ascended straight into the sky, and the sun belongs to one and the moon to the other" (D. Tedlock 1985:159–160). Dramatically, the *Popol Vuh* answers its own question, "How should it be sown, how should it dawn?"

It is significant that throughout the Guatemalan highlands, maize is not ground into flour. Instead, maize is ground wet into *soa*, or dough. There is, however, an important exception. In Santiago Atitlán, at the time of sowing, maize is ground into flour in preparation of the ceremonial drink maatz (as mentioned above). In this process, the maize seed is ground after having been toasted in an oven. Described in this section of the *Popol Vuh* is a veritable recipe for the making of maatz, in preparation for the subsequent regeneration from death of the multiple aspects of the Hero Twins.

The *Popol Vuh* offers clear imagery of the Hero Twins as polymorphous, their aspects guided by a process of Jaloj-K'exoj. Portrayed simultaneously are the stories, not only of the deified twins, but also of seeds underground and of the changing of the seasons. Paralleled by the cycles of maize are the cycles of life, of the sun and moon, of living time. Entwined in trees are the shadows of deified ancestors, ancestors who continue being "fulfilled" in their descendants. The *Popol Vuh* is an ingenious story of death, of transformation, and of regeneration: cycles of sacred change in an ancestral form. The world described in the *Popol Vuh*, like that of the Working People, is dictated by the sometimes fierce laws of this change which bind plants, humans, and gods alike. But for how long has the Mayan world been thus?

Because of the date of its transcription, circa A.D. 1700, as well as its association with the Post Classic K'iche' Mayas, scholars have often attributed a near-Conquest origin to the *Popol Vuh*. However, new data, in part reflecting advances in Mayan epigraphy, as well as the reevaluation of extant data, have led most Mayanists to accept that some form of the *Popol Vuh* has been central to Mayan religion since at least the Maya Late Classic period. Besides evidence from the *Popol Vuh*, other categories of data also suggest that what the Working People call Jaloj-K'exoj has helped shape Mayan culture ever since the Maya Classic period. One such body of evidence comes from Palenque, Mexico, a site whose stone monuments have been described as illustrating "the basic structure of Mesoamerican religion" (Cohodas 1976:155). Motifs found in Palenque include sophisticated depictions of vegetation sprouting from the heads of humanistic figures; of maize and trees growing from skull-like deities; of ears of maize with transposed human faces; of deceased rulers in a tree-related form and in the process of descent into the underworld.

On the basis of iconographic and epigraphic evidence, it is proposed here that a symbolic statement sculpted in stone at Palenque is similar to that described above for traditional Atiteco culture and for the *Popol Vuh*. Indeed, it has been argued that certain figures depicted on the Palenque panels must be incarnations of the Hero Twins (Lounsbury 1985:51). For now, we consider evidence which identifies the principal characteristics of Jaloj-K'exoj, beginning with the belief in ancestral regeneration according to a model based on vegetation.

Consistent with Atiteco mythology, the central design element in all of Palenque's major temples (except the Temple of the Sun) and on the sarcophagus lid of its most noted ruler, Pakal, is the World Tree (Schele and Miller 1986). In the Temple of the Foliated Cross, the tree takes form as maize. In all of its representations this axis mundi is portrayed as growing out of the head of skeletonized deities. For the Temple of the

8. The central icon in much of Palenque's monumental art is the World Tree. For the Temple of the Foliated Cross in Palenque, as depicted above, this axis mundi *is in the form of a maize plant which issues from the top of a seed/skull. In this, Palenque iconography is consistent with later Mayan understandings. (From Schele and Miller 1986.)*

Foliated Cross, Eric Thompson (1970:208, 227) characterizes the deity, often called GII, as both an ancestral and a vegetation deity. And Linda Schele (1976:24) describes it as a god of "generations, ancestry, and lineages." Perhaps most significantly, David Freidel (n.d.:14) identifies this god as a "seed from which a corn plant containing the Ancestors grows."

Important epigraphic evidence supplements these identifications. For instance, leaf motifs found in all of the major temples at Palenque and on Pakal's sarcophagus also make the glyph *le*, which as Linda Schele notes, has the "double meaning of 'leaf' and 'generations' (ancestry)" (1976:22). This is consistent with the leaf/generation association cited earlier for the Atitecos. Additional glyphic evidence indicates that, as with the Working People, the hand may have figured in this ancient Mayan association. Prominent in the "completion" glyph is a hand incorporated into a person's face. This glyph stands for the number 20,

Chan-Bahlum   Chaacal I   Lady Kanal-Ikal

9. The artistry of the Maya ruler Pakal's sarcophagus is dominated by the depiction on its lid of the deceased ruler's descent along the World Tree into the underworld. The exterior sides of the sarcophagus, however, furnish evidence of Pakal's ultimate fate. As represented above, the sarcophagus sides testify to a Classic-period Mayan understanding that the death experience can culminate in rebirth according to a model based on vegetation. Depicted are ancestors of Pakal, identified by hieroglyphs (translated into English letters below each figure), in a process of rebirth as trees. Other evidence indicates that regeneration of Mayan rulers may also have entailed a solar "dawning." (From Schele and Miller 1986.)

which to the Classic Mayas meant "person," as it does to the Atitecos. It should be recalled that to the Working People, there is an association between the fingers as children and the "completeness" of a person. Moreover, depicted prominently in common variants of the "parentage statement" glyphs is a hand holding a "curl," which Karl Taube (1985: 178–179) shows may be a sprout. As noted previously, in Santiago Atitlán infants are thought of as sprouts.

As depicted in Figure 9, on the sides of Pakal's sarcophagus are portrayals of humans who have emerged plantlike from cracks in the ground. From the head of each grows a tree. Included are various *le* glyph leafs. Under the humans' rootlike torsos are what appear to be germinating seeds but are probably representations of the *kaban* glyph, which signifies "earth." Significantly, glyphs associated with the human/ tree combinations identify the individuals as ancestors of Lord Pakal (Schele and Miller 1986:285). In short, the accumulation of evidence drawn from Palenque's most important monuments testifies to the deep historical centrality of the Mayan belief in ancestral renewal founded in the life cycle of plants.

To conclude the argument that adherence to what the Working People call Jaloj-K'exoj guided the culture of Palenque, we consider how this paradigm permeates and informs the operation of multiple cultural phenomena. It has already been shown that depicted in the central iconographic elements at Palenque are deities which combine seed and skeletal qualities, and that together with the World Trees that grow from those "seed skulls," aspects of human and vegetal life are combined. Furthermore, the Palenque iconographic complex combines not just humans and vegetation but also political rulership. Schele and Miller (1986:72) have even associated kingship itself with the axis mundi, the World Tree. Moreover, according to these scholars, this relationship can be expanded to include, among other elements, an association with the sun. This interpretation is supported by the common glyphic reference to Mayan kings as Mah-K'ina, or "He of the Sun" (Lounsbury 1985:47). For instance, Schele and Miller argue (1986:269) that the depiction on the sarcophagus lid of Pakal's death, of his "falling down the *axis mundi,*" is "metaphorically equivalent to the sun at the instant of sunset." They add that "like the sun, which rises after a period of darkness," the Mayas believed that Pakal too would rise again. Reincarnation is demonstrated.

In an article which discusses the centrality of Mayan understanding of cyclic death and rebirth, Clemency Coggins (1989:66) states that "the poor were probably not entitled to the same afterlife [as the elites], although resurrection following an agricultural model . . . might in theory have been accessible to all." The *Popol Vuh*, like the Atiteco data, demonstrates that this was indeed the case.

Included in the symbolic statement of the Palenque panels, as has been shown, are the elements of rulership, of the sun, of vegetation, of ancestry, of birth and death, and seemingly of "dawning" and "sprouting." The abilities of Palenque's artisans cannot be doubted. Had those artisans desired to portray a series of discrete processes, singular images of accession to office, of the cycles of maize, of birth and death, and so on, they would have done so. Apparently they did not want to. Instead, the mix of otherwise unrelated processes and elements and their integration through the Jaloj-K'exoj paradigm, as revealed in traditional Atiteco culture and as described in the *Popol Vuh*, seems also to have underwritten the iconography of Palenque's monuments.

As if ignoring the timeline of history, the Mayas conceive of a sacred past which sustains, is replicated in, and symbolically informs the present and the future. Through the mechanism of what in Tz'utujil is called Jaloj-K'exoj, an indigenous understanding of circular time permeates Mayan culture and is revealed in economic, political, and religious institutions. To the Mayas, the pull of the past is often given religious expression, in what is referred to here as the "flowering of the dead." The concluding section shall consider another avenue through which the Mayas' ancestral past continues to guide the present and the future; by which the dead continue to flower.

THE CONVERSION OF THE SAINTS

This chapter has shown that post-Columbian highland Mayan culture exhibits continuity with the pre-Columbian past; that some contemporary Atitecos represent points on a cultural continuum which extends deep into a pre-Columbian past. While such stability need not entail salient "survivals" (M. E. Smith 1982), this chapter has identified a significant exception. I propose that what Atitecos call Jaloj-K'exoj survived the Conquest, that it helped to shape the "reconstituted" Mayan culture of the Colonial period, and that it continues to have relevance. This is not intended, however, to suggest a culture somehow frozen in time. Quite the contrary. Given that cultures constitute adaptive responses to open and changing environments, their stability demands flexibility. To remain stable, cultures must add, and will subtract, attributes. It follows that to survive, any guiding paradigm, such as Jaloj-K'exoj, must itself be able to accommodate change. Before we elaborate on the dynamics of this adaptive process, an example from contemporary Santiago Atitlán will serve to illustrate this position. Let us turn to the Atiteco "cult of the saints."

The saints of Catholicism undoubtedly constitute one of the most salient aspects of post-Columbian Mesoamerican religiosity and are therefore an appropriate element on which to base consideration of the highland Mayan response to Hispanic intrusion. In Santiago Atitlán, the cult of the saints is incorporated into the town's cofradía system. Collectively, the system can be referred to by its members as R'kan Sak R'kan Q'ij ("Footpath of the Dawn, Footpath of the Sun") and is concerned with effecting the smooth movement of the seasons and of the sun (Prechtel and Carlsen 1988). On another level, the ten public cofradías pertain individually to particular aspects important to the town (Douglas 1969:83). The qualities associated with these aspects and attached to the saints afford a window into local religiosity. Examples include Concepción (impregnation and planting), San Nicolás (shamanic doctoring), San Juan (midwifery), and San Francisco (death). For the present, however, let us consider Santiago, Saint James, the patron saint of the town. This "saint" has a processual association whose characteristics, appropriate to his central position in the community, should by now be familiar. In native taxonomy, Santiago is categorized as a *bokunab*, an antiquated and esoteric term now used only in the cofradías. Derived from the word *bokul*, "so many," the etymology of *bokunab* is easily understood. According to legend, Santiago's *bokunab* quality became apparent when as a soldier he created twin enemies out of one with a strike of his sword. Fortunately for the Atitecos, this ability to effect regeneration and multiplicity (i.e., Jaloj-K'exoj) from the death of the original was better applied toward agricultural fecundity. Santiago joins other *bokunab* in the Atiteco pantheon as a fertility deity.

Santiago's integration into the Atiteco religious configuration supports the contention that local "folk Catholicism" derives from a reinterpretation of intrusive elements according to characteristically Mayan paradigms.[9] As demonstrated above, these have been formulated on the basis of everyday experience. All cultures include such empirically based and seemingly self-evident paradigms. From these paradigms are derived secondary and logically consistent postulates. Santiago's "conversion," like other aspects of the local religion (e.g., see Tarn and Prechtel 1990), attests to post-Columbian Atiteco manipulations in these derivative levels of the local culture, manipulations which have led to the elaboration, addition, and subtraction of cultural attributes. In short, the Atitecos have conformed to the general human tendency to attempt to process information according to previous experience, on the grounds of routinized paradigms. Only when these prove inadequate might they be discarded. It must be kept in mind that the competing paradigms carried by the conquering Spanish incorporated the Catholicism of the day, a fanatic expression grounded in a history and a geography distant from the Mayan highlands. Adding to the resulting irrelevance of these paradigms was the fact that the Mayas' place in this Spanish scenario was to be as cultivators of pig food (maize); as wayward desert dwellers—the "lost tribe" of the despised Jews. So discordant were Spanish and indigenous conceptions it is unlikely that paradigms on the order of Jaloj-K'exoj were ever challenged by the Conquest. Rather, the resulting crisis may have been aetiological. A need to explain why the old gods had failed to deter the Conquest would have been answered by the incorporation of the foreign invaders' gods, the saints (Early 1983).

From this perspective, the Mayas' adoption of select elements of Catholicism helped to maintain cultural stability, may actually have had a revitalizing effect, and above all was adaptive. Given, however, that adaptation is a function of environmental disturbance, that such disturbances can overwhelm the adaptive capacity of any social system, and that the Conquest and all that it entailed might be understood as the prime example of such overwhelming environmental disturbance, it must be asked how, in spite of all that has been argued above, could

Mayan culture have retained its stability from the pre-Columbian into the post-Columbian era?

That question underlies much of the following chapter; for the present suffice it to say that the Spanish incursion into Mesoamerica entailed variable degrees of disturbance, with some areas far less affected than others (MacLeod 1973; Orellana 1981, 1984; Lovell 1985; Jones 1989). The economic and geographic marginality of Santiago Atitlán served as a buffer against strong Catholic influence. From 1620 until just a few decades ago the town rarely had a resident priest (Madigan 1976). It is not surprising, therefore, that as late as 1967 only 7.1 percent of the town's population was identified (by the Church) as being Catholic (*Guía de la Iglesia* 1967:343).

Coupled with these kinds of historical circumstances, the ability of some groups of Mayas to regain cultural stability following the shock of the Conquest must also have involved dynamics intrinsic to social systems. Admittedly, in all cases post-Columbian Mayan communities have been subjected to varying degrees of manipulation. Yet it is fallacious to assume that even the toppling of native priesthoods and of indigenous political systems must have led to cultural collapse. To survive, core cultural elements, such as Jaloj-K'exoj, need not be linked to the specific control mechanisms operated by social hierarchies, mechanisms such as creeds or systems of codified laws. To the contrary: The more focal such an element is "the more strongly it is rendered invariant by the aggregate pressure of all the other activities and interests dependent on it" (Nadel 1953:267). In terms of the present study, local modes of production, understandings of lineage, legends, indigenous language, and so on, have formed a pervasive and durable system of nonspecific controls which have buttressed Jaloj-K'exoj. Moreover, the entire Jaloj-K'exoj–centered nexus has in turn provided a mechanism to integrate intrusive elements into Atiteco culture, converting them to a form acceptable to the local Mayan population. We submit that when revealed in their obvious contrast to highland Mayan culture, Hispanic cultural intrusions have triggered indigenous responses which have ultimately resulted in the modification and normalization of the original practices and beliefs.

These dynamics explain what Robert Carmack has called the Mayas' "fierce resistance toward acculturation" (1983:218). One very important element in this process, however, needs to be considered. Although Mayan "fierce resistance" may at first glance seem to be exclusively an activity of the living, in fact the repetitive patterns of the cultural complex represent the equivalent of a memory, by and large founded on past activities of the dead. Through the activities of the society's living members, themselves having been integrated into their culture through normative socialization, the structure and the function of the system embodies its own history. The relationship between the associations of World Tree with kingship and cofradía organization comes to mind. Whether the convergence of symbolism with civil-religious structure represents direct continuity (Early 1983), or not (Chance and Taylor 1985), may not be of vital importance. Even granting the latter interpretation, it has been demonstrated above that Mayan civil-religious structures are institutions which store paradigmatic information, in this case related to Jaloj-K'exoj and symbolized by the World Tree, and are not themselves the source of that information. Given that such information is stored elsewhere in such diverse forms as cited above, direct continuity in particular cultural components is not necessary for indigenous responses to have effected a reworking to the point where pre-Columbian and post-Columbian forms bear a close resemblance.

Throughout much of the post-Columbian period a predominant bias represented in the literature on Mesoamerica reflects Hispanic myths of lazy and childlike Indians. These self-serving ethnic myths have contributed to the assumption that Indians are incapable of taking meaningful and significant action. As a result, the huge indigenous population has, until recently, been highly conspicuous in its near absence from the pages of the historical literature. When Indians have appeared on the printed page they have typically been presented either as the targets of charges of mindless "paganism" or as subjects of paternalistic claims promising to advance them toward a "civilized" state along the liberating path of forced manual labor. Yet, despite conventional history, the indigenous population has not cooperated in an imposition of cultural amnesia. In the case of the Working People of Santiago Atitlán, we have demonstrated that the past can be recorded in ways other than conventional written history. Moreover, we have argued that this alternative recording of the past has been integral to the continuity of local indigenous culture. Drawing for support on recent ethnohistorical research (MacLeod 1973; Carmack 1983; C. Smith 1984; Hill and Monaghan 1987), we submit here that the post-Columbian Mayas have not been the functional equivalents of billiard balls, mindlessly submitting at every historical juncture to the agendas of their European masters. Instead, the Mayas have interacted with their environment as thinking human beings, and they have been largely successful in their cultural adaptations.

PART TWO

*History, Peripherality,
and Social Pluralism*

4

Conquest and Adaptation in Santiago Atitlán

"The [Mayas] do not want anything Spanish, neither religion, doctrine, nor customs."

GUATEMALAN ARCHBISHOP CORTÉS Y LARRAZ (1770)

SCHOLARLY ANALYSES OF THE POST-COLUMBIAN HIGHLAND MAYAS seem to drift effortlessly toward questions of sociocultural continuity and change. Yet, despite the overtly historical nature of the topic, historical detail has not always received enough attention. It is difficult to escape the conclusion that in too many instances assumptions and theory take the lead over historical data. John Hawkins, for example, writes that "the Saussurian perspective of meaning analysis *forces* [my italics] us" to conclude that what might otherwise appear as a unique Mayan culture is really part and parcel of Guatemala's dominant (Hispanic) culture (1984: 12). Fortunately, enough solid research by scholars such as Carmack (1981, 1995), Cambranes (1985), and McCreery (1994) has now accumulated that ahistorical approaches to explicitly historical questions about the Mayas need no longer be turned to.

Building on the previous chapter's largely cognitive approach, which demonstrated *that* significant Mayan cultural aspects survived the Conquest, I continue with a more conventional historical analysis to show *how* this was possible. Two related factors are of particular importance. First, a lack of significant readily exploitable natural resources in highland Guatemala correlated with scant Spanish interest in the region, particularly in the more peripheral areas. Second, in Santiago Atitlán the consequent limits on physical, social, and cultural contact limited the foreigners' capacity to control Atiteco behavior. In Atitlán, as throughout much of highland Guatemala, the resulting autonomy, like the few points of articulation with the Spanish world, was carefully monitored and negotiated by local Mayas.

To provide a baseline against which the change wrought by European contact can be gauged, and ultimately to establish a context in which to evaluate existence in Santiago Atitlán today, I begin by considering institutional aspects of pre-Columbian Atiteco society.[1] Particular consideration is given to variables related to social organization, economic production, and religion. The focus then shifts, first to the Conquest in 1524, and then to the "reconstituted" indigenous culture that was to emerge from that event. Consistent with what has been argued above, I show that the circumstances unleashed by the arrival of the Spaniards were such that extinction of the local culture, as measured in the considered variables, was neither necessitated nor occurred. As exploitative as the interaction with the dominant culture may have been, the people that we now call Atitecos were far from powerless in determining the nature of post-Columbian relations and the course and design of their own existence. Although over time almost no aspect of the local culture was left untouched by contact with Guatemala's dominant sector, reflecting Atiteco adaptive capacity, most cultural components could nonetheless be traced to the pre-Columbian past.[2] Following this discussion, the book continues by explaining that changes in the Atitecos' socioeconomic environment have undermined the stabilizing capacity to integrate and normalize intrusions, with all too evident results.

THE PRE-COLUMBIAN PERIOD
Tz'utujil Political Organization

The literature on pre-Columbian highland Mayan political organization abounds with references to "tribes," "chiefdoms," "kingdoms," and "nations" (e.g., Recinos 1950:171n; Recinos and Goetz 1953:4; Edmonson 1971:155, 156n). While at first glance this might seem to indicate a wide range of regional political types, it often reflects a troublesome lack of consistency in the application of translated terms. In most cases, underlying this verbiage is a single indigenous source word, *chinamit* (or the equivalent *calpul*).[3] One reason for this state of affairs is that indigenous terms for political organization signify rather complicated non-Western constructs. As has been noted by various scholars, even the Mayas' Spanish overlords never did fully understand either pre-Columbian or post-Columbian Mayan social and political organization (MacLeod 1973:29; Lovell 1985:80; Hill and Monaghan 1987:30). As a result, the early Spanish primary sources are themselves generally unclear or in error.

The somewhat complicated nature of earlier forms of highland Mayan political organization, together with the confused historical documentation on the topic, has led to an important scholarly debate. Prefigured some decades ago by Sol Tax (1937:424), this debate questions whether or not linguistic groupings such as K'iche', Kaqchikel, or Tz'utujil also represented pre-Columbian political groupings. Tax's question notwithstanding, it has long been assumed that until the Conquest in 1524, the major highland Mayan language groups corresponded to individual state societies. A related assumption is that the micro "closed corporate" Mayan communities described in the historical records and observed by anthropologists resulted from the devastation of the Conquest. These assumptions are now under question. More recent interpretations argue that the highland Mayan language groupings are just that, and that they never corresponded to unified political groups, in fact, that the closed corporate community was dominant on the political landscape long before the arrival of Europeans. Clearly, a continuity of atomistic polities, rather than the extinction of unified kingdoms, would have considerable implications in gauging the impact of the Conquest.[4] I find that the more recent theories best account for the historical data pertaining to Santiago Atitlán.

Among the scholars who have addressed ancient highland Mayan political organization are Pedro Carrasco[5] (1982a), John Fox (1987), and Robert Hill and John Monaghan (1987). Robert Carmack (1966, 1981), however, was the first to give systematic consideration to the topic, attempting to explicate the indigenous system using social science terminology and theory. Basing his interpretation on the segmentary lineage model identified by Evans-Pritchard for the Nuer of Sudan (1940), Carmack writes that the clans and lineages were "segmented in various arrangements of opposition and dispute" which "would segment during disputes and arguments" as well as "for the administration of important matters" (1966:44). According to Carmack (1981:162), the K'iche' state was structured with "minimal lineages" at the bottom. These would then segment into "principal lineages," which then formed "major lineages," which subsequently formed "moieties." The moieties then formed "groups" which finally segmented into the "kingdom." Carmack, like Carrasco, argues for the exogamous nature of the configuration. Elaborating on Carmack's model, John Fox (1987) reduces emphasis on the higher end of the proposed political organization, the kingdom. Instead, he concerns himself more with lineage autonomy. According to Fox (1987:15), "as the irreducible atom of Quiché [K'iche'] sociopolitical organization, the segmentary lineage was a fundamental landholding corporate body of kinsmen who exhibited unmistakable degrees of autonomy at various levels." He adds that the segmentary lineages would "aggregate into wider alliances as occasions may dictate, after which bonds of unification may [have been] somewhat loosened."

Clearly, the highland Mayan "kingdom" described above was quite different from its Old World counterpart. If nothing else, one is left wondering what happened to the king during the extended periods of loosened bonds. Motivated by anomalies in the segmentary state model, Robert Hill and his colleague John Monaghan (1987) note that the "juxtaposition of these radically different forms of organization [the segmentary lineage and the state] makes this interpretation difficult to accept." Those two scholars focus their study on indigenous conceptions and terms. With the transposed European-based paradigms put aside, they observe that "a cause of persistent difficulty in the study of local, social, and territorial subdivisions has been the use of [foreign] as opposed to native terminology" (1987:11). Hill and Monaghan's study considers the same native unit on which other scholars founded identifications of tribes, lineages, and moieties—the chinamit. The authors argue that chinamits were neither clans nor were they based on kinship or descent, but rather that they constituted landholding units of political organization and social identification (1987:xvii, 35). They note that the presence of a common surname among chinamit members explains both early Spanish and later ethnographic identifications to the contrary, arguing that "the significant criterion of chinamit membership was to be subject to and take the name of a leader" (1987:32). They add that while exogamy was common among chinamit leaders, endogamy was the norm among the rank and file, in fact that the chinamit was both closed and corporate.

Building on their findings about the chinamit, Hill and Monaghan focus on more inclusive levels of political organization, particularly a native unit called *amak* (*amaq*). Following early Spanish mistaken identifications (e.g., Ximénez [c. 1710] 1985:71), this unit is typically identified as a kind of hamlet or dependency (e.g., Orellana 1984:78). Hill and Monaghan, however, identify it as a group of confederated chinamits. They conclude (1987:74) that the amak was probably the most inclusive type of political integration among the highland Mayas of the period. Hence, an overarching state organization which united all the speakers of a given language group did not exist.[6] The authors concede that on occasion, an exceptional leader of a particular chinamit or amak may have exerted disproportionate control, leading to the appearance of more inclusive political organization. Such anomalies were not institutionalized. The bottom line of Hill and Monaghan's argument is that such polities as a K'iche' kingdom, a Kaqchikel kingdom, or a Tz'utujil kingdom never existed.

To date, Sandra Orellana has given the most consideration to political organization among the Tz'utujil-speaking Mayas. Orellana founds her interpretation on unquestioned acceptance of Carmack's model for K'iche' political organization. She argues that a Tz'utujil kingdom was composed of two moieties, the Ajtz'iquinajay and the Tz'utujil, and that these in turn were each made up of various "lineages" (1984:81). A 1563 legal document which mentions a (seemingly pre-Columbian) folio depicting fifteen "lordships" that were dependent on the Ajtz'iquinajay corroborates Orellana's arguments about the dependent groups (see P. Carrasco 1982b:72). As was the custom among the highland Mayas, the names of these lordships simultaneously signified individual chinamits (or calpuls) and the leaders of those organizations. Another document, the 1571 *Relación de los caciques y principales del pueblo de Atitlán*, lists similar information (1952:435). While Orellana is on solid ground in claiming that the Ajtz'iquinajay and the Tz'utujil each comprised various subgroups, her argument that those two entities somehow formed a unified Tz'utujil state is problematic.

Orellana compares the proposed combined Ajtz'iquinajay/Tz'utujil polity to the K'iche'-speaking Tamub. The Tamub was but one of the several groups which, according to Carmack, segmented to form the K'iche' kingdom. Either Orellana is in error, or the Tz'utujil kingdom was not at all equivalent to its purported K'iche' counterpart. Even more problematic is a letter written by the friar Pedro de Betanzos to the King of Spain in 1559 which states that in the pre-Columbian past there had been two independent Tz'utujil polities, almost certainly the Ajtz'iquinajay and the Tz'utujil (P. Carrasco 1982c:51–57). That letter compared the two Tz'utujil groups to four K'iche'-speaking counterparts (the Kavec, Ninhaib, Ahauquiché, and Kalezaquic) and included statement of the sovereignty of those four. Incidentally, *El Título de Totonicapán* identifies three of the four of those K'iche' entities as amaks (Carmack and Mondloch 1983:131). Similarly, *Relación de los caciques y principales del pueblo de Atitlán* establishes that the Ajtz'iquinajay was independent from the Tz'utujil and specifically identifies the latter group as being an amak (1952:435).

Of considerable importance for evaluating ancient political organization is that the relationship between the two Tz'utujil-speaking polities was hostile. *The Annals of the Cakchiquels* states that in 1521 the Tz'utujil amak even succeeded temporarily in expelling the Ajtz'iquinajay from the south lake area (Recinos and Goetz 1953:117). In summary, it appears that then, as now, the primary linkage of the Tz'utujil groups was the common language, not a unified system of political organization. The plural and hostile relationship between the Tz'utujil-speaking polities continued well after the arrival of Europeans.

Tz'utujil Territory

It is possible to assess the limits of the pre-Columbian area held by Tz'utujil speaking groups. Legend has it that before the arrival of several Kaqchikel groups, Lake Atitlán was the exclusive domain of Tz'utujil speakers (Recinos and Goetz 1953:77–78). This legend is supported by the ethnographic evidence. The 1583 *Título de los indios de Santa Clara la Laguna* notes that until the middle of the fifteenth century, the north lake area around Sololá was Tz'utujil (Recinos 1957:172–181). At that time, Sololá, like Panajachel, was probably seized by the K'iche' leader Quikab (Orellana 1973). By the time of the European contact, the Lake Atitlán area had assumed the approximate ethnic configuration that continues to the present, though there would be gradual Kaqchikel encroachment to just east of Tolimán and modest Tz'utujil expansion along the western shore.

The existing documentation is also useful in reconstructing the pre-Columbian lowland boundaries of land held by Tz'utujil speakers. Tz'utujil landholdings in the coastal region lay between the Coyolate and the Nahualate rivers (Orellana 1984:54). Mirroring the events of the period in the lake region, on the eve of contact, the lowland Tz'utujil area was under increasing pressure from Kaqchikel expansion. While at one time the eastern landholdings of Tz'utujil speakers may have bordered territory of the Nahua-speaking Pipils, by the time of the Spanish *entradas* Kaqchikel speakers had seized land to just outside of the eastern Tz'utujil community of Patalul (Orellana 1984:56). To the west, the boundary of the Tz'utujil land was near contemporary San Antonio Suchitepequez. Following the Conquest and into the early seventeenth century the boundaries of the former pre-Conquest Tz'utujil landholdings remained largely intact, though that landholding configuration was gradually to change (Orellana 1984:133). In part, those changes reflected shifting boundaries with non Tz'utujil-speaking Mayan neighbors. The most significant factor, however was population loss due to epidemics. In fact, that loss would eventually lead to the virtual abandonment of the coastal

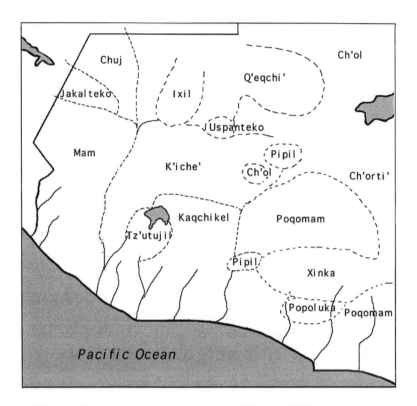

10. This map depicts the approximate boundaries of Guatemala's language groups as they existed at the time of Spanish contact. (Based on Miles 1983.)

area by Tz'utujil speakers.[7] In contrast, around Lake Atitlán, where the effects of disease were not as severe, population pressure eventually even led to the creation of at least one new Tz'utujil-speaking community, Santa María la Visitación.

As indicated above, pre-Columbian Tz'utujil landholding patterns were associated with chinamits and/or amaks. While land around present-day Santiago Atitlán was certainly included in chinamit holdings, the best documented descriptions are for the coastal and piedmont regions. For instance, in 1571, the *Relación de los caciques y principales del pueblo de Atitlán* noted that the two Tz'utujil amaks maintained possession of the locations which, after the Conquest, were named San Bartolomé, San Andrés, San Francisco, and Santa Barbara (1952:435). According to the document, those areas surrendered tribute to the amaks. A 1563 document cited by Pedro Carrasco contains similar information (P. Carrasco 1982b:72). Unfortunately, the existing documentation does not allow a comprehensive reconstruction of which Tz'utujil areas were aligned with which particular chinamits or amaks.

PRE-COLUMBIAN TZ'UTUJIL PRODUCTION

Describing pre-Columbian highland Mayan agriculture, *The Annals of the Cakchiquels* (Recinos and Goetz 1953:81) states "it was then that we began to sow our corn. We cut down the trees, we burned them, and we sowed the seed." Clearly, the Mayas of the period utilized swidden technology (slash and burn) for the production of maize. According to Carmack (1981:87), the K'iche' Mayas used a form of hatchet (*ikaj*) and hoe (*xoquem*) to clear the land. Contemporary findings around Santiago Atitlán of similar ground stone tools are fairly common and confirm swidden use in that area (see S. Lothrop 1933:26, 87). The 1585 *Relación de Santiago Atitlán* states that local agricultural products included plums, zapotes, avocados, beans, squash, tomatoes and chile (Betancor and Arboleda 1964:95, 103). It is likely that fish and crab from the lake were harvested, as well, perhaps with sod traps (as shown in S. Lothrop 1928: 392) and/or basketry traps (as depicted in McBryde 1947:Plate 22d).

It was maize, however, that was by far the most important component of the local diet. As Carmack notes (1981:87), the pre-Columbian highland Mayas (like their contemporary descendants) used maize in a multitude of food products, including tortillas, tamales, gruels, and beverages. It is significant that the *Relación de Santiago Atitlán* states that because of the "sterile" land around the town only a little maize was produced locally, therefore it had to be imported (Betancor and Arboleda 1964:95). Yet, as I noted earlier, the soils around Santiago Atitlán are naturally rich; the condition of the soils written about by Betancor and Arboleda apparently reflected damage due to overuse. Given that the population at contact may have approached 50,000 (Madigan 1976: 177), higher than it is today, pressure to maximize local maize production would have depleted the soil. That situation is being replicated today.

A primary source of imported goods was the lowland area, which provided tribute to the Tz'utujil amaks. The *Descripción de San Bartolomé* (1585), which describes a rich lowland Tz'utujil holding about fifteen miles from Atitlán by way of the Chicacao road, cites that area's fertile farmlands (Betancor and Arboleda 1965:266). According to that document, the area annually produced three maize harvests. In addition to maize, other lowland Tz'utujil commodities brought to Atitlán included honey, feathers, and cotton, the latter woven into clothing in the highlands (*Relación de los caciques* 1952:435; Betancor and Arboleda

1964:104). Perhaps the most important agricultural product of the low-land region was cacao. Not only was cacao used to prepare a beverage, but it was a primary commodity of trade as well. Moreover, as Betancor and Arboleda note (1965:266), it also served as the monetary standard. It is notable that following the Conquest, most of the cacao groves were retained by the Mayas, though much of the harvest in one way or another was transferred to the Spaniards as tribute. This pattern continued largely intact until demographic collapse led to the Mayas' large-scale abandonment of the lowland piedmont region (MacLeod 1973:87; Lutz and Lovell 1990:40).

PRE-COLUMBIAN RELIGION

In the previous chapter I showed that the Jaloj-K'exoj paradigm, which in contemporary Western culture would be categorized as "religious," permeated and integrated otherwise disparate socioeconomic elements of ancient and contemporary Mayan culture. In fact, it is difficult and somewhat artificial to abstract a category "religion" from its greater context in Atiteco culture, as evidenced by the lack of a Tz'utujil word for "religion." Recognizing this limitation, I discuss several aspects of ancient Atiteco culture which pertain either to distinctly religious structure or to characteristically religious ritual.

Mirroring the political landscape of pre-Columbian highland Guatemala, the pantheon of the various polities was atomistic. As cases in point, the *Relación de Santiago Atitlán* mentions the Ajtz'iquinajay god Kaquibuk (Betancor and Arboleda 1964:98), and the *Descripción de San Bartolomé del Partido de Atitlán* states that San Bartolomé, a lowland Tz'utujil town, had a primary god named Ziuateutl (Betancor and Arboleda 1965:269). This sort of particularism in the Tz'utujil region was characteristic of the central Guatemalan highlands in general. In the *Historia de la Provincia de San Vicente de Chiapa* Ximénez writes about the tendency for individual *parcialidades* in the region (*parcialidad* is the Spanish word for *amak* and *chinamit* alike) to have their own "idols" ([c. 1730] 1977 1:45). In fact, the Tz'utujil area seems to have been in conformity with a widespread pattern in Mesoamerica as a whole. Writing about the Aztec counterpart of the chinamit, the *calpulli*, Alfredo López Austin observes that "the most cohesive force for the *calpulli* was the belief in a patron deity, the *calpulteotl*. . . . Those in the group were born under the shelter and the power of this god" (1980: 1 77–78). In the Guatemalan highlands, the patron deity of a chinamit sometimes had its own temple staffed with its own priests (Carmack 1981:162).

This leads to another important characteristic of pre-Columbian Me-

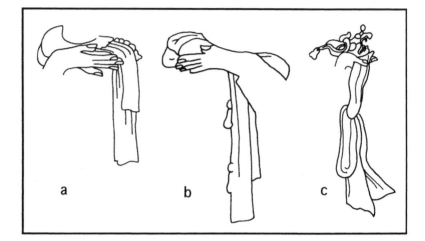

11. *The antiquity and importance of bundle cults in the Mayan area is underscored by numerous late Classic period (c. A.D. 600–900) depictions. Representations a and b are from Palenque, while representation c is from Bonampak. (From Schele and Miller 1983.)*

soamerican religion. López Austin writes that "the power of this deity [the *calpulteotl*] was centered in an effigy and in the rare contents of a bundle carried by the priests." For the Mayas, the importance of bundles can be established back to the Classic period, where bundles had an association with "kings," even with the "burden of office" glyph (Schele and Miller 1986:72; Freidel et al. 1993:416). The cult is also described in both of the Post-Classic texts *Popol Vuh* (D. Tedlock 1985:198) and *El Título de Totonicapán* (Carmack and Mondloch 1983:185). The specific bundle written about in those texts was named Pizom Gagal (Bundle of Flames) and was associated with the Kavec amak as well as with human lineage.

Representing a most significant continuity with the pre-Columbian past, the bundle cult remains very much alive in the Atiteco cofradía system.[8] The antiquity of the cult is demonstrated by the age of the cloth of some bundles, cloth which predates existing Guatemalan textiles in the world's museum collections. In most cases (perhaps all), Atiteco cofradía bundles have a symbolic association with both human and agricultural fertility, as indicated in the names for the two bundles located in Cofradía San Juan, Heart of Food and Water (R'kux R'way Ya) and Heart of the Placenta (R'kux Alaniem). Atiteco cofradía bundles constitute the heart (*r'kux*) of a more inclusive deity (another aspect of which

12. *The most important of the sacred bundles in Atitlán is located in Cofradía San Juan. Though that bundle has various esoteric names, including calendrical identifications, its public name is simply Martín. Martín is a* bokunab, *a category of deity which underlies human, plant, and animal fertility. As shown above, Martín can only be danced by its personal bundle priest, the* nabeysil. *(Photograph by Paul Harbaugh, 1988.)*

may be embodied by a "saint's" image located on the cofradía altar). In what probably represents direct continuity with the pre-Columbian past, Atiteco bundles are associated with a priesthood. In Atitlán, bundle priests are called *nabeysils* and are the technicians of their bundle's power. Certainly one of the most interesting cofradía positions in all of Guatemala, this sacerdotal position requires celibacy and is theoretically held until either death or retirement in old age.

Primary historical sources allow the reconstruction of aspects of ancient highland Mayan rituals. For instance, Roman (in Ximénez 1977: 89; also see Early 1983) states that the ancient highland Mayas would "decorate their idols for fiestas with much gold and jewels, wrapping them with numerous richly decorated cloths. They would then put the idols on litters and, accompanied by music, parade them through the streets." Roman (in Ximénez 1977: 94) states that fiestas included dances in front of the idols and that for ritual reasons the *principales* were often compelled to become drunk. These descriptions bear a remarkable similarity to both the Colonial and contemporary cofradía, an institution reportedly "so perverted, that piety is converted into pernicious tyranny, saintliness into interest and greed, and sacredness into sensuality and drunkenness" (van Oss 1986:110, from a 1740 document). Similarly, in 1690 Fuentes y Guzman wrote that "in the prohibited dances they tell of the histories and acts of their ancestors and of their false and lying gods" (1932–1933 1:212). Dances such as the Deer-Jaguar dance, which no doubt would have received comparable reviews, continue to be performed in Atitlán.

Another aspect of considerable importance in the local Mayan religion was human sacrifice. The *Relación de Santiago Atitlán*, for instance, states that ceremonies to Kaquibuk included cutting open a human victim's chest and then burning the victim's blood in censers (Betancor and Arboleda 1964:99). The document also mentions the prevalence of autosacrifice. Likewise, the *Popol Vuh* is clear that the highland Mayas, including Tz'utujil groups, engaged in human and (nonlethal) autosacrifice.[9] Birds, food, and even cotton could be objects of sacrifice (Orellana 1981:163). The historical sources indicate several motives behind sacrifice, including propitiation of the gods and/or the fueling of human and agricultural fertility. While lethal human sacrifice survives in Santiago Atitlán only in legends, and then in a negative context, primary sources suggest that such sacrifices were performed by Atitecos long after the Conquest (Cortés y Larraz 1958 2:280.) As is indicated in the title "Working People," a concept of sacrifice as a means of promoting fertility and the continuity of existence underlies Atiteco cofradía ritual to the present.

To restate an earlier point, given the tight symbolic bonds of Tz'utujil culture, to the members of its subscribing community the component parts were probably not reducible into discrete units, as delineated above. Through Jaloj-K'exoj and similar cultural avenues, local modes of production, understandings of lineage and territory, legends, indigenous language, and so on, have formed an adaptive cultural nexus, the integrating elements of which were at once stored in the component

13. The Deer-Jaguar dance in Santiago Atitlán reenacts a mythological account of the death of Wind Jaguar at the hands of an Atiteco demigod (Nawal Acha). Although it cannot be determined if the myth is entirely of pre-Conquest derivation, major elements of it certainly are. (Photograph by the author, 1990.)

parts and hidden in the collective mind of the cultural community. Importantly, "any ideology is powerful to the extent that it hides itself in the unmarked reflexes of everyday life, and vulnerable to the extent that it becomes open to scrutiny and argument" (Comaroff and Comaroff 1991:78). Determined as they may have been to undermine the very cultural foundations of the highland Mayas, the Spaniards who invaded the Lake Atitlán region were to be confronted by a functioning culture which would prove far more durable and impenetrable than the area's fortified cities.

THE POST-COLUMBIAN PERIOD
THE "CONQUEST" OF ATITLÁN

Unlike the legendary siege of the Aztec capital Tenochtitlán (Díaz del Castillo [1568] 1968), or even the sack of the K'iche' citadel Kumarakaah (D. Tedlock 1985), the Tz'utujil defeat in April 1524 by the Spanish forces under Pedro de Alvarado was a rather ignoble affair.[10] That incident, which lasted mere hours, is best described by Fuentes y Guzman (1932– 1933). The following summary is based on his account.

While there is no evidence that the highland Mayas mistook the Spaniards for gods, as had the Aztecs (D. Carrasco 1982), they must nonetheless have been awed by tales of the approaching conquerors' military prowess. This did not, however, keep those people that we now call Atitecos from killing four messengers sent by Alvarado to attempt a negotiated settlement. No doubt only further motivated by this incident, Alvarado and an army composed of some sixty horsemen, one hundred and fifty foot soldiers, and several thousand Indian allies advanced on Atitlán. Although Fuentes y Guzman writes that Alvarado's Indian auxiliaries were primarily Kaqchikel speakers, as shown in Panel 28 of the *Lienzo de Tlaxcala* some of the Tlaxcalans who accompanied Alvarado from central Mexico must also have been included. Arriving from the east to an area just outside present-day Atitlán, the Spanish Army encountered the defenders in entrenched positions. Yet attacks by Spanish crossbowmen quickly flushed the defenders from their positions, where once in the open they made easy targets for the advancing force. Taking flight, the defenders jumped into the lake and attempted to swim to an island. By that time, however, the Spaniards' Kaqchikel allies in some three hundred canoes had arrived and quickly dispatched many of the fleeing Mayas.

A general surrender was negotiated the following day. Yet, as the area was poor in readily exploitable resources, the Spaniards quickly departed to pursue other adventures. Meanwhile, the local population was left to carry on much as it had before the Conquest. The Tz'utujil speakers retained possession of their land, their leaders (foreheads hardly dry from baptism), still in power. For instance, the leader of the Ajtz'iquinajay at the time of contact was Voo Noh Quicap, later baptized Don Pedro (perhaps after Pedro de Alvarado), who remained the leader of that amak. This type of hit-and-run military campaign was typical for the Guatemalan highlands, and has led to the observation that the conquest of the region bears "more resemblance to a large raid than to an occupation" (MacLeod 1973:47).

LIMITING AND GUIDING FACTORS IN THE SOCIOCULTURAL EVOLUTION OF SANTIAGO ATITLÁN

Santiago Atitlán suffered its own painful birth in 1547, twenty-three years after contact. At that time, Spanish forces "congregated" several Tz'u-

14. From the "Lienzo de Tlaxcala," this figure depicts the defeat of Atitlán in 1524. This representation, by Diodoro Serrano, was made in the middle of the last century from an original copy of the Lienzo. As with the two other original copies of the Lienzo, the manuscript on which Serrano based his work has been lost. As is shown, the forces of Pedro de Alvarado in his assault of Atitlán were composed of both Spaniards and their Indian allies.

tujil speaking chinamits and amaks onto the site of the contemporary community. Soon after its *congregación*, Atitlán became the focus of a spasm of Spanish activity. By then, the meager gold reserves in the central highlands had given out, driving the Spaniards to scramble for a replacement commodity. That search culminated in the discovery of an ancient New World agricultural product, cacao (MacLeod 1973:80-96). Some of the fledgling colony's richest cacao holdings were in the lowland Tz'utujil area, hence Atitlán was established as a regional administrative center. While this was no doubt a period of considerable social disruption for the Atitecos, that turmoil would be short-lived. Scarcely two decades after the inception of the cacao boom, competition from elsewhere in the empire turned boom into bust, with profound conse-

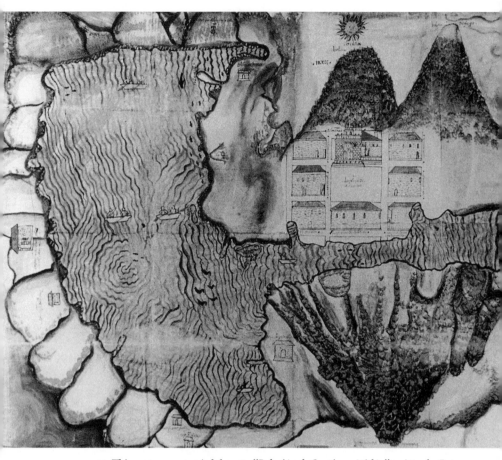

15. This map accompanied the 1585 "Relación de Santiago Atitlán" written by Betancor and Arboleda. Prominently depicted is Santiago Atitlán as it existed several decades after its reducción to its current location. Reducción was a process in which the Spanish forced dispersed communities to move to a central location, thus forming a new town. (Courtesy of the Benson Latin American Collection, University of Texas at Austin.)

quences for local cultural evolution. Certainly not the least significant was the abandonment of Atitlán's regional administrative activities.

Socioeconomic Peripherality

For the Spanish, the Conquest was a maximizing capitalist venture, hence "being entrepreneurs, lay Spaniards were drawn to areas where environmental conditions or natural endowments would maximize material enrichment" (Lutz and Lovell 1990:36). Accordingly, a correlation existed between colonizing intensity and the wealth that an area possessed, with those areas lacking precious metals tending to receive scant attention. Significantly, in Guatemala only a few areas possessed known reserves of such resources, and even those were soon depleted (MacLeod 1973). As exemplified by cacao, attempts to find substitutes were seldom successful. Within decades of contact, Guatemala had become an economic backwater in the emerging world economic system, a status that has proven durable. Many of the first Spaniards in the area were eventually to pursue their lust for wealth elsewhere. Others settled into one of several Spanish population centers in Guatemala, where most managed only to scratch out meager existences.

The Colony quickly settled into a configuration of relative economic cores and peripheries (Lutz and Lovell 1990). Yet, considering the economic reality of Guatemala as a whole, core status in that configuration actually entailed being the core of a periphery in the world economic system. As shown in Figure 16, Atitlán lay squarely in the Colony's economic periphery. While throughout the history of the Colony there existed economic fluctuations, the general trend was toward even greater peripheralization, to the point that Guatemala was eventually abandoned "by not only most commercial houses, but by the Crown itself" (Wortman 1975:251). This fact is thrown into high relief by figures on the Colony's ship traffic with Europe, its primary connection to the outside world. In the seventeenth century, fully a decade might pass without a single such ship putting in to Guatemala's port in the Gulf of Honduras (MacLeod 1973:382). Similarly, from 1729 to 1751 only two ships arrived from Europe (Wortman 1975:255).

No doubt adding to Atitlán's peripherality was the Colony's population decline. The primary source of exploitable wealth in Guatemala was (and continues to be) indigenous labor. As such, catastrophic decline in Mayan population levels due to European-introduced diseases contributed to socioeconomic peripheralization throughout much of the Colony. In its extreme manifestations, that decline would lead to the extinction of entire lowland communities. At the same time, however, it contributed to the Spaniards' loss of interest in distant rural areas, in that way reducing acculturative pressure on the surviving indigenous population. Importantly, in places like south Lake Atitlán where the immediate pre-Columbian population had seemingly outstripped the local carrying capacity, European diseases seem to have restored a more sustainable ecological balance. Ironically, in Atitlán the conquerors' germs may actually have contributed to Mayan cultural survival.

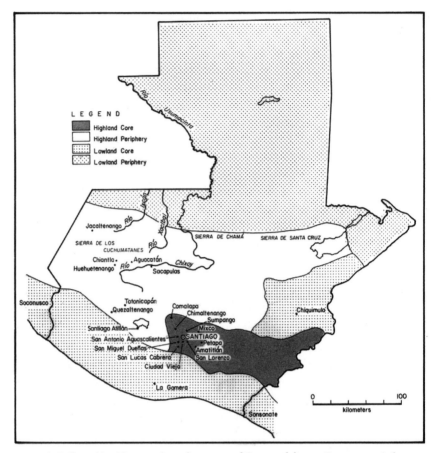

16. As indicated in this map, throughout most of Guatemala's post-Conquest period, Santiago Atitlán lay in a socioeconomic periphery of the highland region. (From Lutz and Lovell 1990, modified by Carlsen.)

A fundamental requirement of Atiteco cultural survival was the accommodation of Spanish demands for tribute payments, which in the Lake Atitlán area were begun by 1528 (Orellana 1984:114) and were primarily in the form of cacao (MacLeod 1973:129).[11] Following contact, the initial form of Spanish exploitation of the indigenous population was known as *encomienda*. In its simplest form, the term *encomienda* indicates a granted right to Indian tribute. It was *not* a land grant. Most often encomienda served as an economic reward for the efforts of the conquerors. Madigan points out that in Atitlán, as elsewhere in the Colony, during the span of approximately one century in which encomienda was viable, the institution evolved through distinct phases (1976:65-69). He notes that the first *encomenderos* probably viewed this institution as a means of achieving rapid wealth and upward mobility. Accordingly, the initial period of encomienda corresponded to large-scale and unregulated exploitation. The second phase, according to Madigan, saw increased restrictions, and even certain obligations, placed on the encomenderos. Finally, in the seventeenth century, *encomienda* came to signify "little more than a modest pension plan for colonists incapable of providing for themselves."

After the conquest, Pedro de Alvarado assigned to himself one-half of the area around what would become Santiago Atitlán and its dependent tributaries as part of his personal encomienda. The other half was assigned to Pedro de Cueto (*Relación de los caciques* 1952:437). De Cueto's encomienda soon passed to Sancho de Barahona. Demonstrating his notorious audacity, Alvarado unsuccessfully attempted to seize Barahona's half and give it to his brother (Sherman 1969:205). Eventually, the Crown was to annex Alvarado's Atitlán encomienda. The Crown and the Barahona family subsequently retained encomienda rights over Atitlán until the early part of the seventeenth century, when the Crown assumed full rights to the area (Madigan 1976:68). By that time, the system of encomienda had for all practical purposes given way to *repartimiento*, in this case an exploitative mechanism whereby demands were placed on a town for a certain number of workers each month.

Even tribute in Guatemala was subject to the constraints of the Colony's core and periphery configuration. Specifically, tribute discriminated geographically in that "the nearer a village was to a major Spanish city or agricultural settlement the more subject it would be to the pressures of the labor draft" (MacLeod 1973:295). In comparison with the Indian communities near the capital, Santiago de los Caballeros (contemporary Antigua), repartimiento in Atitlán was considerably less abusive. In his demographic history of the area, Madigan argues that repartimiento was viewed by rural communities such as Atitlán as a tolerable pay-off to deter Spanish meddling in the community's internal affairs (1976:241–242). The author acknowledges the class implications of this situation, pointing out that summons for repartimiento labor were sent to town leaders. Few indigenous leaders registered themselves to fulfill the labor obligations.

Equally important in the assessment of Guatemalan tribute is that it was subject to the fluctuations of the Colony's unstable economy. In short, there was an inverse relationship between the health of the economy and the demands placed on the indigenous population. Accordingly, the region's Mayan communities often "flourished more in bad times for the Spanish economy, and vice versa" (MacLeod 1983:

208). Although the relaxation of demands on Mayan labor would have theoretically freed that labor for expenditure within the local communities, the Indian and Spanish economies may not have been that closely linked. Despite economic fluctuations in the dominant sector, the minimizing economies of the Mayan communities would have remained largely static. This is indicated by the *barlovento* (lit., "source of the wind"), or "Indian tax," which was a tax received in Guatemala City on goods bought from and sold to Indians. Figures studied by Miles Wortman show a fairly consistent level over time of that tax, suggesting that the "Indian economy was only marginally affected by the fluctuations in Creole commerce" (1975:273–274, 286). Once again, social pluralism between the Colony's two primary ethnic sectors is evident.

Political Ecology

Key to the cultural configuration which was to emerge in Santiago Atitlán was the Atitecos' political organization. It is highly significant that the base unit of pre-Columbian indigenous political organization, the chinamit, continued as the base unit of post-Columbian indigenous political organization. The amak structure was to survive the Conquest as well. Not only did the leader of the Ajtz'iquinajay amak at the time of contact, Voo Noh Quicap (Don Pedro), continue as leader of the amak, but for several generations his descendants followed in line (P. Carrasco 1982b:73). Although the Spanish use of native rulers in indigenous political administration may at first have been informal, in 1542, the "New Laws," propagated by Charles V and inspired by the Dominican friar Bartolomé de Las Casas, gave legal sanction to the practice (MacLeod 1973; Wasserstrom 1983:16–21). As late as 1681, the publication of the "Laws of the Indies" (*Recopilación de las leyes de los Reynos de las Indias*) reinforced that status (García Añoveros 1987:101–126).[12]

Despite the survival of Tz'utujil chinamits, local political organization certainly underwent significant transformation. It is clear that *congregación* was largely ineffective in the integration of the various chinamits. Instead, throughout highland Guatemala, many chinamits continued to adhere to what Lovell (1985:80) calls "aboriginal patterns of discrimination" (also see Hill 1984, 1989; C. Smith 1984; Hill and Monaghan 1987). Rather than townships, the resulting settlement pattern was more an accumulation of chinamits existing in forced proximity. Post-Columbian Atitlán was consistent with that pattern.

In 1609 there were eighteen chinamits (calpuls) in Atitlán (Orellana 1984:176). Interestingly, most of the chinamit leaders signed documents with the Spanish title *don*, demonstrating their descent from pre-

Columbian royalty. Of particular importance is that the far from congenial relations between the pre-Columbian chinamits and amaks continued well after contact. This is evident from a 1563 document studied by Pedro Carrasco (1982b), the basis of which is a lawsuit brought by the Tz'utujil amak ("parcialidad") against the Ajtz'iquinajay amak ("parcialidad"). Claiming that they had always been separate from the Ajtz'iquinajay, the Tz'utujil demanded a reinstitution of what they felt to be their declining economic and political sovereignty. That the litigation was won by the Tz'utujil is highly significant for the determination of both the pre-Columbian and post-Columbian relationships between those two amaks.

The Spaniards' tolerance of Mayan political organization raises several considerations. First, the structure helped the Crown, which lacked Spanish administrators, implement its agenda. In Atitlán, for instance, chinamits directed tribute-raising activities, such as repartimiento. (Madigan 1976:242; Orellana 1984:230). Yet to hold that the Spaniards forced chinamits on the indigenous population would be to ignore the numerous historical data which show Mayan enthusiasm for the institution. In fact, the institution was symbiotic. While the Spanish used the structure to further their own ends, Mayan leaders employed it in means that were distinctly anti-Spanish, and certainly self-serving. In 1770 Archbishop Cortés y Larraz wrote that chinamit leaders routinely spread rumors that the Spaniards were deceivers, and that the religion of their own Mayan ancestors was the true religion. He added that whatever the chinamit leaders demanded, whether it be to engage in idolatry, to avoid mass, or to ignore Christian doctrine, the Mayas eagerly heeded (1958 2:173; also see García Añoveros 1987:94).

Religious Ecology
Guatemala's increasing global peripheralization and its resulting internal core-periphery social configuration had a direct impact on the religious instruction and administration of the rural Mayan population. MacLeod writes that a feature of the late sixteenth and early seventeenth centuries was "a gradual change in the geographical distribution of the secular and regular clergy . . . we find more and more of the clergy living in the Spanish towns, or in the fairly ladinoized villages near them, and correspondingly fewer living and proselytizing in the poorer, remoter, and higher Indian villages" (1973:230).

Fully two decades after the Conquest, the total monastic population in the Colony was just four Mercedarians, four to six Franciscans, and perhaps eleven Dominicans (van Oss 1986:14). By 1555, however, the

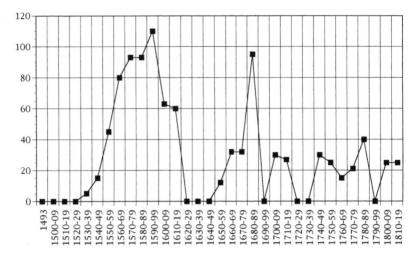

17. *The number of Catholic missionaries who arrived in Guatemala by decade.* *(Source: van Oss 1986:8.)*

Colony could count six Mercedarians, thirty-seven Franciscans, and forty-seven Dominicans. As shown in Figure 17, this rise in the number of clerics continued until near 1600. Nonetheless, a movement of the clergy to Spanish population centers was underway. Importantly, this reshifting of clerics soon gave way to a dramatic net loss in their numbers. By 1620, the number of new missionaries sent to Guatemala fell to near zero. While this situation no doubt reflected economic vicissitude, it also corresponded to a loss of evangelical fervor. According to David Carrasco (1982:17), the first missionaries to the New World "were driven by an especially intense spiritual vision. They wanted to establish a new world and new church in America that would imitate the primitive church of the Apostles of Christ." In the jargon of the day, they sought to create the "New Jerusalem." [13] Within a few decades of contact, however, financial limitations, as well as the Indians' refusal to cooperate in the priests' otherworldly ambitions, had dashed such enthusiasm. Just a few short decades after having arrived in Guatemala, the Church, by and large, conceded to most rural areas their religious peculiarities.

Santiago Atitlán was entirely consistent with this pattern. In conjunction with the town's establishment as a regional administrative center, a Franciscan monastery had been built (Madigan 1976:58). Given the presence of the monastics, that must have been a period of intense proselytization. [14] However, with the rapid bust in the cacao market, Atitlán's monastery went into decay, and was eventually abandoned (Madigan 1976:60). That abandonment would underscore the Church's involvement with the Atitecos for centuries to come.

While the parish history of Santiago Atitlán is not complete, historical records indicate that by 1638 the physical condition of the church had deteriorated to the point that financial help was requested for its reconstruction. Reportedly, the church's wood was rotten and its walls were broken in places (Orellana 1984:200). Reflecting the Church's near-abandonment of the rural areas, almost a century later, in 1735, the requested financial help had yet to be received. Although it is likely that during this period there were times when the parish was without a priest (O'Brien 1975:20), when Archbishop Cortés y Larraz conducted his survey of the dioceses in 1770, Miguel Medina was in residence (Cortés y Larraz 1958 2:280). Within a few years, however, the Atitlán parish was to be abandoned. Until 1964, when the parish was adopted by the archdiocese of Oklahoma City, the clerical presence in the town would be limited to periodic visits by roving priests. Incidentally, Medina reported to Cortés y Larraz that despite their tendency toward drunkenness and lust, and an aversion to attending mass, the Atitecos of the day displayed few serious problems of morality. In his report on Atitlán, Cortés y Larraz noted rumors of human sacrifice in the area.

From the outset of the post-Columbian period, a dearth of Spaniards, compounded by a preference for the company of their own countrymen, insured a high degree of Mayan religious self-administration. About the use of Indian auxiliaries in the administration of religion, Adriaan van Oss (1986:21–22) writes that "by approaching the conversion of Indian communities through their traditional leaders, missionaries insured that the persons who played an active role in the establishment of the new cult, for example as sacristans, acolytes, catechists, etc., would in many cases be exactly the same individuals who before the conversion had occupied comparable positions in the spiritual life of the community, with obvious implications for the kind of Christian observance which took root."

Central to the "Christianity" that took root in Atitlán, in fact to the evolution of Atiteco society in general, was the Spanish introduction of cofradías. In their orthodox form, cofradías are religious sodalities dedicated to a particular Catholic saint. It was hoped that the New World cofradías would be similar to those of the Old World, where the institution had existed since at least A.D. 1151 (Foster 1953:12). Introduced into Guatemala by 1527 (Rojas Lima 1988:59), cofradías were intended to facilitate the Indians' integration into the Church and to serve as mechanisms for the collection of revenues from the indigenous population.

While the former motivation proved to be a failure, the latter was to be significant. Specifically, the priests came to rely on the funds paid by cofradías for the saying of mass on saints' days. Importantly, in many cases the priests, who were often itinerant and living in distant towns, neither had direct control over the cofradía funds nor over the amount of the stipend received (e.g., García Añoveros 1987:69). It is not surprising that throughout the Mayan area, indigenous leaders came to utilize cofradía funds as an instrument of barter with the priests, in fact to buy a degree of cultural autonomy (MacLeod 1973, 1983; Farriss, 1984, writes of the same strategy for the lowland Mayas). According to MacLeod, "one is led to suppose that these cofradías existed, at least in part, to provide bribes or presents to potentially intrusive outsiders." If a priest refused to be "bought off" he might well "face protests, appeals to the *audiencia* from the Indian community, refusals to pay, or even attacks on his person" (1983:192). Importantly, in this way cofradía barter maximized the peripheralization already underway in the rural Guatemalan hinterlands.

Because cofradía payments came to be a primary source of clerical income, the Church would not aggressively attempt to regulate the institution (e.g., van Oss 1986:111). More important, to attempt to have done so would have risked Spanish loss of control over the Colony's Mayan population. Cortés y Larraz, for instance, stated that tampering with the cofradías would have led to indigenous revolts, the Mayas' wholesale abandoning of their towns, as well as their disowning of the very name "Christian" (in García Añoveros 1987:72). The archbishop cited an incident in Sololá in which suppression of the local cofradía system led the Kaqchikel population to abandon the church and refuse even to have their children baptized until the Church had reversed its policy. This incident is particularly significant in that it exposes Mayan subterfuge and demonstrates purposeful resistance to the dominant culture.

Just as notable as cofradía barter was what MacLeod identifies as its "barrier" function (1973:328). As the cofradía system was ostensibly Catholic, as long as idolatrous gear was kept from sight the system was on the whole at least minimally acceptable to the Church. Which is certainly not to say that "idolatry" disappeared. To the contrary, it flourished, and in important ways, the cofradía system offered the platform for that survival. On the one hand, enough of the accouterments of Catholicism were present in the cofradías to deflect Spanish intervention. Yet this barrier provided a venue for the celebration of distinctly non-

Catholic ritual. This was engineered in one of two ways. First, conforming to what Nancy Farriss terms the "chameleon nature" of Mayan gods
(1984:313), the saints lining the walls and altars of the cofradías and parishes in many cases merely came to represent aspects of far more inclusive Mayan deities. According to Farriss, "the addition of one more guise
to the multiple permutations each deity already possessed would hardly
have fazed the Maya theologians." Images might also merely be carted
off to nearby caves, or simply hidden in the cofradías and parishes (e.g.,
Gage [1648] 1958:281).

Various stone images, at least several of definitively pre-Columbian
origin, are of considerable importance in Atiteco cofradías even today.
One image, so notorious that several decades ago it was stolen by Catholics and never returned, offers an interesting case. That image, typically
referred to as simply the "stone of the brujos" (Mendelson 1956:43), was
used by Atiteco shamans (*aj'kuna*) in a technique called *yol chay*, or
"giving the obsidian." *Yol chay* is prescribed for curing the "bad blood"
of a pulse area, and entails bloodletting using obsidian flakes (Douglas
1969:157–158; Carlsen and Prechtel 1994:94–98). Although in most
cases the actual bloodletting is performed in a patient's house, the blood
may be extracted in Cofradía San Nicolás. Resonating with a chameleon
nature, Aklax, a.k.a. San Nicolás, is the patron deity of *aj'kuna*, and in
fact is sometimes referred to as simply Chay, which means obsidian.
Traditionally, the *yol chay* blood was eventually removed to a location
near the back edge of the town, where the shaman poured it into the
mouth of the stone image. Since this image was stolen, a cave located
behind the town cemetery has served for the disposal of "bad blood."

Despite the barrier function, Spanish complaints about cofradía
activities were legion and flow from the pages of the chronicles and
documents of the Colonial period. Orellana (1984:213), for instance,
cites a 1637 document stating that:

> [I]n view of the growing number of cofradías in Indian towns
> and of the excesses committed during dances and feasts cele-
> brated during the day of the patron saint, it is ordered in the
> confines of the Audiencia . . . that all cofradías not authorized
> by the bishops be suppressed . . . for the offenses which are
> made against God our Lord with drunkenness and feasts which
> are celebrated the day and night of the fiesta when it is custom-
> ary for many drunken Indians to gather together in the house
> of the Indian *mayordomo* of the cofradía . . . where with dances
> and fiestas they recall their antiquity and idolatry.

18. *Certainly one of Atitlán's more interesting cofradías is the private Cofradía San Martín. San Martín is owned by the family of the last of Atitlán's great prophets, Aplas Soguel. A most interesting aspect of this cofradía is its abundance of stone figurines, which some critics would no doubt identify as "idols." For centuries, this sort of cofradía ritual paraphernalia has triggered Catholic condemnation. (Photograph by the author, 1988.)*

19. Perhaps the most important religious object in Cofradía Ch'eep San Juan is this pre-Conquest jaguar, generally simply called Tigre. (Photograph by the author, 1991.)

Similarly, in 1648 the apostate Catholic priest Thomas Gage wrote of highland Mayan cofradías, "they yield unto the Popish religion, especially to the worshipping of saints' images, because they look upon them as much like unto their forefathers' idols" (1958:234).[15] And nearly a century and a half later Cortés y Larraz noted that "upon leaving the church, the *cofrades* gather in the house of the *mayordomo*, where there is food and liquor . . . they eat and drink until drunk, and they have their music and dances called '*funes*' or '*zarabandas*,' and they pass all the day and night in grave excesses" (in García Añoveros 1987:72).[16]

ASSESSING ATITECO CONQUEST AND ADAPTATION

The conquest of Mesoamerica was a highly varied process, with some areas being affected far more than others. At the time, highland Guatemala was dominated by culturally sophisticated and functioning societies, and was not otherwise disposed to momentous sociocultural change.

20. *It might be difficult to find a clearer depiction of the "chameleon nature" of Atiteco saint/deities than the San Juan in Cofradía San Juan. Adorned with the characteristic cofradía headcloth (x'kajkoj zut), the "saint" is holding a baby lamb (a characteristic of Saint John the Baptist). Upon closer inspection, however, the lamb can be seen to have black spots and whiskers, as well as fangs protruding from its mouth. In fact, it is no lamb at all, but a baby jaguar. Consistent with the widespread "conversion" of the saints in Atitlán, Saint John is but one characteristic of a far more inclusive deity, one of whose characteristics is Lord of the Wild Animals, Rjawal Pek'chila Chkop. (Photograph by the author, 1992.)*

The change unleashed by contact, far from being an internally generated process, stemmed from an event imposed from without. In assessing the transformations which occurred it is important to realize that change *of* social systems must proceed from one of three factors: total force; the failure of an existing system; or, at least in theory, a system's exposure to obviously superior novelty. In the Guatemalan hinterlands the Conquest entailed none of these.

Reflecting that fact, the changes which occurred were *within* the area's Mayan societies, what might otherwise be understood as adaptive change. In Santiago Atitlán and elsewhere, such changes represented the Mayas' rejection of Spanish culture, combined with their adaptation to that

21. This c. 1865 etching from the French periodical Le Monde Illustré *brings to mind Spanish complaints about drunken cofradía ceremonial dances. The drawing, by Firmin Bocourt, is titled "Dance of the Devils," and depicts a ceremony in Cobán.*

same culture through the adoption of certain Spanish cultural elements. Yet, as is underscored in the Atitecos' successful "conversion" of the Catholic saints, this type of adaptation was itself a form of resistance. Far from integrating elements of Spanish culture in order to emulate the foreigners, the Mayas did so in ways that preserved important aspects of their own culture. The net result was gradual evolutionary change. In Santiago Atitlán, as throughout the region, the cultural configuration which emerged reflected a particular set of conditions. Had any of several primary factors been different, that cultural configuration would have assumed an entirely different form. As I have demonstrated, indigenous culture maximized the Mayas' potential power and subsequently played a pivotal role in the region's socioeconomic profile. Nonetheless, no factor was more important than the limited foreign activity in the area. In the following chapter, I explain what happened when the foreign interests raised their level of intervention in highland Guatemala.

5

On Enlightenment,
Liberalism, and Ladinos

*"Not far from Sololá we passed a group of Indians working on the road.
Two or three soldiers, rifles in hand and with bayonets fixed were supporting the operations. Convicts? Not a bit of it: taxpayers and volunteers. Most Indians still pay taxes in labour, and when any considerable
job needs doing, the authorities send word to the neighboring villages
that they are in need of so many volunteers. The soldiers are there to see
that the volunteering spirit does not cool down."*

ALDOUS HUXLEY, *BEYOND THE MEXIQUE BAY* (1934)

THE CLOSE OF THE EIGHTEENTH AND THE DAWN OF THE NINETEENTH
century in Guatemala represented a time of significant social pluralism.[1]
In the newly established capital, la Nueva Guatemala (Guatemala City),
preoccupation with the crash of the indigo market reigned, again underscoring the region's economic insignificance (R. Smith 1959). Outside of
the capital, the highlands remained demographically and culturally Mayan. Most indigenous communities were without Catholic priests, and
many were virtually without any non-Indian representation at all. Until
1877, most non-Mayas inhabiting indigenous communities were able to
do so legally only through the *censo enfiteusis*, a type of long-term rent
available at the discretion of the indigenous municipality. Towns usually
extended the *censo enfiteusis* to raise funds for taxes or for special needs
such as natural disasters or public works (see McCreery 1990:99–100).

Perhaps the single most representative feature of the Colony at that
time was "the failure of the elites to penetrate the countryside as land-
owners or producers" (McCreery 1990:98). Just as the Spaniards tended
to remain sequestered in the larger towns, the Mayas tended to maintain ownership of the rural hinterlands. According to one scholar, as
late as the middle of the nineteenth century, more than a thousand villages owned over 70 percent of Guatemala's best agricultural land (Cambranes 1985:88). Moreover, until rather late in the last century the lati-
fundios so characteristic of contemporary Guatemala were quite rare.

Importantly, while at first the relationship of Indian countryside to Spanish urban centers was a matter of facility to the latter, the relationship eventually became institutionalized and reflected the legal difficulties of outsiders in acquiring the Indians' (corporately held) land. And when a dispute over land would arise, "the members of the community would make it perfectly clear that the land had been theirs 'since time immemorial,' . . . they did not permit their neighbors to trespass on 'a single inch of property' which did not belong to them, and when this occurred, endless court action ensued" (Cambranes 1985:88; also see McCreery 1990:99).

In short, the Colony had settled into an inherently conservative ethnic balance, which left the rural Mayan population in possession of the primary mode of production, agriculture. Once established, it was in neither the Spaniards' nor the Mayas' best interest to seriously test the limits of the status quo. In Santiago Atitlán, when laissez-faire Spanish administration was violated "the community was prepared to react, regardless of whether this entailed litigating lands, burning a hacienda, suing or attacking a local government official, or running a zealot priest out of town" (Madigan 1976:276). At other times, Spanish violation of the line demarcating Mayan sociocultural autonomy led to indigenous revolts (Fried et al. 1983:24; Carmack 1983; C. Smith 1984:201; García Añoveros 1987:187). Mayan excesses, of course, could also lead to Spanish reprisals (Hill 1989:179–187). Other mechanisms were also instrumental in the maintenance of the Mayan and Spanish social pluralism. While not as pronounced as in the Mayan lowlands (Farriss 1984; Jones 1989), highland Mayan flight from resident towns was a mechanism which mediated extremes in Spanish economic or cultural demands. Specifically, the Spaniards had to weigh any benefits from such extremes against a potential loss of tributaries. Yet many Mayas did take flight. In Atitlán, such flight began as early as 1571 (*Relación de los caciques* 1952:438). By 1770, according to Cortés y Larraz, fully one-third to one-half of Guatemala's population was dispersed (García Añoveros 1987:21–25). The archbishop cited both the desire to evade tribute payments and refuge from Christianity as motivating factors for the Colony's disenfranchised population, a group which he described as a "congregation of people subject to neither God, the Church, nor to the King" (Cortés y Larraz 1958 1:288).

In the Mayan hinterlands, the costumbres, the Old Ways, constituted the primary law of the land (e.g., McCreery 1990:98). To be sure, the costumbres were themselves undergoing fundamental changes in the latter half of the Colonial period. In Santiago Atitlán, such change was evidenced in the vicissitudes of the cofradía system. By the late eighteenth century the cofradía had emerged as the single most important Atiteco social institution, supplanting chinamits. In fact, by that time there is absolutely no evidence of the continued existence of the town's chinamit structure. That is certainly not to say that it had disappeared without a trace, as important aspects of the earlier institution, such as the bundle cult, were absorbed into the cofradía system. An association in Guatemala of cofradías with chinamits can be documented to fairly early in the post-Classic period. The (c. 1650) Coto dictionary (Kaqchikel) notes a relationship between chinamits (parcialidades) and cofradías (1983:393). Similarly, in 1690 Fuentes y Guzman (1932 1:349) cited a patron relationship between chinamits (calpules) and *guachibales* (a name used in the Colonial period for private cofradías). Nonetheless, the two institutions tended to maintain identifiable degrees of separation. While the existing historical documentation does not allow an exact reconstruction of the ascendancy of the cofradía system as the central feature in Atiteco sociopolitical organization, the town's demographic collapse must have been a primary factor.

By 1770 the population of Santiago Atitlán had fallen to around a mere 800 inhabitants (MacLeod 1973:131). Not only must some chinamits have lost virtually all of their members, but continuing repartimiento demands on the surviving Atitecos would have increased general impoverishment. As such, both the capacity of surviving chinamit leaders to finance rituals and the authority which they had derived from that sponsorship would have been undercut, hence putting pressure on the community to assume ritual responsibilities and to share expenses. The annual changing of cofradías from one sponsor to another addresses those requirements. Regardless of the specifics of this chinamit-to-cofradía transition, the organization that eventually emerged in Santiago Atitlán would display many of the appearances and functions of the preceding one. In addition to the bundle cult and its associated priesthood, important aspects of civil organization and control were also transferred. Primary among these were the control of communal lands and the delegation of labor.

There were important differences as well. For instance, the eventual emergence of a unified cofradía civil and religious hierarchy based on a ladder of ascending offices apparently had no direct antecedents (see Chance and Taylor 1985). Certainly another primary difference was the disappearance of what was described earlier as the conformity to "aboriginal patterns of discrimination." Specifically, in Santiago Atitlán, micro-identifications on the level of the chinamit gave way to macro-

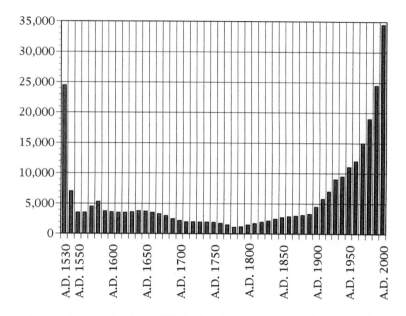

22. *The population of Santiago Atitlán by decade, A.D. 1530–2000. (Source: Madigan 1976, modified by Carlsen.)*

identifications on the level of the town itself. Quite simply, Atitecos came to think of themselves as just that, residents of Santiago Atitlán. Accordingly, Atitlán's cofradías drew members from throughout the town, regardless of micro-affiliations, such as *cantón* (neighborhood) residency. Similarly, sponsorship of individual cofradías, reportedly numbering eight in 1804 (Gleto Montiel, in Orellana 1975:853), moved freely from one part of the town to another.[2]

The emergence of the cofradía system as the central feature of local political organization is of particular importance to this book's larger discussion on adaptation, and testifies to the Atitecos' continued fierce resistance toward acculturation. It should be recalled that Atiteco Working People envision Atitlán's cofradía system as a manifestation of the World Tree, an identifiably pre-Columbian component which is itself symbolically informed by what in Tz'utujil is called Jaloj-K'exoj. The symbolic transformation of cofradías into the World Tree demonstrates the local Mayas' continued capacity to integrate intrusive elements into Atiteco culture, converting them to a form acceptable to the local indigenous population. As indicated in the symbolic conception of Atitlán's various cofradías as branches of the World Tree which support the people of the town, who are represented by fruit and flowers, the local cofradía system consolidated the Atitecos' sense of membership in their community. In turn, the largely unified community continued to wield the capacity to mediate external exploitative interests through means ranging from barter to rebellion. As I shall explain, such local adaptations, multiplied a thousandfold throughout the Guatemalan hinterlands, would prove formidable obstacles to the consolidation of a soon-to-be-conceived Guatemalan state.

INCIPIENT CONDITIONS OF GUATEMALAN SOCIAL CHANGE

Near the time of its independence in 1821, Guatemala's prevailing social relations were so entrenched that the possibility of momentous change must have seemed remote indeed. Yet several factors were quietly engaged which were to effect profound changes for all Guatemalans. Those factors were significant ethnic and demographic changes within the Guatemalan population and the rise of "Liberal" politics.

ETHNIC AND DEMOGRAPHIC CHANGE

Despite the decline in the size of the Indian population throughout most of the Colonial period, that sector nonetheless remained considerably larger than the Colony's Spanish (mostly Creole) population. Madigan (1976:238) writes that during the Colony's history it is unlikely that the ratio of Indians to whites ever dropped much below 14:1. He adds that at the close of the Colonial epoch, the number of Guatemalan *vecinos* (adult white males) was near five thousand, which was only about twice the population of Santiago Atitlán alone. However, the emergence of an entirely different ethnic sector of the Guatemalan population would soon dramatically alter the region's demographic structure and character. That emergent group was the *casta* population, a group now called Ladino.[3] The casta population was composed largely of mulattos (slaves and free)—the offspring of disenfranchised Indian servants (*naborios*) with Spaniards or blacks—and Indians who no longer identified themselves as Indian (Lutz nd.a, nd.b). Around 1700, a time when the Indian and the Spanish population levels were either stagnant or in decline, the casta population began to increase rapidly in sparsely inhabited areas, particularly the coastal piedmont and the oriente regions. During the century which followed, in some areas of the lowland zone the castas became the dominant sector (Lutz nd.b). At the time of its devastation by earthquake in 1773, the capital city (modern Antigua) was overwhelmingly populated by castas, who by then were generally called Ladinos.

By the middle of the seventeenth century the phenotypical blurring characteristic of contemporary ladinoization was already well underway. Simultaneous with that blurring, a continued Spanish input into the casta gene pool led to its increased "whitening." As a result, routes were opened "via biological and cultural *mestizaje* towards the lower echelons of Spanish society" (Lutz nd.b:9). The child of a Spaniard and a *castiza* (female casta) for instance, was considered a Spaniard. This is certainly not to say, however, that such a person might have been considered the social equal of someone of pure or almost pure Spanish blood, the so-called *personas de calidad conocida*. As late as the 1830s, the social limitations of even the most accepted of those Guatemalans of mixed blood were underscored by their total absence from the young Republic's ruling aristocracy. Instead, atop Guatemalan society was a two-tiered structure made up of Creoles and peninsular Spaniards. According to Woodward (1972:46), at the pinnacle was the extended family of the House of Aycinena, known regionally as simply "the family." They were followed in power and status by a group called the "middle sector," which as Woodward notes was an inaccurate term, given that group's actual close proximity to the upper social echelon.

In addition to changes in the ethnic makeup of the Colony's population, by the nineteenth century an equally dramatic shift was underway in its size. After having declined since the Conquest, the indigenous population had entered into a period of steady growth. That growth, which continues to the present, has had tremendous social implications. In Santiago Atitlán, the period from 1780 to 1880 was to see an approximate doubling of the population. As in the rest of Guatemala, Atiteco population growth in the twentieth century has accelerated to truly explosive levels. Exemplifying this growth, between 1930 and 1959 Guatemala went from doubling its population every one hundred and forty-four years to doubling it every twenty-one years, one of the highest rates of change ever recorded for a national unit (Early 1975:276). Fueling this growth has been increased access to Western medicine (Douglas 1969; Sexton and Woods 1982:199). In the latter part of the eighteenth century, emergent progressive elements in Guatemala actively embraced concern with the modern medical practices of the day, even at that early date, in the widespread dissemination of the smallpox vaccine. The emergent progressive element came to form the Liberal party.

THE RISE OF GUATEMALAN LIBERALISM

To many, the terms "Liberal" and "Conservative" in their Latin American context are familiar only through the inane perpetual wars that provide a comical backdrop to the writings of García Marquez. Yet, even to those somewhat familiar with the major political trends of post-Independence Latin America, these binary terms can be confusing. Certainly a primary reason is that the terms correspond to quite different types of political behavior than in their Anglo usage. In fact, "neo-Liberals" today constitute a primary faction of the political right wing in Central America. Another source of confusion has been the acceptance by some scholars of the rhetoric associated with the Liberal and Conservative agendas, at the expense of considering those factions' actual behavior. For instance, in their best-selling book *Bitter Fruit*, Schlesinger and Kinzer (1982:29) praise the "enlightened reforms" of the arch-Liberal of Guatemala Justo Rufino Barrios, including his purported attempts to seize land from the wealthy to give to peasants. As I will show, nothing could be further from the truth.

To understand the historical development of Liberalism in Guatemala, it is important to consider the late eighteenth century Bourbon reforms of Spain's King Charles III (Rodríguez 1978). During the reign of Charles III moves were undertaken to improve agricultural production throughout the Empire, largely through the implementation of an Adam Smith–type of laissez-faire capitalism. Included were attempts to break state and regional monopolies and to improve infrastructure in the colonies, particularly through the building of roads. And most important to the present discussion, initial steps were taken to break up communal landholdings. Part and parcel of the Crown's economic agenda was the implementation of the philosophy of Enlightenment (*ilustración*) then popular in Europe and the United States. That philosophy was characterized by a rejection of traditional social, religious, and political ideas, and by an emphasis on rationalism. In short, the Crown believed that through the removal of all that was economically retrograde, coupled with the implementation of modern thought, the Empire could be thoroughly revitalized (Rodríguez et al. 1972). Importantly, reflecting the Crown's interest in accommodating an increasing demand by North Atlantic states for raw materials, in Guatemala it was the rural producers of agricultural raw materials who were particular targets of this agenda (McCreery 1983:735). That, of course, meant the indigenous Mayan population.

A primary instrument for the dissemination of the doctrine of Liberalism in Guatemala was the Royal Economic Society and its journal, the *Gazeta Oficial* (later to become the *Gazeta de Guatemala*). Articles in the journal ranged from arguments for incorporating new cash crops into the economy to whether Indians should be made to learn Spanish and wear European-style clothing. Descartes, Locke, Montesquieu, and

Rousseau were favored sources for citation. Indicative of the day's idealism, in his prospectus to the journal, the editor wrote that he intended to "goad inactive spirits into thinking, discussing, and inventing useful things" (Rodríguez 1978:21). Basic to the agenda was that Guatemala's indigenous population be integrated into the mainstream of civilized Hispanic society. Reflecting the general tenets of the Enlightenment, it was professed that the Indian was not inherently inferior. Spanish "suckers and parasites" were even blamed for the Indian condition (Rodríguez 1978:23–24). Accordingly, many Liberals of the period held that the economic development of the Colony necessitated the emancipation of the Indians, hence leading to the abolishment in 1812 of the policy of repartimiento.

Given that the Enlightenment underpinnings of Guatemalan Liberalism were founded on a rejection of the past in favor of an idealized vision of the future, it is understandable that the regional movement anticipated independence from Spain. In Guatemala, the Crown, like colonialism in general, was blamed for the Colony's economic retardation and stagnation. The attempt to redress those economic woes took a step forward on 15 September 1821, the date of Guatemala's independence from Spain.

GUATEMALAN INDEPENDENCE AND ITS AFTERMATH
"APPLIED ENLIGHTENMENT"

The fledgling Guatemalan Republic's first decade was hobbled by fiscal uncertainty, regional problems with the other Central American states, and so on. With the coming to power in 1831 of Mariano Gálvez, however, the Liberals were poised to implement their idealized and untested program, what Rodríguez (1972) identifies as Guatemala's epoch of "applied enlightenment." Consistent with what has already been stated about Liberalism, the Gálvez (*galvista*) agenda incorporated a two-pronged program optimistically expected to quickly direct Guatemala to a place among the world's leading nations. The two primary aspects of this program were, of course, education and economic reform. Exemplifying the first, "a 'protector' system was established whereby those 'lovers of civilization' and those interested in the 'improvement of the Indians' could keep either in their homes or in the *colegios* an Indian boy or girl and furnish food, clothes, and instruction in primary letters and domestic economy" (Williford 1972:35). This type of program, however, was to have little, if any, effect on the Mayan population. If nothing else, few Mayas had either the time or the interest to learn to read, much less to read about Montesquieu and the like.

In contrast to the educational elements of the Liberal agenda, the economic aspects would eventually have dramatic effects throughout the entire Republic. Basic to Liberal economics was the "rationalization" of communal property, the expropriation of holdings which were understood as constituting a feudal barrier, not only for the capitalist development of the Republic, but, typifying the Guatemalan Liberalism of the day, also for the intellectual development of the indigenous population. As such, a series of "land reforms" were enacted which, being most notable for their "ineffectualness and for the hostility they engendered," served to underscore the first-generation Liberals' "inability to reconcile largely utopian theory with reality" (McCreery 1990:100). In particular, underlying the implementation of Liberal idealist policy lay certain age-old realities. Quite simply, any Liberal success was dependent on the behavior of a relatively large, potentially unruly, and generally autonomous Mayan population. Importantly, from that group's point of view the Liberal policies amounted to little more than imposition and theft.

RAFAEL CARRERA AND THE WAR OF THE MONTAÑESES

The galvista approach had sought to confront decolonization headlong. Yet the Guatemalan state at that time was only strong enough to "generate opposition but not to put its policies into effect; it could irritate and injure but it could neither protect nor control, especially in the countryside" (McCreery 1990:101). In short, the galvista approach flew in the face of the entrenched social balance between the Republic's indigenous and Spanish populations, with predictable results. The most notable response was a remarkable popular revolution.[4]

Several factors were instrumental in leading up to the War of the Montañeses ("mountain people"). Among the most important were continued economic depression, a serious outbreak of cholera, and political opposition to the galvistas from the Conservative oligarchy, including the Church (Pinto Soria 1986:209).[5] It was the unrest of the peasant population, however, which was the single most significant variable. The peasant population at that time comprised both Indians and disenfranchised Ladinos. The most activist of the latter group were located in semilegal settlements in the east of Guatemala. Collectively, those settlements were often referred to simply as "Valleys" (Pinto Soria 1986:212). The primary motivation to take up arms in the Valleys was poverty, apparently in contrast with the primary motivation in the Mayan communities. As Carol Smith (1990:79) notes, "attention to the details of the reaction . . . suggests that the [Mayan] rebels were much more concerned about losing their political autonomy than their property. . . . The greatest threat to the community was the 'nationalist program' of the Gálvez period, the attempt to create equal, free, individual citizens within a homogeneous nation. Because the nationalism of this period was an imposition of elite culture on the masses and because it had no respect for local cultural forms, it provoked a popular, cultural reaction."

It is difficult to state exactly when the War of the Montañeses began. As early as 1834, the government's attempts to ban burials within churches led to a significant uprising in San Miguel Totonicapán. By 1837 there was an explosive surge in the number of such Indian uprisings, Woodward citing more than thirty in mid-1837 alone (1993:61). Although there were incidents in Sololá, Verapaz, and Quezaltenango, perhaps the most important occurred in March 1837 in San Juan Ostuncalco. That was followed a few months later by largely Ladino uprisings in the eastern Guatemalan towns of Santa Rosa and Matasquintla, incidents which raised the first mention of the rebel leader Rafael Carrera (Miceli 1974:76). In response to those uprisings Gálvez sent some six hundred troops, which commenced to route the insurgents, and to terrorize and plunder their villages. "Among other excesses, the last outrage was perpetrated upon Carrera's wife" (Stephens [1841] 1969 1:226).

Prior to his role as rebel leader, Rafael Carrera had been a swineherd and a soldier. Although he was certainly a Ladino, racial classifications of Carrera range from Indian to almost pure Spanish. According to the noted author and diplomat John Lloyd Stephens ([1841] 1969 1:224), "his friends, in compliment, call him a mulatto; I, for the same reason, call him an Indian, considering that the better blood of the two." Stephens described Carrera's infantry as being "mostly Indians, ragged, half naked, with old straw hats and barefooted, armed with muskets and machetes, and many with old-fashioned Spanish blunderbusses" ([1841] 1969 2:76).

However shabby, this army, with Carrera at its lead, successfully employed patently guerrilla ambush-and-hide tactics. Stephens ([1841] 1969 1:231–232) describes the consternation and horror of the Creole citizenry witnessing the entry into Guatemala City on 29 January 1838 "of this immense mass of barbarians; choking up the streets, all with green bushes in their hats, seeming at a distance like a moving forest; armed with rusty muskets, old pistols, fowling-pieces, some with locks and some without; sticks formed into the shape of muskets, with tin plate locks; clubs, machetes, and knives tied to the end of long poles." Stephens adds that upon entering the city, the triumphant peasant soldiers proceeded directly to the national cathedral where they "set up around the beautiful altar the uncouth images of their village saints." Although it would be another year before total victory could be claimed, by April 1839 Carrera had defeated the Guatemalan Army.

While Carrera would not officially claim the presidency until 1844, from 1839 he would be Guatemala's de facto ruler. In 1854, he even engineered his own elevation to the position of President-for-Life, which according to the letter of the law, he held until his death on Good Friday, 1865. This is certainly not to claim, however, that Carrera did not have political setbacks. In 1848 he was even driven into temporary exile in Mexico. Moreover, on two occasions the state of Los Altos (composed of the departments of Socunusco, Totonicapán, Huehuetenango, Suchitpequez, Quezaltenango, and Sololá, which includes Santiago Atitlán) declared independence. On both occasions, in 1839 and in 1848, the primary actors were non-Indian Liberals. And on both occasions the actions of the Liberal leaders triggered the negative reaction of the region's huge Indian population, contributing to the failure of the secessions.

THE CARRERA LEGACY

Largely disparaged in Guatemalan historiography as a reactionary setback to modernization, if not an outright fling with barbarism, the Carrera era may have been something of a "golden age" for the Republic's indigenous population (La Farge 1940; McCreery 1990). In 1839, the Constituent Assembly officially recognized the value of Indian customs and culture, stating that by law Indians may "not be molested in the practice and habits that they have learned from their elders which are not contrary to good customs" (e.g., see Rodríguez 1972:1–32; Woodward 1990:67, 1993:135). Moreover, in marked contrast to the galvista agenda, there was a movement back to the traditional division of lands: the state, by and large, recognizing Mayan communal landholdings (Pinto Soria 1986:230). The protection of indigenous culture and land was further buttressed by Carrera's restoration of the Laws of the Indies. Other decrees signed by the President specified that Indians would be paid on time for their work, as well as for travel time to and from their villages; that where there were no hospitals, employers would be responsible for providing medical care; that Indians would not be forced to serve in the military; and that schools would be provided for Indians (Woodward 1993:424).

Although some historians have implied that over the course of his lengthy rule, Carrera gradually abandoned his support for the rural masses in favor of alliance with the Conservative elite (e.g., Miceli 1974, Cambranes 1985), this is largely untrue (see Woodward 1993). To be sure, following 1850, he aligned himself with the Conservative elites. Yet his reinforcement of the rights of Indians demonstrates that this alignment was not at the expense of his relationship with the native population. One reason for Carrera's continued courting of the Indian population no doubt stemmed from the rebellion of 1848, in which Carrera was temporarily deposed. As Woodward (1993) documents so well, prior to that time the President often attempted to play Liberal against Conservative interests, and in that way solidify his own position. Although that strategy was not without its successes, in 1848 it jackknifed on him and he was temporarily forced into exile in Chiapas, Mexico. A reason for Carrera's setback was that he had lost favor with the rural Indian population and hence a pivotal element of support. As one British resident of Guatemala wrote, "by allying himself with the whites and the mestizos, he has in great measure lost his influence among the Indians, who say that he has betrayed them" (in Woodward 1993:190). Significantly, in large part by reestablishing the confidence and support of the Indians, Carrera was able to seize back control of Guatemala in August 1849.

A primary lesson of the Carrera period is that the Republic's Mayan population was motivated neither by national nor partisan loyalty, but by self-interest. As the 1848 revolt demonstrated, if the Mayas in some particular area felt that the President was not serving their interests, he could quickly lose their support, and his political base with it. Conversely, by supporting the indigenous population, which generally meant maximizing village autonomy, Carrera added a potent ally. It is difficult to escape the conclusion that the Carrera period also represented a rejection of "capitalist enterprise by peasants who presumably preferred autonomy to national integration" (C. Smith 1984:202; also see Carmack 1990:133). Underscoring this point, and the importance of Mayan support, upon Carrera's death his successor (Conservative) Vicente Cerna actively promoted agro-export expansion. In so doing, he abandoned support for Indian labor rights and encouraged the expropriation of Indian land. As a result, when a Liberal armed insurrection against Cerna was mounted, it mustered considerable Mayan backing (Woodward 1993:338–339). As the rebellion grew, Cerna was left without the pivotal support the Indians had provided Carrera and was eventually toppled.

While at first glance Cerna's failure might seem to indicate the Mayas' continued potential to exert power, along the lines of the War of the Montañeses, that was hardly the case. Throughout the Carrera presidency significant demographic and economic changes were engaged which would soon neutralize the capacity of even the most remote Mayan villages to check socioeconomic intrusion. From the moment that Carrera and his moving forest of peasant soldiers assumed residence in Guatemala City, the country's Creole population was irreversibly forced into a power-sharing relationship. With the return of the Indian members of Carrera's victorious force to their dispersed communities, the nonwhite participation in that power sharing was exclusively Ladino, although the elites would have to respect rural Indian autonomy for several more decades. Consistent with the example of the President himself, throughout the Carrera period Ladinos gained increasing entree into the higher echelons of Guatemalan socioeconomic circles, particularly the military. Simultaneously, the Ladino sector became aligned with elements of the Creole elite, gradually rearranging the country's peasant/elite balance of power. Notably left behind were the Indians.

These changes eventually had a significant economic impact. The unlikely catalyst for sweeping economic changes in Guatemala occurred in a small European laboratory in 1856 when the chemist Perkin accidentally discovered a process to produce synthetic dyes (McCreery 1986 : 103; Carlsen and Wenger 1991). For several decades Guatemala had been the world's leading producer of cochineal, an insect-derived red dye. In a single accident in a test tube, Perkin undermined the basis of Guatemala's cochineal industry, and its economy as well. Although Guatemalan cochineal exports would actually increase for another decade or so, competition from the new synthetic dyes caused prices to plummet. Once again, the Republic was cast into the search for a new cash commodity, a process which culminated in the rise of Guatemala's coffee industry.

Although Guatemala's commercial production of coffee had begun in the 1830s, it initially met with little success. The early coffee growers were hampered by the dominant Conservative economic interests— particularly those of the powerful Consulado de Comercio—which were wedded to cochineal production (McCreery 1976 : 439–440). Moreover, whereas before 1856 cochineal had provided high profits on low volume and demanded relatively little land and labor, coffee production was both labor- and land-intensive. It has already been noted that at that time the best agricultural lands were under Indian control. Compounding this was a situation in which "the existing village system largely satisfied the material and social-ritual needs of the indigenous population and [therefore] the Indians would not go voluntarily into the coffee fields" (McCreery 1986:103). The demise of the cochineal industry, however, was to force a reappraisal of the economic status quo.

POST-ENLIGHTENMENT LIBERALISM

With economic vicissitude the driving force, many Consulado de Comercio elites came to realize the value of coffee production. By manipulating credit and transport, those Conservative interests sought to maintain coffee production on an artificially low scale and at high profit levels, much as they had done with cochineal. In that way they hoped to retain economic control of the Republic. However, it is understandable that this scheming was a source of great frustration to those coffee growers who were intentionally excluded from Consulado circles. Importantly, by the time of President-for-Life Carrera's death in 1865, foreigners, mostly English and German, had come to dominate Guatemala's import-export commerce and were increasingly numbering among the country's non-Consulado coffee growers. According to Cambranes (1985:117–119), the foreigners' understanding that Guatemala's economic development was being retarded by national policy led to their financing of armed forces for the purpose of toppling the Conservative regime. Demonstrating a changing balance of power in Guatemala, following a series of small battles, on 30 June 1871 a Liberal faction under Miguel García Granados overthrew the Conservative regime of Vicente Cerna and took power. Although the García Granados presidency was to be short-lived, it gave way to the even more staunchly Liberal regime of Justo Rufino Barrios (1873–1885). After a hiatus of some thirty years, the Liberals were firmly back in power. Notably absent from the emergent brand of Liberalism, however, was the Enlightenment optimism of the Mayas' potential.

As indicated above, primary obstacles to the fulfillment of the Liberal coffee growers' entrepreneurial ambitions were the scarcity of manpower to work the land and the scarcity of land to be worked. Key to this situation were the autonomous Mayan villages. While the indigenous communities maintained their communal landholdings, and equally important, while they had the political and social institutions to protect those holdings, there was almost no incentive for Indians to work for low wages on the coffee plantations (McCreery 1976:456; also see C. Smith 1990:79). As Carol Smith (1984:200) notes, "the preservation of the indigenous community represented the greatest barrier to capitalist development." Not to be dissuaded, in 1871 the coffee growers penned a statement which called for the reinstitutionalization of forced

23. For all of Guatemala's Mayas, the final quarter of the nineteenth century was a period of pivotal and debilitating change. Such changes were readily evident in the eroding authority of community cofradía leaders. This late nineteenth-century photograph by Alberto Valdeavellano is of cofradía members from Santiago Atitlán.

labor, the definitive expropriation of communal lands, and the development of the infrastructure needed for improving the coffee economy (Cambranes 1985:121).

While the implementation of that agenda may have seemed straightforward, especially to the newly arrived foreigners, President Barrios realized otherwise. In particular, memory of the Carrera revolution remained strong enough that Barrios at first tended to treat the Indian population gingerly, primarily when dealing with issues of land (McCreery 1976:450; Cambranes 1985:89). Nonetheless, the program of "rationalizing" the Indian lands progressed. Significantly, that progression correlated with a dramatic drop in Indian uprisings (McCreery 1990: 109). Clearly, the socioeconomic rise of the Ladinos, coupled with the influx of foreign entrepreneurs, had neutralized the potential power of the Indians vis-à-vis the Republic's increasingly dominant economic interests. As important, infrastructural advances within the Republic allowed increased control over the Indian communities. By the 1880s, the country was integrated by telegraph and road systems. As such, news of uprisings could be quickly transmitted to the authorities, who would then respond with an increasingly modernized army. In short, the Mayas quickly realized that the balance of power had tilted decisively against them. "What had largely disappeared was the tumulto [riot] as an effective form of resistance by the indigenous community to the state. The primeval Indian, fire and machete in hand, remained a vivid ladino nightmare, though one at least until recently, with less and less basis in fact" (McCreery 1990:112).

That shifting of the balance of power increasingly freed the Liberal interests to implement their agenda, leading to what McCreery (1976: 457) has called "a massive assault upon village lands." In the face of that assault, the Atitecos were particularly aggressive in attempting to hold on to their territory; between 1870 and 1900 they even managed to more than double their share of titled land (see McCreery 1994:254). Any success, however, was far more apparent than real and merely accounted for ownership in the Guatemalan legal sense. In reality, the Atitecos suffered significant loss of nontitled lands that had been theirs since time immemorial, including much of their best agricultural property. Importantly, land made available for foreign ownership did not just entail distant holdings, but included at least 2,500 hectares approximately one mile from the town center (see Madigan 1976:146–158).

Within a few decades, perhaps half of the lands traditionally held by Guatemalan Indian communities had been taken (Carmack 1979:248; C. Smith 1984:204). All told, by 1950, 72 percent of the agricultural land in the country was controlled by slightly more than 2 percent of the farming units, with 88 percent of the farming units controlling only 14 percent of the agricultural land (Handy 1990:1969). It is abundantly evident that Guatemalan landowning patterns have moved dramatically in the direction of latifundia. Importantly, such changes were possible only because of the opening of the previously closed and corporate communities. One of the first wedges in that opening was Decree 170 (1877), which allowed former communal land to be privatized. In many cases, land which Mayas had held since long before European contact but for which they possessed no title was simply confiscated. Other Mayan communities were compensated for prime coffee land with title to distant lands. In any case, once opened the Mayan communities were incapable of mustering their former level of self-defense (C. Smith 1984: 205; Cambranes 1985).

Certainly the most significant of the intrusions into the indigenous communities was the non-Indian–owned commercial estate (*finca*). In

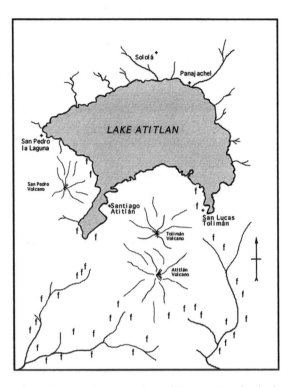

24. This map shows the approximate locations of former Atiteco land subsequently deeded to coffee growers in the form of fincas. As is evident, the expropriated land tends to lie in riverine valleys where most of the region's best land is located.

Santiago Atitlán, *fincas* came to control much of the best land surrounding the town. Other sometimes interrelated intrusions into the indigenous communities were also significant. In 1882, for instance, shortly after having proclaimed the Decree of the Freedom of Liberty and Religion, President Barrios went on a missionary shopping venture to New York, where he successfully petitioned the Board of Foreign Missions of the Presbyterian Church to commence a presence in Guatemala. Thereafter, the Indian villages were opened to Protestant missionization. Barrios' petition had little to do with his personal religious conviction. Instead, demonstrating the web of relations which the Mayan communities were up against, the President's actions represented an attempt to undermine the Church's opposition to his Liberal agenda (Burgess 1926: 214–215). Moreover, Barrios, a Catholic, sought to attract foreign entrepreneurs otherwise ill-disposed toward Catholic countries (Zapata 1982: 28–29).

It should be reiterated that the brand of Liberalism instituted by Justo Rufino Barrios was void of the positive Enlightenment sentiments about the Indians embraced earlier by the galvistas. For instance, Barrios is on record as having stated that "100 foreign families were worth as much as 20,000 Indians" (Cambranes 1985:302). Quite unlike the Enlightenment-era Liberal attempts to improve the Indians' lot, the emergent Liberal policies toward the Mayan population sought little more than to maintain a supply of cheap labor for the large commercial agriculturalists. A statement by Nevin O. Winter (1909:116) is instructive in this regard. The American entrepreneur/author writes that "as an individual the [Guatemalan Indian] peon is not particularly lovable except for his fidelity. He is much like a child in many ways and has to be frequently treated as one. He even fails to resent the chastisement by a knock-down blow from his employer. . . . The personal *mozo*, or body-servant of the master, is especially useful and amiable."

In order to secure a steady supply of Indian laborers, Decree 177, issued in 1877, spelled out a rural labor code which successfully created a vast system of debt servitude from which few Mayas were free. In Santiago Atitlán, for instance, by the beginning of the twentieth century, ninety-five fincas had debt peonage relationships with Atitecos (Madigan 1976:247). And by 1928, only about 20 percent of the Atitecos were free from some patron-debt relationship. To avoid the year-round support of indigenous workers whose labor on the coffee fincas was needed for only several months, enough land was left to the villages so that the "natural economy" of the highlands might continue to reproduce itself (McCreery 1983:738).

While the coffee growers' strategy initially worked as planned with the natural economy of the rural area meeting the most basic needs of the seasonal work force, a factor raised earlier soon changed that. That factor was population growth, and the resulting emergence of a landless peasantry. By the end of the nineteenth century, population growth in Guatemala had become explosive. The resulting population increase has aggravated the land problem to the point that in 1968 fully 86 percent of Guatemala's cultivable landholdings were too minuscule to support their owners (McDowell and C. Smith 1976:274). Once again, the situation in Santiago Atitlán is characteristic. My research shows that even if all available land were under cultivation and planted exclusively with traditional (noncash) crops, at present less than 25 percent of Atitecos have enough land to satisfy their own food needs. It has been estimated that by the end of this decade that number will drop to less than 10 percent (Early 1983:185). Where just a few decades ago Atitlán had been the largest exporter of corn in the Lake Atitlán area, it is now forced to import corn from other areas.

UNDERMINING COMMUNITY

The final quarter of the nineteenth century witnessed a quantum increase in the power of the Guatemalan state (see C. Smith, ed. 1990). That increase was coupled with a marked decline in potential indigenous power. On the one hand, Guatemala's increased integration with the global economy combined with the socioeconomic rise of the Ladino sector to raise the level of centralized power. On the other hand, the confiscation of vast amounts of Mayan land added to exploitative labor practices and debilitating population growth to undercut the "self-reproductive capacity of the indigenous peasantry at both the level of simple economics and at the sociopolitical and ideological levels as well" (McCreery 1986:113). By century's end the Mayas were under tighter control than in any previous period in their history (Carmack 1990:126). Perhaps nowhere were the results more evident than in the eroding effectiveness of the traditional institutions, particularly the cofradías' capacity to "barter" with nonindigenous interests. In fact, in its attempt to integrate the indigenous communities into the national and international socioeconomic systems, the government directly targeted traditional indigenous civil authority. As late as 1945, for instance, constitutional changes mandated open elections in the Mayan towns, thereby effectively outlawing the civil component of the cofradía civil-religious hierarchy. It is notable that even in 1945, when the governing capacity of the cofradías had already been undermined, this reform was not welcomed by many Mayas. As I shall explain, such changes would further open the Mayan communities to nonindigenous and often exploitative interests.[6]

Guatemala's transition to a coffee economy and the Republic's simultaneous integration into the world economic system have brought to bear acculturative pressures on Mayan communities such as Santiago Atitlán that exceed even the conditions triggered by the Spanish Conquest. Since long before contact the culture of the Tz'utujil-speaking Mayas inhabiting the south of Lake Atitlán has rested on an agricultural basis. The primary crop has been maize and the predominant method of agriculture has been slash-and-burn, a method whose success hinges on low population density. In Atitlán, as I have shown, the importance of maize has extended beyond purely economic levels and permeated the culture. On a symbolic level, consistent with the belief in an ancestral life force manifested as a seed/skull, the human body itself was believed to be made of maize (*ixim acha*). Moreover, on a political level rituals associated with agricultural fertility have sanctioned the civil-religious hierarchy—itself simultaneously associated with a sacred maize plant and the ancestors—and have thereby buttressed the community's capacity to negotiate with outside interests. It figures that if such a society is to remain viable, at least in its existing form, a minimum requirement must be its access to sufficient agricultural land. However, for Santiago Atitlán, that requirement has been severely violated, paving the way to what one Maya scholar has called a "revolt against the dead" (Brintnall 1979).

PART THREE

Death of Community,
Resurrection of Autonomy

6

Under the Gun in Santiago Atitlán

"Only he who fights has the right to be victorious. Only he who is victorious has the right to live."

MARTIAL POETICS GRACING THE ENTRANCE
TO A GUATEMALAN ARMY GARRISON, 1990

IN 1932 THE AMERICAN ARCHAEOLOGIST SAMUEL LOTHROP and his wife, Eleanor, stepped from a boat onto the lakeshore dock at Santiago Atitlán and into what was to be a particularly chaotic venture. It was their plan to take up residence in the town while Samuel pursued archaeological investigations of local pre-Columbian Mayan ruins. According to Eleanor (1948:82), they were the first foreigners to have attempted residence in Atitlán since the eighteenth century. The Lothrops' efforts at ending that reign of isolation, however, were hardly welcomed by the Atitecos, a people about whom Eleanor wrote, "of all unfriendly Indians, these were the most so." Consistent with that analysis, several months after their arrival and fearing for their lives the Lothrops beat a hasty retreat from Atitlán. In 1932, Santiago Atitlán remained a community tightly closed to outsiders.

A CLOSED COMMUNITY IS OPENED

During the Lothrops' stay in Atitlán, no Atitecos would befriend them, except for one Pedro Mendoza. In fact, Mendoza actually searched out the Lothrops for camaraderie. Although an Atiteco, he was as much a pariah in his community as were the Lothrops (E. Lothrop 1948:98). The reason for that ostracism was simple: Pedro Mendoza was a Protestant. Though in 1932 the young John Franklin was still several years away from bringing his Assemblies of God ministry to Guatemala, Cameron

Townsend, the eventual founder of the Wycliffe Bible Translators, was in residence in the north lake town of Panajachel (Stoll 1982:38).[1] In that Kaqchikel town he had established the Robinson Bible Institute, and Pedro Mendoza was among the first of Townsend's flock. Back in Atitlán, Mendoza's violation of community norms triggered the townspeople's wrath. He was accused of being a traitor and of selling himself for foreigners' money. In the face of these charges, however, Pedro Mendoza maintained faith. Noting that his family had already converted to the new religion, Mendoza stated that in time others would also learn. Those words would be prophetic.

Two decades later, in 1952, following the directive of his professor Robert Redfield, a young French graduate student from the University of Chicago named E. Michael Mendelson commenced fieldwork in Santiago Atitlán. Mendelson's investigations in that town were successful, culminating in his dissertation (1956) and several scholarly papers (1958, 1959, 1962), as well as a classic monograph, *Los escándalos de Maximón* (1965). According to Mendelson (pers. comm. 1988), in 1952 Santiago Atitlán exhibited little of the reflexive hostility toward outsiders that it had shown the Lothrops.[2] Although the Atitecos' change of attitude may seem rapid, the reason for that transition is evident.

In 1935, just a few short years after Pedro Mendoza had been deemed a traitor and sentenced to community ostracism, Santiago Atitlán's first Protestant mission, the Centroamericana, opened its doors. Approximately a decade later another, quite different, religious group began to promote apostasy within an Atiteco population still largely defined by the Old Ways. The newest breed of reformer, the Catequista, was introduced by a Catholic priest named Recinos. The Catequista movement constituted a reform wing of the Church, and at that time was being implemented throughout rural Guatemala in the hope of rooting out non-Christian elements and of placing community religiosity under Church control (e.g., see Ebel 1964; Warren 1989).

By the time that Mendelson arrived in Atitlán, Recinos' efforts had already taken seed. In fact, it was precisely the religious competition engendered by Recinos' work which provided the catalyst for Mendelson's primary research in Atitlán, what he called the Maximón "scandals." The scandals began during Holy Week 1950 when Padre Recinos came to town to say mass. (The town was still without a resident priest.) Not surprisingly, given the padre's sentiments about indigenous religiosity, Maximón was targeted for priestly wrath. Although Recinos' initial efforts were limited to curtailing Maximón's ritually prescribed presence in the church during Holy Week, on 6 June 1950 he returned with two other priests. Inside the Cofradía Santa Cruz, where Maximón normally resides, Recinos and his companions destroyed the god's head and then proceeded to steal the two masks which graced that head.[3] Included among the events which followed was a temporary civil ban on Maximón worship from the departmental capital, Sololá (see Mendelson 1956, 1957, 1965). In 1953, with the Maximón cult still in turmoil, events took a most surprising turn. On the first day of March, a contingent of Atiteco Protestants interfered on the side of the Working People. That support, which according to the Evangelical protagonists was designed to demonstrate their tolerance of religious freedom (certainly not without a modicum of self-interest), tipped the balance of power enough that the Catequistas were forced to concede to the resumption of the Maximón rituals. Permission to resume those rituals was sealed by presidential decree. Since that time, the Maximón rituals have not been interrupted, and the cult remains vital.

Evident in the "scandals" is that by the early 1950s a process of significant social change was fully engaged in Atitlán. The successful penetration into the community of the Protestants and the Catholics alike suggests that the age-old social mechanisms for rejecting or normalizing cultural intrusions had become ineffective and demonstrates a notable increase of Atiteco receptivity to nonindigenous interests. What is more, having established toeholds in the community, the emergent interest groups actually began to reward various antitraditional activities and in that way established competing spheres of social interaction. As is demonstrated in the scandals, a primary target of the antitraditional agenda was the moral legitimacy of the cofradía system and the Old Ways. This faction-building process entailed what Pérez and Robinson (1983:21) identify as the "Satanization" of traditional culture. Despite the earlier Atiteco Protestant demonstrations for religious freedom, within local Protestant circles (and Catholic for that matter) the Old Ways would soon be branded as evil and the Working People held to be tools of the Great Demon (e.g., Douglas 1969:105). Inevitably, an atmosphere of hostility among Atitlán's religious factions became pervasive and battle lines were drawn.

ATITLÁN'S "REVOLT AGAINST THE DEAD"

Conveniently for my present purpose, the course of Atiteco factionalization, like its sociocultural change, is measurable. In 1966, anthropologist William Douglas conducted a survey in Atitlán of multiple variables. In 1991, I completed a survey which addressed some concerns covered in Douglas' study, thus providing a twenty-five-year perspective on aspects of change in Atiteco society. Data from these combined studies are also useful in addressing questions of continued success in local adaptive behavior. Based on these findings, I am led to argue that sociocultural changes in contemporary Santiago Atitlán reflect the obsolescence and resulting abandonment of earlier cultural behavior and adaptive strategies, that they involve considerable social instability, and that the decisions by Atitecos to pursue some realizable promise of a more desirable existence are of scant value in explaining the causes of the observed changes.

Before elaborating on the results of my study, I should comment on my methodology. In 1966 Douglas surveyed the residents of three blocks (*cuadras*), one block in each of three of Atitlán's five neighborhoods (*cantones*). Interviews were conducted with the heads of households. The individual blocks were chosen because they were home to Douglas' native assistants. For my 1991 study, I surveyed the same three blocks as had Douglas, and also employed resident members of the sample blocks as assistants. In fact, my primary assistant had been an assistant in Douglas' original survey. In order to strengthen my sample, I expanded the survey population. First, as one of the blocks covered by Douglas (in Cantón Panul) contained only fifteen households, I added an adjacent, more populous block. I also included blocks in each of the two nonrepresented neighborhoods (Cantón Tzanjuyú and Cantón Xechivoy). In both cases, my criterion for choosing those blocks was the same as that used by Douglas: They were home to assistants. Although the sample population cannot be considered random, its relatively large size (covering roughly 7.3 percent of the town's total households and providing data on 1,361 individuals) minimizes sampling errors.[4]

RELIGIOUS CHANGE

Perhaps nowhere is recent Atiteco sociocultural change more evident than in the area of religious affiliation. In 1966, Douglas observed that Atitlán's population of Working People (31 percent) remained larger than its combined Catequista (13.8 percent) and Protestant (8.6 percent) sectors (1969:194).[5] Nonetheless, nearly balancing out the Working People, the Catequista, and the Protestant sectors combined was a group under which Douglas included nominal Atiteco Catholics (i.e., those individuals who virtually never participated in religious activities), and those who professed having no religion. That combined group, according to Douglas, comprised 46.5 percent of the total Atiteco population. Douglas noted that despite Atitlán's diverse religious identifications, the cofra-

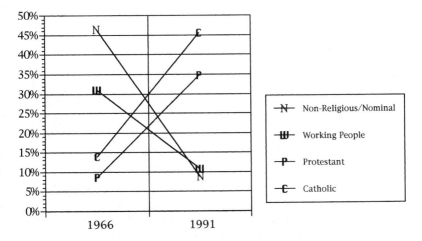

25. *Over the past twenty-five years in Santiago Atitlán, Catholicism and Protestantism have displayed remarkable growth. This growth has been at the expense of the Working People, the nominally religious, and those who profess having no religion. For consistency with Douglas' 1966 data, in this chart the Working People are defined as those who attend cofradía functions. Also for consistency, nominally religious Catholics and Protestants are included in the non-religious category.*

día system remained viable, in fact that it "showed few of the signs of wear apparent in some other pueblos" (1969:62). He added that perhaps only one cofradía in Atitlán was without a full contingency of members.

Twenty-five years later, I considered these same topics. Based on my survey population, and diagrammed in Figure 25, the largest religious sector in 1991 Santiago Atitlán was Catholic, with 45.6 percent of the population identifying itself as members of the Catequista movement Catholic Action. This should be compared to the Church's 1967 figure of 1.6 percent Catholic Action membership (*Guía de la Iglesia* 1967:343). I should note that consistent with Douglas' methodology, my 1991 figure does not include nominal Catholics, but only the 82.8 percent of the total Catholic sample group that claimed regular church attendance, plus the 10.5 percent citing periodic attendance (less than one time a month but more than once every three months). The next largest religious group in 1991 was Protestant, with 34.9 percent of the sample population claiming to regularly or periodically attend one of Atitlán's approximately twenty Protestant churches. Based on the total Protestant sample, 88.3 percent of Atiteco Protestants are regular church attendees, while another 10.4 percent attend periodically. Computed for the town, the number of Protestants would be just under seven thousand members. To better gauge the growth of the Protestant sector, it might be noted that in 1926 there were only about two thousand Indian Protestants in all of Guatemala (Stoll 1982:35).

In contrast to Catholic and Protestant growth in Atitlán, according to the sample population the no-religious-affiliation category had shrunk to only 8.7 percent. Perhaps most significant for the task at hand, the number of current or recent cofradía members was only 2.5 percent, a figure which rises to 10.7 percent if adjusted to include those who sometimes participate in cofradía rituals. Further underscoring the decline in importance of the Working People is that in 1991 only two of Atitlán's ten public cofradías (Cofradías Santiago and Santa Cruz) could boast complete contingencies of members.[6]

In short, these figures demonstrate that since 1966, both the Catholic and the Protestant sectors in Atitlán have experienced remarkable growth. That growth has come at the expense of the Working People, the nominally religious, and the nonreligious. Furthermore, I am prepared to argue that these figures demonstrate that the growth of Atiteco Catholicism has outstripped the otherwise impressive Protestant gains. A pantheon of "converted" saints notwithstanding, I contend that the religion of the Working People is *not* Catholic, "folk" or otherwise. My contention is supported by inclusion in the Old Ways of Maximón, the "stone of the brujos," and countless other such figures; the defining and identifiably Mayan religious principles at the center of the Old Ways; and the Working People's own proclamations about the topic. Significant differences in economic patterns and behavior between Atiteco Catholics and the Working People further buttress my contention. In addition, given that church attendance rates in Atitlán for both Catholics and Protestants are high, and that the nominally and nonreligious sector has declined dramatically, it appears that Atitlán has become more devoutly religious than it was a quarter-century ago. This trend may well reflect Atiteco solace from violence and social turmoil and a related sense of their inability to significantly do anything about it.

Brief consideration of a 1990 episode which addresses Atiteco religious solace in the face of large-scale powerlessness should be helpful for putting into perspective the relationship between Atitlán's social and political instability and the local religious ecology.

KIKS ON THE SOCCER FIELD

For several weeks in February 1990, fliers announcing a "Meeting of Atiteco Unity" to be held on the town's soccer field appeared on storefronts and lamp poles throughout Atitlán. In fact, what transpired at that meeting was a celebration of unity between the local "Association of Pastors" and the Army.[7] Attendance was standing room only, including Uzi-laden soldiers who ringed the soccer field. The event commenced with each member of the Association of Pastors taking a long-winded pass at the microphone. Finally, they all had their say, and it was the Army's turn. The primary speaker for the Army cut a formidable figure, the tight fit of his short-sleeved camouflage shirt exaggerating his muscular build. His distinctly European face remained noticeably grim throughout his talk. As such, it rang hollow, at least to me, when with lips drawn tightly he confessed to the congregated Atitecos an overwhelming joy at being filled with Christ's love. (My skepticism was reinforced two weeks later when the very same soldier conveyed a message of support for the Old Ways to a group of Atiteco Working People.) The subsequent presentation, which intertwined military propaganda with religious proclamations, included a statement of the military's hope that Guatemala would soon be entirely Protestant. Concluding the Army's portion of the get-together was a declaration that the Atitecos could sleep soundly at night knowing that the streets were being vigilantly patrolled.

The Meeting of Unity was closed by an Atiteco pastor, who seized his moment at the podium by letting loose with a boisterous "Hallelujah," and then thanking God "for allowing us *still* to live in Liberty" (italics indicate original emphasis). The overtly pro-Army and antiguerrilla sentiment of the statement was obvious to all of those present who could speak Spanish, which may well have been a minority. Finally, there were hymns, beginning notably with the symbolically loaded "I'm Going To Hide Myself In The Rock Of Jesus," and including another constructed around the line "In the cross of Jesus there is power, there is power, there is power, . . ." Upon departing the event, I noticed that on the wall surrounding the soccer field soldiers had painted graffiti which proclaimed: "God and the Army are with you." Underscoring an irony of that message, during the next few months the Army would be directly implicated in the murders of numerous civilian Atitecos. In fact, due to that violence, in mid-1990 the Association of Protestant Pastors severed its relationship with the Army.

OCCUPATIONAL CHANGE

According to the Seventh Census of the Population (1964), 79.2 percent of heads of Atiteco households claimed agriculture as their primary occupation. Similarly, in 1966, just over 90 percent of Douglas' sample population listed its occupation as farmer or laborer, most of the latter

26. *During Atitlán's occupation by the Army, graffiti such as this example, which pro-claims "God and the Army are with you," was common. While it is difficult to imagine that this sort of message was intended to sway Atiteco thinking, such graffiti, which typically appeared during the night, certainly underscored the fact that anyone caught in the streets during the curfew hours should be prepared to meet his maker. (Photograph by the author, 1990.)*

category being wage-earning agriculturalists (1969:193). Clearly, a quarter century ago Santiago Atitlán remained a primarily agricultural community, as it always had been. By 1991, however, that designation could no longer be claimed. As shown in Figure 27, in 1991 only 29.6 percent of Atiteco heads of household listed farmer as their primary occupation. Even when laborers are added, that figure rises to only 42.3 percent. I should note that a private 1987 survey of the entire Atiteco population found the combined farmer and agricultural laborer sector to be 49.4 percent (P.C.I. 1987:38). In any case, it is certain that the figure is now under 50 percent of the total for local heads of household.

Much of the transition away from agriculture is reflected in an expansion of Atiteco mercantilism. The typical Atiteco merchant engages in buying and selling commodities outside of the community. Such a *comerciante de fuera* might, for instance, purchase dried fish on the coast and then transport them by bus for resale in Guatemala City. In both the 1964 census and my 1991 survey, merchants constituted the second most numerous category. In 1964, that figure was 11.2 percent. By 1991, however, according to my sample, the rate for merchants had jumped

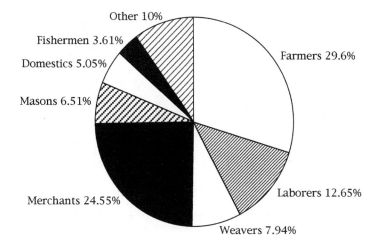

Other 10%

Fishermen 3.61%

Domestics 5.05%

Masons 6.51%

Farmers 29.6%

Laborers 12.65%

Merchants 24.55%

Weavers 7.94%

27. This figure diagrams the occupation types for the (generally male, but also widowed female) heads of Atiteco households in the 1991 survey. Compared with earlier studies, it is clear that the frequencies of the various occupation types among Atitecos have undergone significant change.

to 24.5 percent. In short, it appears certain that the category merchant will soon overtake farmer as the primary occupation-type in Santiago Atitlán.

Another aspect of occupational change covered in my survey addresses correlations between religion and occupation, a topic which I shall demonstrate shortly is of considerable value in explaining local cultural change and identifying potential adaptive advantages. As shown in Figure 28, such correlations are rather as might be expected. In a word, the Working People, followers of an agriculturally based religion, are more likely to engage in agriculture than are Catholics or Protestants. Conversely, Protestants are the least likely to engage in farming, but the most likely to engage in mercantilism. Having stated this, I should note that mercantilism is hardly a novel expression of Atiteco livelihood. In the mid-1930s Felix McBryde observed that Santiago Atitlán was a "merchant-agricultural community depending upon the crops planted on the ample, fertile slopes of the volcanoes and upon returns from the trade voyages of the middlemen who penetrate far into Highland and Lowland alike" (1947:85). Considering that one of Maximón's multiple permutations is Lord of Merchants (R'jawal Bnoi Aj'bijer), that occupation, like all other such traditional endeavors in Atitlán, was once widely associated with the religion of the Working People and symbolically informed by the Old Ways. Aside from the fact that Atiteco mer-

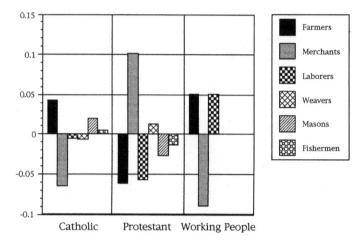

28. *This figure charts occupation types for male Atiteco heads of household, as sub-divided according to categories based on religious identification. Zero represents the average for the town as a whole.*

chants once transported their wares atop their backs and now use buses, what differentiates modern Atiteco mercantilism from its earlier form is its far greater representation in the local population, and certainly its correlation with Protestantism.

Landownership

A relationship between religious affiliation and occupation type stands out in even higher relief when set against a backdrop of changes in land-ownership patterns. McBryde noted that at the time of his 1935 investi-gations, the average Atiteco head of household owned between fifty and a hundred *cuerdas* of land (1947:95).[8] In contrast, by 1966 a mere 36 per-cent of the Atiteco population owned the twenty-nine cuerdas required to support its own agricultural needs (Douglas 1969:33). Douglas' cal-culation of the amount of land needed for a family reflected the fact that in 1966 there was no use of chemical fertilizers in Santiago Atitlán. Over the past twenty years, however, virtually all Atiteco farmers have come to utilize such fertilizers regularly. As a result, the amount of land needed to feed the average Atiteco family of 5.15 persons has fallen to only ten and one-half cuerdas. Nonetheless, based on my sample population, by 1991 only 24.3 percent of Atiteco families had even that amount.[9] Of that figure, 24.3 percent of Atiteco Catholics, 23.5 percent of Protestants, 33.3 percent of Working People, and 25 percent of those who profess no religious affiliation are land-sufficient. These data, however, may be as remarkable for what they do not show as for what they do.

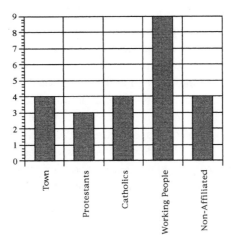

29. This figure shows the median amount of land for a sample population of Atitecos in 1991. According to the sample, Working People tend to possess significantly more land than do other of Atitlán's religious factions. (Measurements are in cuerdas.*)*

According to my sample, the mean average of land owned by Atiteco heads of household is 7.5 cuerdas, or roughly three quarters of that required for food sufficiency. Of that figure, the Working People average 8.8 cuerdas, and tend to own more land than do those of the other religious groupings. That figure compares with 7.6 cuerdas for Catholics, 7.4 for Protestants, and 6.7 for those Atitecos professing no religious affiliation. When these data are computed for the median, however, the pattern for landownership is given new meaning. The median for the Working People is 9.0 cuerdas, the similarity between mean and median indicating land owning consistency within that group. In contrast, a comparison between mean average and median for Catholics, Protestants, and those of the no-religious-affiliation group demonstrates a marked lack of such consistency. For both Catholics and those Atitecos claiming no religious affiliation the median drops steeply to four cuerdas, and to only three cuerdas for Protestants.

These figures illuminate important characteristics of the Atiteco religious ecology. First, the wide discrepancies between the mean and the median for Catholics, Protestants, and the no-religious-affiliation categories indicate that a relatively small number of well-landed individuals skews the mean average for each group and that in reality the average members of each tend to be land-poor. Second, even though only 33.3 percent of the families of Working People may be fully land-sufficient, most members of that group own almost enough land to provide for their food needs. Finally, the difference in subsistence patterns between the Working People and Catholics indicated by these figures adds to my argument that there are fundamental and defining differences between the two groups. Together with data presented earlier, these figures are indicative of a linkage between land, occupation type, and religion. Specifically, the cited data indicate that Working People in Santiago Atitlán tend to own significantly more land and that they are more likely to engage in agriculture as their primary means of subsistence than are local Catholics, Protestants, or those claiming no religion. Conversely, according to my figures, there is a correlation between Protestantism, a lack of land, and a decreased likelihood of engaging in agriculture.

ATITECO POPULATION GROWTH

The reason for the rapidly diminishing average size of Atiteco landholdings is abundantly evident. Adding to the earlier loss of Atiteco land to Guatemala's coffee economy, the immediate cause is explosive population growth. At the time of Douglas' research in Atitlán, the population of the town proper (*aldeas* and *caserios* not included) stood at 9,393. Twenty-five years later in 1991, that figure had risen to 18,430 (P.C.I. 1987:34; 1991 adjustment based on 3 percent annual growth). As indicated in the figures cited above for landownership, the consequences for agricultural production have been catastrophic. In his demographic history of Atitlán, Madigan (1976:197) observed that the town was "experiencing a population explosion of major proportions which [threatened] to surpass the resource capacity of this traditional society." In fact, after noting that in the mid-1970s there were neither external nor internal factors engaged to alter the direction in which Atitlán was headed, Madigan (1976:203) forecast a likely Malthusian collapse.

Although Madigan did not foresee the impact that chemical fertilizers would have on averting Malthusian collapse, it is nonetheless relevant to ask how a society's population level could reach the point where that society might actually teeter on the brink of severe crisis. Clearly, in the decades and centuries past Atiteco existence demanded numerous children. The Atitecos' labor-intensive agricultural existence required children to help work the fields and, equally important, consistently high mortality rates placed pressure on couples to produce children throughout their potential child-bearing years. As late as 1950, mortality rates for Atiteco children ages 0 to 4 remained over 50 percent (Early 1970a:180). Yet, as I explained earlier, the Atitecos' increased access to Western medicine has led to significant drops in infant mortality rates, to the point where by 1987 fully 55.5 percent of Atiteco women reported having never lost any infants (P.C.I. 1987:56). What is more, Atitlán is no longer a primarily agricultural community, hence the need to rear children as agricultural workers has been greatly reduced.

So why do Atitecos continue to reproduce as fast as they do? My direct queries to Atitecos on that question have generally failed to elicit satisfactory answers. For instance, men sometimes state that the problem lies with the women, who they say "lack self-control." Such queries aside, the answer to this question is fairly evident; children remain a necessity. The Atitecos' transition to mercantilism notwithstanding—I will argue shortly that this transition has, by and large, been unsuccessful—Atiteco existence is generally hand-to-mouth, with the accumulation of economic surplus being impossible for most. Hence, children serve as one's old-age pension. Simply put, an aged Atiteco without children, or at least extended family members capable and willing to offer economic support, is likely to have to turn to begging as a means of subsistence.

Compounding this necessity to have children is that, although most Atitecos are no longer agriculturalists, the economy remains labor-intensive. For one thing, the labor required for contemporary Atiteco domestic existence—hauling water from the lake and firewood from the mountains, grinding corn, making tortillas, weaving, and so on—has changed little since times past. For another, the decreasing importance of agriculture has merely forced most Atitecos, young and old, to take up any of a number of supplementary petty commercial enterprises. Such labor-intensive enterprises range from braiding "friendship bracelets" destined for fad-markets in the United States and Europe to daily sending off one's children to sell peanuts to tourists in Panajachel. The clamoring of underemployed Atitecos to engage in this limited number of activities insures that profits remain small. Nonetheless, as marginal as this neo–penny capitalism might be, it typically contributes to the survival of the individual Atiteco family unit.[10] As has been found in the neighboring Tz'utujil-speaking communities of San Juan and San Pablo (Loucky 1988:321), in Santiago Atitlán "children are an implicitly recognized and visible means of securing provisions and income." In short, though parents may be fully aware of the importance of birth control, they may not be able to afford to limit the size of their family (Sexton and Woods 1982:199).

A scant use of modern birth-control methods by the Atitecos is consistent with this continued need for children. Although some Atitecos claim that they do not utilize such methods because of ignorance, those individuals are in the minority. The regional director of the private family-planning organization APROFAM, which maintains a presence in Atitlán, told me that there is a widespread lack of interest among the Atitecos in learning about birth control. This conforms to the 1987 Project Concern study of the Atiteco population, which showed that 80.8 percent of Atiteco women claim to have no interest in learning about the topic (P.C.I. 1987:61). That figure should be compared to the mere 9 percent who say that they do not use birth control because of a lack of knowledge and the remaining 10.2 percent of women who were either using birth control at the time of the survey or had used it in the past. However, despite a lack of modern birth-control practice among the Atiteco population, there has been a notable decline in the average number of live births per female, indicating that other methods are being used. For the mid-1960s, John Early reported an average of eight live births for the average Atiteca (1970b: 161). At present, that figure is under five (P.C.I. 1987:53). Not only does this trend belie those Atiteco men who would attribute population growth to women's lack of control, but in a situation of decreased infant mortality it indicates rationality as a primary factor underlying the decision whether to have children. In any case, it is the number of surviving children and not the number of live births that dictates population growth.

THE DYNAMICS OF CHANGE IN SANTIAGO ATITLÁN

The survival capacity of any society is dependent on its success in adapting to its environment. I have argued that in decades and centuries past Atiteco society was largely successful in that regard. At that time, successful subsistence and a relevant ideology combined to strengthen the Atitecos' capacity to mediate with nonindigenous cultural interests, allowing the maximization of sociocultural autonomy from Guatemala's dominant sector. However, as I have also shown, subsequent changes in local and external dynamics have undermined the adaptive capacity of Atiteco society. On the one hand, Atiteco demographic change and landlessness reflect global factors, particularly an increased international demand for Guatemalan agricultural products and the availability of Western medical technology. But internal factors have also been significant. Most notably, population increase within Santiago Atitlán has contributed to greatly diminished landholdings for the average Atiteco. This scarcity of land has correlated with a transition away from agriculture as the primary means of local subsistence, even to the obsolescence of the

Old Ways. In this light, that Atitecos have abandoned the Old Ways in droves becomes understandable.

RELIGIOUS CHANGE AND ECONOMIC ADAPTATION

That Atiteco society and culture are changing partly because of economic demand and access to advanced medical technology, factors that some would argue to be ultimately beneficial, points to a most important consideration. Simply stated, might not Atiteco novel behavior be associated with some superior mode of adaptation? In other words, released from the functional bonds of ritually prescribed wealth-leveling, cut free from what the Comaroffs (1991:62) call "enchanted entanglements," and with their passions and vices harnessed by proper religion, are the Atitecos free at last to excel?

For the community as a whole, this possibility is easily dismissed. My indexing of the price changes between 1970 and 1990 of fourteen of the commodities most used by Atitecos, and a comparison of those changes with the index change for wages illustrate the Atitecos' plight. The average index rise for the commodities was 236, while the index rise for wage labor was only 201. Virtually all of this decline has occurred since 1980 and even at that time the Atitecos were hardly affluent. While 1980 figures for poverty in Santiago Atitlán are not available, the Atitecos' situation was certainly close to that of Guatemala as a whole. CEPAL, the Comisión Económica de América Latina y el Caribe, reports that in 1980 only 28.9 percent of Guatemalans lived above the poverty line (CEPAL 1982:20–21). By the end of 1991, according to the same agency (in Loeb and Stolzman 1992:10), that figure had dropped to a meager 13 percent. Incidentally, in a 1993 update to the tracking of commodity prices and wages in Atitlán I found that since 1990 there had been a further decline of nearly 15 percent.

In contrast to the relative ease in assessing the direction of recent economic change for Santiago Atitlán as a whole, microanalysis of local wealth is considerably more complicated. To be sure, over the past decade or so a few Atitecos have managed to attain considerable personal wealth. Perhaps no one better than Juan Pablo serves as a case in point. For most of his adult life, Pablo had been a minimally successful Atiteco merchant, engaging in commerce in the coastal and piedmont regions. Rather suddenly, however, he came to have substantial wealth, enough that he was even able to found a bus company, the Transportes de Atitlán. Since the source of Pablo's wealth was a mystery, many Atitecos came to suspect *pak rxinjuyu,* "Mountain Gold." According to Atiteco legend, a blast of blinding light sometimes shines down in the mountains. If a person marks a cross on the ashes produced on the ground by that light, eight days later *pak rxinjuyu* appears on the spot. It is cautioned, however, that if the recipient becomes fat, he or she will turn into a pig. Although Juan Pablo did become rather portly, his fate was quite different. On 22 May 1990, along with three other Atitecos, Pablo was pulled off his bus and brutally murdered. Investigations of the incident by internationally known researcher Ambrose Evans-Pritchard (pers. communication 1990) point solidly to the Army as being the murderers.

Far more meaningful than isolating individual cases of capital accumulation, such as that of Juan Pablo and his purported *pak rxinjuyu*, is assessing patterns of successful subgroup adaptation. Toward that end, during the course of my survey I attempted to establish figures for relative wealth within the sample population. One method was simply to ask my assistants who was the most wealthy person, the second, the third, the fourth, and finally the fifth. Then, replacing poverty for wealth as the primary variable, I repeated the question process. The results of this endeavor were generally unsatisfactory. Establishing patterns for poverty was rather straightforward, indicating that the poorest families were those headed by widowed mothers. The data on positive wealth, however, were far less conclusive. In the six blocks that I surveyed, there were no truly wealthy families, i.e., those owning a car, truck, huge amounts of land, or so on. In short, the typical response from my assistants was that, other than the poorest residents of the blocks, "the rest of us are all the same." Although having no particular reason to doubt the general accuracy of those assessments, I nonetheless turned to other methods which might isolate superior adaptive behavior, beginning with consideration of education.

Education and Adaptation

Atitecos have traditionally held the pursuit of formal education to be of scant value. Indeed, to Atiteco horticulturalists, formal education has been largely irrelevant. Moreover, as noted by Douglas (1969:59), it opened few channels for meaningful employment. Given the evolution of Atiteco society, however, it might seem that education would now be both advantageous and desirable. If nothing else, it would seem that literacy must be essential for mercantilism. Yet, when compared to earlier figures recent data on education trends in Santiago Atitlán reveal only mixed improvement.

According to my survey, the 1991 literacy rate among Atiteco heads of household was 21 percent, to be sure, a considerable improvement over the 9.4 percent rate detected in Douglas' survey (1969:196). Even more significant is the change in the total number of students enrolled in school. Douglas reports that the total 1964 attendance was 213 students. Based on a 1990 survey of all of Atitlán's schools, I established that figure to be 2,056. When adjusted for population growth, these figures demonstrate an approximately fivefold increase in school attendance between 1964 and 1990. Other considerations, however, demonstrate that the current state of education in Santiago Atitlán is not so bright as these data might indicate.

Citing data from the 1964 census, Douglas (1969:53–57) writes that in that year there were 38 percent fewer students in second grade than in first. And by sixth grade, the minimum grade through which Guatemalan law states that children must attend school, that number had fallen to 89 percent fewer students than in first grade. As shown in Figure 30, the situation in 1990 was little improved. The total number of 1990 second-graders was 47 percent less than the number of first-graders, a worse drop than in 1964. The number of sixth-graders in 1990 was fully 78 percent less than the number of first-graders. Although this statistic represents an improvement over the 1964 figure, it remains terrible. In short, despite some improvements in formal education in Santiago Atitlán, high dropout rates and widespread illiteracy support an earlier contention: as a group, Atitecos are not adapting well to the demands of the modern world. Nonetheless, the question remains, might more microanalysis of educational data isolate the superior adaptive behavior of some segment of Atiteco society?

To address that possibility I surveyed the town's eight public schools and two parochial schools: the Catholic school for orphaned children and the Colegio Alfa y Omega, operated by the Centroamericana church.[11] Unfortunately, as the Catholic school only goes through second grade, data from that source are of limited value. A comparison of the Protestant Colegio with the combined public schools is more meaningful. (In the interpretation of these data, it need be kept in mind that Catholic and Protestants alike attend the public schools and therefore that these figures compare a mixed population with a Protestant population.) As depicted in Figure 31, for 1990 the Protestant school's second grade was 51 percent smaller than its first grade, while for the public schools that drop was 39 percent. By sixth grade, however, the positioning of the two is reversed. For that grade the Colegio shows a drop of 65 percent from the size of its first-grade class, while the combined public schools show

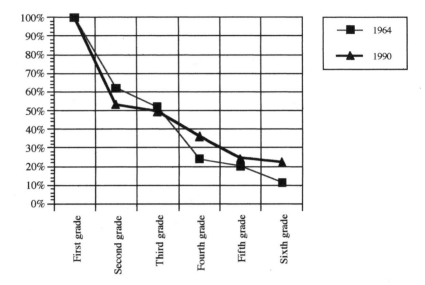

30. *A comparison of the figures for school attendance in Santiago Atitlán for 1964 and 1990 reveals mixed change. The 1990 change from first to second grade is more severe than that of 1964. By 1990, however, the sixth-grade figure is 11 percent improved from that of 1964. In any case, the figures for both 1964 and 1990 are grave.*

an even worse decline of 76 percent. Additional data supplement these figures.

According to data gleaned from my 1991 survey of Atitlán's five neighborhoods, literacy for Atiteco heads of households as subdivided into religious grouping is as follows: 21.2 percent of Catholic heads of household are literate, 25 percent of Protestants, 9.5 percent of those reporting no religious affiliation, and 0 percent of Working People (with a larger sample size, that figure would certainly show a marginal rise). These figures should be compared with the 1991 town average of 21 percent. The average number of years of school for literate Atiteco heads of family in the sample population was 3.2, a figure which typically includes a year of preschool Spanish-language education (*castellanización*).

In concluding this section, I am reminded of an incident told to me by Atitlán's Catholic priest, Tom McSherry, an account which somehow puts these figures into perspective. Among the myriad minidramas characterizing McSherry's parish population is a boy who habitually faces his father's wrath. The crime: sneaking *into* school. In Atitlán today, hunger for education must give way to the family unit's survival imperatives, which generally means children's commitment to full-time work.

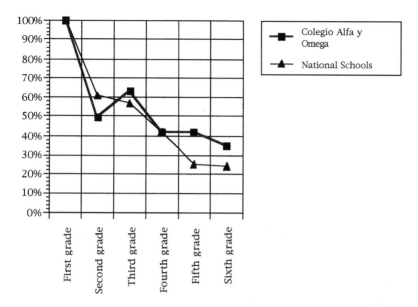

31. *This figure charts the 1990 school attendance rates for the Protestant Colegio Alfa y Omega and the combined public schools of Santiago Atitlán. Although the Protestant school exhibits a steeper decline between its first- and second-grade populations than do the combined public schools, by sixth grade the situation is reversed. The net increase of third-grade students at the Colegio reflects its awarding of a number of scholarships.*

MERCANTILISM AND FARMING

Before assessing the broader significance of these data, it should be helpful to consider figures on two particularly vital sectors of the Atiteco population, mercantilism and farming. In contrast to Atiteco farming, which clearly represents a declining mode of subsistence that may even become virtually obsolete, mercantilism is the fastest growing occupation within the local work force. As such, a comparison of the two should speak to the relative success of Atiteco adaptation to the community's changing environment.

To continue for the moment with education as an indicator of adaptation, only 33.9 percent of the merchants in the 1991 sample reported being literate. Of that figure, Catholic merchants show a greater tendency toward literacy (34.5 percent) than Protestant merchants (32 percent). The percentage of literate merchants compares with 22.8 percent literacy for farmers. Despite the roughly 10-percent advantage of merchants in this comparison, it must be kept in mind that for Atiteco farmers, literacy is perhaps more a luxury than a necessity. That the opposite is true for mercantilism offers initial evidence that as a group, local merchants lack essential cultural capital for adaptive success. That conclusion is supported by other data.

Whereas merchants and farmers differ considerably in education, the average number of surviving children for the two is surprisingly similar, with farmers reporting 3.5 and merchants 3.4 surviving children per family. These figures compare to a town average of 3.4 surviving children. When combined with a final statistic, these data on children offer particularly important information. In the 1991 survey, only 28.8 percent of the farmers reported having secondary or tertiary occupations. This figure differs widely from the 72.4 percent reported by merchants, as well as the 46.4 percent for the town as a whole. In the interpretation of these data, the question arises: accepting that Atiteco agriculture is considerably more labor-intensive than is Atiteco mercantilism, why the similarity in the number of children? I contend that this similarity reflects the relative levels of labor required in the family livelihoods of each, an interpretation supported by the data on supplementary occupations. As indicated above, merchants are far more likely to have multiple occupations than are farmers. Many of those second and third occupations, which incidentally often entail low status and remuneration, demand intensive labor. In conformation with a pattern for the community as a whole, children no doubt provide supplementary labor. So why then do not Atiteco merchants merely abandon these supplementary occupations? It is difficult to escape the conclusion that if they were satisfactorily employed through mercantilism, they would not turn to those occupations in the first place.

Assessing Atiteco Social Change

All told, the above data indicate that as a group Atitecos recognize the need to change, indeed, that they are changing. Nonetheless, the same data indicate that successful change may continue to be hampered by factors over which the local populace has limited control. For instance, the Atitecos' transition to successful mercantilism would no doubt be greatly facilitated by improved formal education. Yet, just as the majority of local merchants have had virtually no such education, poverty and the direct and indirect costs of education all but guarantee that neither will their children be satisfactorily educated.

To be sure, the above data demonstrate variability within the Atiteco population. Yet it should be kept in mind that the analysis of virtually any relatively large social group will detect variability, and that to isolate the higher end of that variability may be of negligible value. I believe that this caution is particularly applicable to contemporary Santiago Atitlán, and that to make much of the more positive aspects of the associated data risks being unjustifiably optimistic. For instance, the approximate 65 percent dropout rate by the sixth grade in the Colegio Alfa y Omega is hardly grounds for optimism, even if compared to the more severe rate in the public schools. Similarly, although the 33.9 percent literacy among Atiteco merchants might exceed the town average, other data indicate that on the whole Atiteco mercantilism does not constitute superior adaptation. Rather, the cited figures indicate that Atiteco mercantilism alone tends to be an inadequate means of family support, even that it is simply another petty economic activity. In a word, I submit that the data on contemporary Atiteco socioeconomic behavior merely tend to isolate levels of inadequate adaptation.[12]

Based on all of the above, I am led to argue that due largely to the increasing obsolescence of their former culture, including agriculture, most Atitecos are being pushed toward sociocultural change. Conversely, very few are being pulled forward toward that change by some realizable promise of a more desirable existence.[13] That is, external and internal factors have combined to undermine the viability of their traditional modes of subsistence, and the Old Ways alike. Yet to date, neither external nor internal solutions have proven capable of satisfying the demands of contemporary Atiteco existence. The results of this situation are to be seen in greatly heightened social instability, and in a greatly reduced desire and/or capacity to resist sociocultural intrusions. The successful penetration of Evangelical missionaries, or even Chuck-the-Gringo and his cable television system, serve as cases in point. Clearly, those factors are interrelated. Perhaps nowhere in Atitlán has this causal interplay of increased instability with sociocultural intrusions been given more prominent and tragic display than in local political violence. To underscore that point, this chapter concludes with consideration of Santiago Atitlán's "decade of violence."

"LA VIOLENCIA" COMES TO ATITLÁN

In June 1980, the recently formed guerrilla group ORPA entered Atitlán, where its members began the open and successful recruitment of Atitecos. The following month, strangers in civilian clothes commenced asking some Atitecos questions about town residents. On occasion, those residents' addresses were demanded. In October, with the Atitecos powerless to do anything about it, the Army began its occupation of the town. Scarcely two weeks later, two Atitecos disappeared. By the beginning of December, the total had risen to ten. And in 1981, the number of victims soared. Included were sixteen Atitecos murdered in a coffee plantation, as well as the resident Catholic priest, Oklahoman Stanley Rother. Virtually all Atitecos remain convinced that the perpetrators of those killings were elements of the Army. (Paul and Demarest [1988] discuss similar occurrences for the neighboring town of San Pedro la Laguna.)

ORPA, the Organization of People in Arms, initially enjoyed considerable popular support in Atitlán and elsewhere in southwestern Guatemala. That support, however, was undermined by a successful counterinsurgency strategy implemented by head of state Ríos Montt, the born-again Evangelical general who professed to transform Guatemala into a moral beacon of light and its citizenry into something he called "new Israelites." This call to spiritual arms certainly appealed to elements of the religious right in the United States who, encouraged in part by the agency International Love Lift, contributed large sums of money to Ríos Montt's effort. As noble as it may have sounded, the toll in human corpses demonstrates otherwise (e.g., see Stoll 1990). Realizing that a guerrilla army can be successful only if it is supported by the local civilian population, Ríos Montt responded to incidents of guerrilla activity with what one scholar has called "total war at the grassroots" (Jonas 1991:148). Following guerrilla activity in a particular area, violence rained on the local Mayan population. Amnesty International recorded some 6,000 killings by security forces during the six months following the March 1982 coup that brought Ríos Montt to power (Simon 1987:108). Responding to the violence, in May 1982 the Guatemalan bishops stated, "Never in our national history have we come to such grave extremes. These murders are . . . genocide."

In Atitlán, as elsewhere, this counterinsurgency certainly did not endear the Army to the people. But it did succeed in neutralizing popular support for ORPA. As the counterinsurgency around Atitlán progressed, the frequency of guerrilla actions diminished, until by 1988 they had virtually ceased. Yet, rather than loosen its grip, the Army actually ratcheted up the level of violence. The evidence indicates overwhelmingly that by 1989 the Army in Atitlán was clandestinely engineering robberies, kidnappings, and murders (Carlsen 1990; Loucky and Carlsen 1991). Information was then disseminated bolstering claims of continued rural "terrorism," thereby not only justifying the Army's continued high pro-

file presence, but derailing legally mandated negotiations with the guerrillas at the same time. As one small example, the burning in 1990 of several highway-department trucks on the road into Santiago very nearly
undermined pending discussions between the representatives of Guatemala's major political parties and guerrilla leaders. Lost on journalists
covering the story was that the initials EGP that had been painted on the
trucks belonged to a guerrilla organization that operates exclusively in a
distant part of the country.

ENGINEERED INSTABILITY

A secondary Army goal in Atitlán has been to destabilize, and thereby
undermine any capacity for community resistance. One mechanism was
the Army's implementation of the Patrulla de Autodefensa Civil (PAC),
otherwise known as civil patrols. These units were composed of Atitecos
who were forced to police the community, purportedly to protect it
from "terrorists." In fact, through the civil patrols, Atitecos were drafted
into being agents of the Army within their own community. A couple of
schemes insured the patrols' vigilance. First, the Army typically made
the patrols directly responsible for subversive activity in the area. (Also
see Cultural Survival 1988:11–17; Wilson 1991:33–61.) Second, the Army
hired local Atitecos to administer the patrols. Those administrators, the
notorious *comisionados militares*, received the license to violate the law.
If the comisionados were not corrupt to start with, this encouraged
them to become so. In Atitlán, that license translated in everything from
demand for firewood to sexual coercion to murder. Certainly the most
notorious of the local *comisionados* was Nicolás Pedro Mendoza, whose
actions were rewarded by an assassin's bullet in 1987. Not content that
justice had been served, several Atitecos reportedly later dismembered
his disinterred body. That same year, the Atiteco citizenry took the bold
step of demanding that the local civil patrols be disbanded and the military commissioners dismissed. Although the Army was forced to acqui-
esce, as late as 1990 it was clear that a goal of military violence was to
make the Atitecos reconsider their decision.[14]

Even the education system in Atitlán was targeted for violence. One
day late in 1987, anonymous messages were left at the houses of each of
the teachers in the town's largest public school advising their immediate
and permanent departures from the town. Realizing fully the implications of that sort of message—according to a report published by the
United States Army (Nyrop 1983:158), in 1980 some 326 elementary and
secondary school teachers were murdered in Guatemala—all the teach-

ers left the following day. The Army has even supported gangs of Atiteco robbers, this certainly to fuel instability, division, and mistrust within the community. An observation by one of the more insightful contemporary anthropologists, Michael Taussig, is instructive in this regard: "The Armed Forces in an age defined by Pentagon theorists as one of 'low intensity warfare,' have as much to gain from disorder as from order—and probably a good deal more" (1992:17).

ATITECO SOCIETY UNDER THE GUN

Ultimately, the disparate mutations of military control subsumed or undermined all other sources of formal Atiteco civilian authority. Left to the mercy of the grim reapers in battle fatigues, and with few sources of defense, by 1990 the town came to be paralyzed by the fear born of unrestrained military violence (Carlsen 1990). Even my family and I were directly affected. On 30 May of that year, perhaps not wanting to have a foreigner around whose job it is to ask questions, soldiers moved into my yard in Atitlán and set up a substantial camp. Following a couple of uncomfortable encounters with the commander of the local garrison, and understanding too well the *modus operandi* of the Army, I acknowledged the evident message for me to leave the country. (Only exceptional conditions allowed my return in December 1990.) Shortly after being run out of Guatemala, I penned a report for the *Guatemala Scholars Network News* about the state of affairs in Atitlán. To convey a sense of the destabilizing fear in Atitlán, I quote from that report:

> At night in Atitlán, a de facto, though not officially declared, curfew prohibits honest Atitecos from venturing from their homes between 10 P.M. and 4 A.M. This curfew is so rigid that should a child become ill during these hours, the child's mother must wait until 4 A.M. before going to the clinic. It is curious then that bands of Atiteco robbers operate with apparent immunity during the curfew hours. The most blatant example of this sort occurred on 9 March [1990] when, over a two hour period, an entire block was systematically looted. Although most of the members of these gangs are known to the local populace, complaints to the police have been fruitless. I should note that in a meeting on 11 January, *before the robberies had started*, an Army spokesperson informed the heads of the town's ten public cofradías that "we have heard that there is going to be a wave of robberies in the town and we think that it would be tragic if any of the cofradía relics were stolen. So be careful."

Lo and behold, *the following day*, the robberies started. A few days later, posters appeared throughout the town which both condemned La Delincuencia Terrorista and used it as a pretext for the local Army presence.

As may already be evident, lurking behind much of what happens in Santiago Atitlán is the Army presence. While soldiers typically vacate the town during the morning when the tourist hordes descend from Panajachel, by early evening they are back. And at night, the soldiers are omnipresent. The fact is that at any time of the day one need only look a few hundred yards to the hillside behind the town to see soldiers peering down from a recently constructed observation post. With their telescopic devices, the soldiers can and do watch the very faces of anyone that they choose. Stated simply, nothing is done in Santiago Atitlán without first considering the Army factor. One case among many is particularly illustrative.

During the afternoon of 30 May a local widowed Maya who lived directly next door to Atitlán's military base was shot dead as she was walking into town. The woman's husband, a military commissioner, had been killed several years back (probably by ORPA). In order to help support herself, she washed clothes for the Army. On the surface, this case might seem to have been the work of the guerrillas. However, the fact is that shortly before the murder, as he was walking home a neighbor of the victim was approached by several soldiers. That nineteen-year-old Atiteco school teacher was instructed to deliver a letter to the woman, a letter which ordered her immediate presence in town. On her way into town, the woman was killed. Shortly after, the school teacher was picked up by the Army for subversion. He joins a long list of the Atiteco "disappeared."

Contributing to the repressive climate in Atitlán is that disappearances are keeping numerous Atitecos from venturing to their maize fields or from cutting firewood. While the mountainside behind Atitlán has been off limits to all but soldiers for several years, the danger of venturing outside of town now extends in all directions. As a result, not only have many Atitecos been cut off from the sources of their livelihood, but various ancient rituals which require Atiteco presence in the mountains have had to be abandoned.

Given the reality of Atitlán, it is understandable that most Atitecos harbor a suspicion of all but their most trusted friends. Sadly, lest suspicion be raised, many are careful not to give outward expression of their own fear. With spies (*orejas*, lit. ears) known to be lurking about, there is even fear that fearful behav-

32. It has been common that following a murder in Atitlán the Army disseminates fly-ers such as this. Generally, one side depicts ORPA "terrorists" brutalizing honest Atite-cos. The other side cites, in Tz'utujil, the name of the victim and the date of the killing, and offers a general description of the incident. Such flyers aside, in most cases it has been the Army itself which has been responsible for the terrorist actions, to justify its continued high-level presence in the south Lake Atitlán area. This flyer was issued fol-lowing the 31 January 1990 murder of Salvador Sapalu Cojtin.

ior itself might be construed as deriving from "unallowable" behavior. By way of example, after having just voiced an emo-tional testimony of his own general sense of fear and frustra-tion, a longtime confidant explained that "upon stepping out onto the street a smile comes to my face. If anyone asks me how I'm doing, I say 'great.' And if they ask me what I think about some incident, my reply is 'I don't know anything about it.' I then tell them 'if you want to find out, you should talk to the family. I'm just on my way to pray at the church.'"

The totality of this situation, and many others like it throughout Gua-temala, is conveyed in the words of the cultural geographer W. George Lovell, who writes (1988:48), "In recent years, the people whom Mi-guel Angel Asturias immortalized as *hombres de maiz* ["men of corn," from the ancient/contemporary belief that flesh is corn] have actually had to seek permission from military personnel to tend their plots and raise the very crop that created Maya civilization." Under these condi-tions, the Atitecos have been forced to conceal their own terror under smiles, and seemingly have been reduced to diverting their anger into church prayers. While this situation certainly represents considerable erosion of the Atitecos' earlier autonomy, and might otherwise indicate their spiritual conquest, in late 1990 the Atitecos would demonstrate in remarkable fashion the error in prematurely dismissing their capacity for self-determination.

7

When Immortals Die

"Atiteco Friends, the Future of Your Village Is in Your Own Hands."

A SIGN ERECTED BY THE GUATEMALAN ARMY ON THE SPOT WHERE
DAYS EARLIER ITS SOLDIERS HAD KILLED THIRTEEN ATITECOS, 1990

THE CAR APPEARED TO BE RACING the descending darkness as it sped along the south lake road toward Santiago Atitlán.[1] Not until it approached the town's outskirts did it finally slow, and then stop. One of the passengers took out a black *gorra*, a hoodlike knit cap with eyeholes, and pulled it over the head of the man seated between himself and the other backseat passenger. Despite the dusk, the driver turned off the headlights, and then proceeded slowly into town. As he passed groups of Atitecos walking home from their *milpas* (maize fields), the driver, the sole occupant of the front seat, carefully avoided eye contact. Similarly, his three passengers lowered themselves in the backseat. After traveling nearly through town, the car veered right and proceeded slowly down a side road, toward the lake. Although that road was designed for vehicles, such traffic was rare enough that almost everyone in the street turned to look. Reaching the end of the road, the car turned, continued several meters onto a boulder-strewn footpath, and finally halted directly in front of the stone gate to a family compound. Immediately, several waiting Atitecos stepped out from the shadows, opened the car's rear door, and hustled the hooded passenger inside the compound. On the evening of 21 February 1990, Jerónimo Quieju Pop, the great shaman and Maximón's *telinel*, returned to Santiago Atitlán.

MAXIMÓN'S SHOULDER, MAXIMÓN'S NOSE

For weeks, Jerónimo would not leave his family's compound. Not only was he convalescing, but he was afraid. Jerónimo's earlier prediction of dreaming the identities of his would-be assassins notwithstanding, those individuals were still on the loose, and perhaps still in town. Fortunately, Jerónimo's stealth return had paid off, as few Atitecos suspected that he was back. In fact, most still assumed that he had died from the "fourteen" gunshot wounds. Compounding Jerónimo's anxiety was a somewhat less immediate though equally pressing concern. More than any other of the Working People, as telinel Jerónimo had ritual obligations. And the most public, most high profile, and most important event of the ritual calendar was quickly approaching. As noted earlier, the telinel is the personal shaman (aj'kun) to Maximón. Much of a telinel's time on the job is spent inside Cofradía Santa Cruz performing rituals to the deity.[2] Yet, while such duties are time-consuming, they are not the job's most important. As the derivation of the word telinel (from telek, "shoulder") implies, a telinel's most important function is to carry the deity on his shoulder through the streets of town during Semana Santa (Holy Week).

According to the Old Ways, the rituals performed during the five days of Semana Santa in which Maximón is of central importance are vital in fueling the transition of the dry season into the wet, and similarly of the cycles of death into life. It is a cosmically unstable few days that has been associated with the uayeb period (the five "delicate" days) of the ancient Mayan solar calendar (Mendelson 1965). Moreover, this time is inextricably linked with fertility, agricultural and otherwise. During Semana Santa that fertility is given ritual display in the nocturnal running through the streets of San Juan Carajo (Saint John the "Prick"), in the songs of Atiteca virgins to the hole called R'muxux Ruchiliew (Umbilicus of the World) located in the church floor, and certainly in the ritually prescribed sexual intercourse of the alguaciles (cofradía "policemen") with their wives. In a literal sense, however, it is Maximón himself that takes center stage. As the R'jawal R'kux Ruchiliew, the Lord of the Middle of everything that is (including the human body), during Holy Week Maximón represents a primary sexual organ whose task it is to reinseminate the world and hence pave the way for the coming of the rainy season, as symbolized by the resurrection from death of the Christ figure. Accordingly, the pivotal and certainly most dramatic event of the week occurs on Good Friday. With many thousands of Atitecos looking on, the telinel shows Maximón to the crucified and dead Christ, represented as the carved wooden figure Señor Sepultado. Perched atop the telinel's shoulder and jutting above the crowd, Maximón bows to the World's four corners and then rushes full speed through the crowd of onlookers and back to Cofradía Santa Cruz. Under the shaman's guidance, the cofrades finally hide the deity in the attic, hence curbing his potentially disruptive and now unnecessary hypersexuality.

As might be suspected, besides providing a vehicle for Atiteco ritual performance, Semana Santa now serves as a platform for community dissension. Ever since the 1953 legal resolution to the Maximón scandals, Semana Santa has forced the new ways of the Catequistas to interface with the Old Ways of the Working People. Adding to the tension, the Catholics have wrested away from the Working People, who used to control the event entirely (e.g., see McDougall 1955) important aspects of the event, particularly as they concern the persona of Jesus Christ. In a power play underscoring that point, during the rituals of 1989 the Catequistas humiliated the Working People by making them wait for almost two hours before piously bringing Señor Sepultado down the church's front steps, finally allowing the confrontation with Maximón to proceed.

A year later, that incident seemed forgotten. Clearly, there was a more pressing matter: what to do about the telinel situation? For their parts, many Catholics and Protestants alike were gleeful. With the recently shot "witch" (*brujo*) believed either to be dead or incapacitated in the hospital in Sololá, hope reigned among the antitraditionalists that Maximón's spasms of Holy Week evilness might finally be squelched. In contrast, those Working People who knew that Jerónimo was in town worried that he would not be enough healed from his wounds to undertake the grueling rituals. Yet, even as Jerónimo returned to Atitlán, he had begun to prepare for Semana Santa, starting with the ritually prescribed sexual abstinence. Within days, word began to filter through the cofradías that not only was the telinel back, but that he intended to fulfill his ritual obligations. It soon became evident, though, that Jerónimo may have been too optimistic about his convalescence.[3]

The first important ritual during Semana Santa occurs late on Monday evening when the telinel mounts a large bundle of Maximón's clothes atop his back and dances it across town to the lakeshore. Amid clouds of incense and copious amounts of liquor, the clothes are ceremonially washed by cofradía members. The grueling part of the ritual is the return trip when, accompanied by guitar music, the telinel must dance the bundle of sopping wet and now extremely heavy clothes back through town. Despite Jerónimo's determination, when Semana Santa finally arrived he conceded to a stand-in. As it was, the telinel's test would commence Wednesday. Early in the afternoon of that day, the telinel shoulders Maximón to the town hall (*alcaldía*) and in a highly esoteric ritual performance, lays the deity in a circle of fruit portered up from the coast by the alguaciles in a two-day pilgrimage. Evidence suggests that this fruit represents female slaves, with whom Maximón symbolically copulates (Tarn and Prechtel 1990). Several rounds of liquor and a couple of hours later, Maximón is shouldered to his private chapel where, until midday on Good Friday, he is hung on a pole adorned as a tree.

Not only would this event mark Jerónimo's first public exposure since being shot, but even under optimum circumstances the days of hauling the deity, of virtual sleeplessness, and the incessant mouthfuls of ritually prescribed and gut-wrenching "canyon water" (*ptsiwanya*, moonshine liquor) present a formidable test of any telinel's strength. In fact, the Working People say that pretenders to the position will be unmasked by the demands.

If Wednesday's events were indicative, Jerónimo was clearly worthy of his title. Far from withering, throughout the day he actually seemed to gain strength. As is mandated by the Old Ways, Jerónimo spent Wednesday night accompanied by various Working People in Maximón's chapel, all the while drinking canyon water and periodically strumming his guitar while meditatively singing traditional songs to the deity.[4] Semana Santa was the first time in months that the Army had relaxed its curfew, and while the telinel sang, a constant stream of the faithful and the curious passed by to watch and to listen.

> . . . *O son of the tree,*
> *O son of cord.* [Reference to Maximón's manner of construction]
>
> *He blesses the corners,*
> *He blesses the ancient thrones* [palimal] *of the rain deities.*
>
> *O son of Juan, son of Diego.* [Reference to the Martín bundle]
> *O son of María Heddle,*
> *O son of María Lease Stick.*
> [Continues with acknowledgment of all of the deified loom parts]
>
> *Mama mam achi, mama mam acha . . .*

Thursday followed with more of the same. Food, canyon water, and of course tobacco (Maximón is inventor and lord of tobacco) were brought to Maximón and his entourage. Yet it must be understood that pleasure was not a primary factor. The Working People (as their title specifies) realize that rituals such as this demand "sacrifice" and pain to be efficacious. Accordingly, by midday, the atmosphere inside the chapel was defined not only by the copal incense and song, but also by nausea, sweat, heat, and dust. To be sure, synesthesia, a euphoric blending of the senses brought on by the intensity of sounds, smells, sights, liquor, and fatigue occasionally led to ecstatic wailing. More commonly, however, that intensity merely caused the participants to pass out on a bench or on the floor. Understandably, concern lingered about Jerónimo's endurance. After all, a full day remained until the confrontation with Jesus and the subsequent shouldering of Maximón back to the cofradía. And it is common knowledge among the Working People that over the course of Semana Santa the deity's increased spiritual potency translates into increased weight.

Good Friday began with the telinel taking leave of the candles and incense of the chapel. Perhaps as a test of his own strength, he wandered through the early morning darkness to the town center. There he mingled with the crowd watching the running of San Juan Carajo. As those in the crowd talked, every few minutes young Atitecos portering the "Prick" would appear out of the darkness, race up to the image of María Andaloor (San Juan Carajo's concubine), and amidst shouts thrust their sacred cargo phallically into the night sky. The porters of the carved wooden image, who had paid hard-earned money for the honor, would then turn around and race back into the blackness from whence they had come. All the while, a group of Working People stood to the side singing Tinieblas, a haunting chant about darkness and abysmal ignorance. Although teams of runners would continue until near dawn, after an hour or so the telinel returned to Maximón, where he prepared for the Semana Santa climax.

Though the climactic confrontation between Maximón and Jesus (Señor Sepultado) does not occur until well into the afternoon on Friday, the crowd on the plaza between the church and Maximón's chapel invariably begins to form much earlier. After all, the confrontation may be the day's major event, but the mingling among friends and neighbors is certainly a major attraction. As the spectators arrive, many dressed in exquisite outfits woven especially for the occasion, inside the chapel the incense, the canyon water, and the song continue unabated. "Strum strum boy, strum strum man . . . Knock knock boy, drum drum mama, drum drum Lucha."[5] Uniting those inside—who by this time feel tightly connected to what Mircea Eliade (1971:4) identifies as *illo tempore* (mythological primacy)—with the spectators in their fancy clothes is a growing sense of excited anticipation. In a way, that sense is self-fulfilling; the excitement is generated by the anticipation of a climactic

33. From midday Wednesday through midday Friday during Holy Week, Maximón is hung from a post adorned with willow branches. During that time the deity represents the tree at the center of the world, the axis mundi. *(Photograph by Paul Harbaugh, 1990.)*

event, a climax which invariably satisfies because of the pent-up excitement. This year would be no different.

By mid-afternoon, thousands of spectators were jammed into the plaza. On cue, a contingent of young Catequistas bearing Señor Sepultado exited the church. With their precious cargo held aloft in an elaborate glass-sided coffin, the nicely dressed young men advanced to the spot where, according to custom, they gently swayed back and forth while awaiting the appearance of Maximón. At that point, however, something very significant happened: absolutely nothing. For a minor eternity, the contingent of swaying Catequistas waited. But still no telinel and no Maximón. By the time that the lull reached its first hour, most of the exhausted entourage holding Señor Sepultado aloft had to be replaced. Rumors began to spread through the crowd that Jerónimo, who by now was widely known to have returned, had collapsed. Yet the Working People in the crowd seemed suspiciously unconcerned. When a nonchalant telinel finally appeared at the doorway of the chapel, it became apparent what was happening. Stealing a chapter from the Catholics' playbook, the Working People had taken back control of this most important of Semana Santa rituals. Determined to emphasize the victory, even then Maximón's contingent was in no hurry. While the crowd of onlookers became more restless, the still swaying Catholic porters worked at mediating anger, fatigue, and piety. Suddenly, Maximón and his telinel were off and running. Amid a roar of excitement the duo rushed up to the coffined figure, performed the pulsating bows to the World's four corners, made a final thrust at Señor Sepultado, and then flew full speed through the crowd. In a flash, it was over.

Even as the multitude started to collect itself, a Ladino onlooker began screaming "Maximón es paganismo. Paganismo es Maximón." The numerous Working People in the crowd were hardly fazed by the outburst. They were accustomed to Ladino rudeness. More important, they were reveling in the day's events. Well into the evening conversation throughout Atitlán's cofradías centered on Jerónimo's victory. Not only had the old shaman engineered a coup for the Old Ways, but on a more personal level, he had also triumphed over those that would have had him be dead. The possibility that his would-be assassins were actually watching in the plaza that afternoon was lost on nobody, and only made the victory more enjoyable. Soon after Semana Santa, the violence began to reassert its grip on the town. Barely a month later when Cofradía Santa Cruz and Maximón made the annual transfer to a new sponsor (alcalde), the town had entered fully into a reign of military terror not experienced since the days of Ríos Montt. Adding to that terror, late one afternoon in October hooded gunmen burst into the cofradía and turned their weapons on the new telinel and the deity seated to his left. The telinel, Martín Kik, was riddled by multiple shots and died instantly. For his part, Maximón had his nose blown off. Yet, in a miraculous occurrence that the Working People now claim prefigured the remarkable series of events soon to occur, within days Maximón's nose grew back.[6]

THE RESURRECTION OF ATITECO AUTONOMY

On 3 December 1990, word began to trickle out of Guatemala of a significant massacre the day before. The initial reports in the international media singled out the Army as the perpetrators and cited an unnamed western Guatemalan town as the locale. The town, of course, was Santiago Atitlán. Over the next few days, extensive media coverage allowed a piecing together of the incident. (Also see Loucky and Carlsen 1991; Cockrell 1991.) Along with several of his subordinates the commander of the Atitlán garrison had passed the afternoon of 1 December drinking in a local cantina. In the early evening, the drunken group moved on to another bar, where the heavily armed soldiers beat a few Atiteco clients. For the next few hours, the soldiers roamed the streets, abusing passersby, wounding a nineteen-year-old Atiteco, and attempting to break into a store. The soldiers eventually focused their energies on a private home, where they reportedly sought to rape the owners' daughter. However, a crowd of local Mayas was able to overpower the bunch and severely beat them with hand-held rocks.

At that point the events took a most significant turn. Seemingly pushed over that line which separates hopeless terror from the courage born of desperation, aroused Atitecos spread out through town, waking the mayor and the mayor-elect, and ringing the church bells. Several thousand Atitecos massed in the church plaza. Though a decade of violence had taught the Atitecos the likely consequences of their actions, they decided to confront the Army with their grievances. With their only defense being white flags carried overhead, in the early hours of 2 December between 2,000 and 4,000 Atitecos marched on the local garrison. As the crowd approached, a soldier on a loudspeaker called out in Spanish: "What is happening, people? What is your problem? We can resolve it." When the town's mayor-elect, the leader of the Atiteco marchers, responded, a soldier fired into the air. Immediately, other soldiers commenced shooting directly into the crowd. The initial thunder of automatic weapons-fire soon subsided into sporadic bursts, which continued for several minutes longer. The indication is that during those few minutes of terror, soldiers chased some Atitecos into surrounding coffee groves, where one bullet-riddled body was found. Twelve others lay either dead or dying on the road nearby, with dozens more wounded.

The aftermath of the Atitlán massacre has been most significant. It triggered the December 1990 decision by the United States to curtail all military aid to Guatemala.[7] It led to a censure of the country by the European Economic Community. Indicative of the unprecedented criticism heaped on the military, the Guatemalan Catholic Archdiocese Human Rights Office issued a scathing report on the affair, concluding that the Army was guilty of crimes of genocide and recommending major changes in military policy. Perhaps most remarkable, as a result of the national and international condemnation, on 20 December 1990 the Guatemalan Army vacated its Atitlán garrison.[8] With that exit, the town became one of the very few Guatemalan communities of over 10,000 inhabitants not to have a permanent military base or garrison, in fact the country's only community entirely free of any military presence whatsoever.

At first glance, there seems little which would account for the remarkable outcome to the events of 2 December. The fact is that this incident pales in comparison with many other massacres that have occurred in

Guatemala's recent past. Between May and July 1994 alone, mass graves containing as many as 1,500 men, women, and children were uncovered in Río Negro, in La Libertad, and in Playa Grande. In all cases, the Army has been directly implicated.[9] Yet the Atitlán massacre has been unprecedented in its political impact. Although many Working People attributed the entire event to the shooting of the telinels and Maximón, the more apparent reason lies in the event's immediate publicity and in the testimonies of the numerous witnesses. The reporters and human-rights groups investigating the incident were met by an outpouring of denunciations from the Atitecos, as if a floodgate of emotions had been opened following a decade of deathly silence. Similarly, less than twenty-four hours after the killings, fifteen thousand Atiteco signatures and thumbprints had been collected on a petition demanding the trial and punishment of those responsible. Moreover, the evening following the massacre Atitlán's mayor and mayor-elect gained uncensored access to national television. In a display of free speech rarely witnessed in Guatemala they recounted the details, not only of the massacre, but of the town's entire decade of violence.

Guatemalan President Vinicio Cerezo's announcement three days later that the Army would vacate the town triggered an emotional explosion in the community. It was a profound sense of *communitas* which combined the mourning for those murdered with the lifting of a cloud of paralyzing fear and terror, and which certainly reflected the realization of having partaken in a most unusual occurrence. The catharsis of that moment led quickly to a celebration of freedom and solidarity, a celebration remarkable under any circumstances, but especially so in Guatemala. In memory of the thirteen Atitecos martyred days before, black bows were hung above the doorway of virtually every house and store in town. A photo display commemorating the hundreds of victims of Atitlán's entire decade of violence was mounted in front of the town hall. A "peace park" was even constructed at the site of the former Army garrison and scene of the massacre. As that garrison was itself being dismantled by the Army, the Atitecos delighted in describing the discomfort of the soldiers confined by presidential decree within its barbedwire and stone walls. They made no attempt to hide their glee when describing how thirsty the soldiers must be without the cold drinks that they had previously gotten in town, or how hungry they must be now that their supply of tortillas had been cut. After all, the reign of terror was over, and every act of violence and all that had divided the community and caused such pain over the past decade was being attributed to the *kiks*, the "bloody ones."

34. *Within days of the 2 December massacre in Santiago Atitlán a display appeared in the town's Catholic church naming (on small paper crosses) some of those Atitecos murdered (asesinados), "disappeared" (secuestrados), and injured (heridos) during the town's decade of violence. In addition, a group of thirteen paper crosses (to the extreme right) named those "martyred" in the massacre. The entire display was itself hung above the monument to the American priest Stanley Rother, who ten years earlier was murdered in the adjoining parish by elements of the Army. (Photograph by the author, 1991.)*

Reconstituted Atiteco Power

Clearly, the Atitecos' reaction to the massacre, combined with the unprecedented national and international response, had caught the Army off guard. Only days before it had wielded near total power in Atitlán. By means of a strategic application of violence, the soldiers seemed to have channeled the Atitecos' potential social activism into religious expression, for instance, the pursuit of social justice and material enrichment into prayer. As evidenced by an Atiteco search for empowerment "in the cross of Jesus," as the hymn goes, these attempts at what the Comaroffs (1991:xi) call the "colonization of consciousness" were at least partially successful. Yet, had the soldiers not become arrogantly confident of their power, they might better have assessed important changes underway within the local population, changes which expose an underlying Atiteco "consciousness of colonization." For instance, several months prior to the massacre, the Atitecos had begun to form vigilante groups. On one occasion, following the murder of a Mayan caretaker of a local vacation home, one such group of vigilantes was able to run down and capture the killers. They were soldiers from the local garrison.[10] Several Atitecos caught during robberies and suspected of collaborating with the soldiers were even executed by the vigilantes.

Complementing a rise of overt Atiteco militancy was an increased wielding of "weapons of the weak." In Atitlán, for instance, a decade of living under the gun had taught the populace that by purposefully "forgetting" to attend meetings called by the Army, they merely lived down to the standards for "Indianness" embraced by the Ladino officer corps. In 1990, this type of purposeful inaction derailed Army attempts to reinstate the military-sponsored civil patrols (PACs). In contrast to such strategic inactivity, some applications of weapons of the weak were quite activist, and entailed considerable potential risk. One remarkable incident occurred on the lake just around a bend and out of sight of the town. As a late afternoon boat from Panajachel was approaching, Mayan sentinels on the shore began waving flags to raise the passengers' attention. When the boat slowed, elderly Atitecos in a flotilla of dugout canoes pushed off from shore. Arriving at the boat, they explained that soldiers were at the town dock waiting to conscript the young male passengers.[11] Still out of sight of the town, the Atitecos in the canoes then proceeded to trade places with the young men on the boat. A few minutes later when the fully loaded boat pulled into dock, the soldiers were dumbfounded when not a single young man numbered among the scores of Mayan passengers.

The sudden and entirely unanticipated eviction of the Army, however, posed entirely new survival imperatives for the Atitecos which required an immediate consolidation of the available sources of power. Benefiting from a temporarily staggered military, and taking advantage of their tremendous support across the country, the Atitecos immediately established a security zone of twenty-five square kilometers which they declared off limits to the Army and the ORPA guerrillas alike. To administer their newly gained sovereignty and neutrality, the Atitecos both elaborated on existing institutions and created entirely new ones. Primary among those institutions were the Office of the Mayor, the Development and Security Committee, and the *rondas*.

OFFICE OF THE MAYOR

Until the relatively recent past, local civil government in Santiago Atitlán was dominated by the cofradías and the Working People. Despite a 1945 law mandating democratic elections and designed to curb rural Mayan autonomy, for several decades longer in Atitlán the office of Mayor tended to remain an extension of the cofradía. Yet the mere fact that the town's last four mayors have been Protestant underscores the social changes underway in the town. During the Army occupation few Atitecos looked to the Mayor for protection. Since the massacre, however, local expectations of the job have changed. The position has been transformed into a source of considerable indigenous power and, despite the 1945 law, into an instrument of autonomy. The Salvador Ramírez administration exemplifies the evolution of that office.

From the moment that Atitlán's mayor-elect, Salvador Ramírez, appeared on national television following the massacre, he seemed to delight in deriding the Army. When he became Mayor, a favored forum for Ramírez were the *concentraciones*, town meetings that, in commemoration of the massacre, take place on the second day of every month. There was the time, for instance, when the Army proposed to reenter Atitlán to "help" the Atitecos cope with the 1992 cholera epidemic. Ramírez replied that he would rather contract that disease than allow the Army in town. On a different occasion the Mayor recounted his audience with Mexican President Carlos Salinas de Gortari. "The President told me 'Keep going forward. Now you are strong, and I hope that you will stay united so that the Army doesn't come and invade the town. Because if the Army invades, they will massacre all the people. For the Army, there is no law, no Congress, no human rights.'" On yet another occasion, Ramírez told the gathered crowd that he had received a demand from the regional military zone (Zone 14) that a specified number of young males be turned over for inscription into the Army. Ramírez went to the base in Sololá where he informed the commander that as an elected servant of the people of Atitlán, he *could* not comply. He then stated that having lived in Atitlán for ten years under Army rule, he *would* not comply. He added that the soldiers could kill him but that they would then have "to contend with the consequences." [12]

DEVELOPMENT AND SECURITY COMMITTEE

A second source of Atiteco community leadership and power came into existence following the December 1990 massacre. The Comité de Desarollo y Seguridad, or simply *the* Committee as it is generally called, was organized both to consolidate local security and to administer the considerable funds donated by local and external sources. Since then, it has become the primary entity responsible for the security of Santiago Atitlán. For the first three years of its existence the Committee was under the leadership of Manuel Sisay, a Catholic. In 1994, Sisay was forced to resign amid controversy, including the implication of his brother-in-law in a series of local robberies.

The committee operates on two fronts: inside and outside the town. Inside Atitlán, the Committee is in charge of managing the rondas, which are groups of men and boys that patrol the streets at night. The rondas constitute the primary arm of law enforcement in Atitlán, their authority far exceeding that of the National Police. In fact, following the massacre and the Atitecos' eviction of the Army, President Cerezo had blocked the Atitecos' attempts to oust the National Police. Not to be dissuaded, the Atitecos merely ordered that all National Police actions in and around their town first be cleared by the Committee. As a result, the Police have been largely reduced to consuming cold drinks in the town park, and reportedly offer little trouble.

The other arena of Committee operations is outside the town. Most Atitecos are convinced that because of their resistance to the Army, soldiers have engineered assaults on Atiteco-owned buses on rural highways. In fact, in a couple of instances, Committee investigations have successfully identified the attackers. During one assault, immediately before he was shot dead an Atiteco victim smashed his assailant's head with a stone. Within hours, Committee members found the injured killer, a soldier, in a nearby hospital. On several other occasions, the Committee has successfully interceded on behalf of Atitecos who have been illegally pulled off buses for conscription into the Army. Finally, the Committee directs operations during attempted incursions into the Atitecos' self-declared security zone. If combatants (Army or ORPA guerrilla) are sighted, individual Atitecos are informed to go immediately to the town center. After human-rights groups and the media have been summoned, the Atitecos then return *en masse* to confront the intruders. To date, this strategy has succeeded in repelling all intrusions (e.g., see D. Scott 1991a, 1991b; Carlsen 1994).

THE RONDAS

The Atiteco rondas (lit. "patrols") represent the resurrection and adaptation of a far older institution. Until several decades ago, all Atiteco men who were married in a given year served that year as alguaciles in the cofradía system. In addition to their ritual obligations, described earlier, alguaciles policed the town. At night, armed with whistles and clubs, the alguaciles patrolled the streets in groups called rondas. Reflecting Ladino attempts to draft the alguaciles as personal servants, *mozos*, as well as increasing religious diversification and opposition to the cofradías, rondas were abandoned. Following the eviction of the soldiers, however, the institution was resurrected, albeit in an entirely secular capacity with no cofradía affiliation.

Every night at nine o'clock, ronda members lower a metal gate across the road into town, sealing off all traffic until four the following morning. Each of the town's five cantones, as well as the aldeas Panabaj and Chacaya, are then patrolled by their own rondas. Each ronda includes seventeen individuals. Depending on the population size of the particular cantón, an individual must spend approximately one night per month in ronda service. As in the past, members are armed only with clubs and whistles.[13] All males over sixteen years of age participate, Ladinos included. Participation is virtually mandatory, as refusals are met with orders to leave the town.

THE IRONY OF ATITECO AUTONOMY

The social reality of Atitlán today, as in the past, testifies to the Atitecos' capacity to resist, to subvert, and certainly to adapt. Accordingly, the Office of the Mayor and the Committee have replaced the Working People as the mediator of outside intrusions. In place of cofradía barter, the Atitecos now utilize the telephone and fax, exploiting their global electronic integration with the press and international human-rights agencies.[14] Yet that very integration points out an evident irony in the autonomy for which the Atitecos paid so dearly. Quite simply, that autonomy now hinges on outside intervention in the town's affairs, exactly the opposite of its historical past. While not discounting the Atitecos' considerable role in evicting the soldiers, it was international pressure which tipped the balance in the Army's decision to leave. That decision notwithstanding, consistent with a commitment to the permanent militarization of the Guatemalan countryside, the Army occasionally makes clear its desire to re-militarize Atitlán. Addressing that subject, Army spokesman Col. Homero García Carrillo states that "by law we have the responsibility to protect every part of the national territory" (D. Scott 1991a). The Atitecos are fully aware that the only factor separating them from the nightmare of renewed Army protection is continued international attention.

As symbolized by the ronda's nightly lowering of the gate, this irony of Atiteco autonomy is not the only uncertainty about the contemporary reality of Santiago Atitlán. In important ways the gate not only keeps out undesirable elements, it locks in problems which have taken root within the community. If political violence had been the primary cause of the instability of the 1980s in Santiago Atitlán, then the expulsion of the Army would hold great promise for a bright future. However, as Mendelson's account of the 1950 Maximón scandals documents so well, significant community instability and factionalism were evident long before the entrance of the soldiers. The soldiers who came in 1980 merely exploited an existing situation, and although in so doing they ironically were to pull the community together for the first time in decades, the resulting solidarity has proven to be inherently weak.

As might be expected, complaints about the deteriorating economy have become legion in Atitlán. Evidently, solidarity alone can feed a community for only so long, and the former rips in the social fabric have once again become apparent. This was demonstrated on the level of democratic politics when Mayor Ramírez faced the head of the Committee, Salvador Sisay, in the 1993 mayoral election. Ramírez threatened to invite the Army back into town if he lost. Where the massacre seems to have brought out the best in Ramírez, partisan politics apparently exposed the worst. (A third candidate won.)

A plague of common crime and a resurgence of Atiteco factionalism, particularly religious, are indicative of the town's web of problems. While increasing competition for limited resources is of course fertile ground for factionalism, in Atitlán it has also led to a search, born of desperation, for religious answers to the town's social woes. Unfortunately, the spiritual flaws of the local religious competition are the targets of Catholics, Protestants, and Working People alike. For instance, within Atitlán's Protestant churches and missions explanations for the town's problems typically point to the evilness of its traditional past and to those Atitecos who continue to perform ancient rituals. Underscoring the dynamics of division within the community, the most vicious factionalism is to be found between Atitlán's Protestant sects, perhaps explaining why the pastor of the largest church, ELIM, seldom strays from an escort of bodyguards. In a clear demonstration of how this situation is undercutting the peace in Santiago Atitlán, the members of ELIM now refuse to participate in the rondas. (In order to conform to local mandates, the members of ELIM have formed their own rondas.) Further reflecting the deteriorating state of affairs, following pastoral demands, one faction of Atiteco Protestants refuses to attend the *concentraciones*, saying that those meetings had become a "cult to the dead."

Of even more immediate concern than local factionalism has been crime, particularly robberies. While no doubt reflecting local poverty, the situation has been amplified by the recent legacy of political violence. An entire generation of Atitecos has come of age in an environment of extreme violence; what's more, during its occupation of the town the Army actually encouraged young male Atitecos to prey on the community and in that way justify its own presence. It is hardly surprising that the Army's departure initially did little to curb local delinquency. Instead, that burden has fallen directly on the Atitecos themselves.

In that regard the community has taken effective, albeit heavy-handed, measures to address local crime. Specifically, mid-1994 was characterized by a particularly violent spasm of robberies. Typically, masked Tz'utujil-speakers would rob buses returning to town loaded with Atiteco merchants and their generally meager profits. The crimes often included severe beatings and even murders of passengers, including one seven-year-old boy. Finally, in late October, following a robbery in which the twenty-two-year-old bus driver was murdered, the town exploded into action. Under the direction of the Development and Security Committee and its newly appointed leader, the irrepressible Salvador Ramírez, several suspects were rounded up. Prompted by the strategic application of electric cattle prods to particularly sensitive body parts, the suspects divulged the names of some twenty other gang members. This information led to the retrieval of large amounts of stolen merchandise. Days later, the Committee delivered the group of severely beaten gang members to the regional prison in Sololá.

At least for the present, Atitlán is again an island of hard-earned peace. Yet it is difficult to escape the conclusion that factors which previously undermined the functioning of the Old Ways remain in place and threaten to undermine present efforts at social stability as well. Stated differently, in this case Bibles, like bullets, are at least in part symptomatic of underlying and decades-old demographic, economic, and ecological problems. For Atiteco society to regain acceptable stability, changes will have to be made on the levels of technology, education, and basic subsistence. Yet only inputs from the world outside can be expected to effect such changes. Clearly, the required evolution must affect all levels of Atiteco society, including such areas as language, cosmos, and political consciousness. Returning to an earlier concept, a change *of* Atiteco society is required, and not simply change *within* that society. Lest this prescription raise the ire of some, it need only be noted that changes of great magnitude have already taken place. This century has seen significant and fundamental evolution in virtually all areas of Atiteco social and cultural existence that eclipses even those changes which followed the Conquest. Nonetheless, the activities, institutions, and strategies which have emerged have as yet to lead the way to the adaptive solutions demanded by the Atitecos' circumstances.

Atiteco Culture Is Dead— Long Live Atiteco Culture

The social and cultural transformations of the past few decades in Santiago Atitlán have clearly been exceptional. To some, such as those focusing on the seemingly "spontaneous" expansion of Protestantism, the changes have bordered on miraculous. In contrast, I have proposed a far more mundane explanation. I have argued that contemporary Atiteco existence is influenced by a shifting relationship of local and global socioeconomic factors, a relationship in which the global factors have assumed the dominant role. Involved in the associated changes have been entirely new degrees and types of outside intervention into the town's affairs. Likewise, dynamics internal to the town have been affected. In the past when core cultural aspects such as maize agriculture and the Old Ways contributed to successful social functioning, the Atitecos fought for the maintenance of those aspects. Only as Atiteco culture has become incapable of fulfilling the society's most vital needs has much of the populace looked elsewhere for solutions. For some, that search has ended at the front door of the local Assemblies of God mission. For others, it has led to the camps of the ORPA guerrillas.

In drawing this discussion to a conclusion, I am reminded of the initial *fiesta titular* in Atitlán following the massacre, particularly the procession for the town's patron saint, Santiago. Aside from its normal symbolic importance, the 1991 procession was a celebration of the ejection of the Army, and hence held exceptional significance. Underscoring that, television crews from Mexico, Venezuela, Spain, and Belgium were present to capture virtually every inch of the procession on video. Moreover, the crowd which lined the streets to watch the goings-on was the largest in some years and numbered several thousand.

On one level, the procession (Stiniem Santyaag) is really just a stroll around Atitlán's central block. (For a comprehensive accounting of the procession, see my description in D. Carrasco 1993: 223–237.) Yet, symbolically, it is a pilgrimage from the center of the world (R'kux Ruchiliew), located in Atitlán's Catholic church, to the world's corners, which symbolically lie at the corners of the block on which the church sits. Consistent with what has been stated about the Old Ways and Atiteco cosmology, the proper fulfillment of this ritual demands sacrifice and requires many hours to complete. In this case, that sacrifice includes stops at each of the four corners and at the north/south axis which bisects the block. At each stop, truly remarkable amounts of canyon water are imbibed. All of this is meant to fuel the world's essential operations.

A pivotal point in the procession each year occurs when it reaches the halfway mark. That spot lies in the middle of the block directly behind the church and represents the space which divides the world and its associated pairings of binary opposites, such as male/female or wet/dry. Most important in this case is the space which divides death from life and the past from the future. Leading the procession to the midway point are members of the old Cofradía Santiago, which for the past year has been in charge of the town's patron saint and primary bokunab. Once the procession arrives at the midway point, its snail-like pace grinds to a complete halt, and the litters which bear Santiago and several accompanying saints are lowered to the ground.

At first, this stop seems little different from the several others which have preceded it: The town elders offer prayers; clouds of incense billow through the huge crowd; and, of course, canyon water flows. After awhile, however, a dramatic nuance occurs. Amid a barrage of explosive rockets (*bombas*) launched high overhead, a group of men and women in their ceremonial finery approaches. In fact, the group of newcomers form the cofradía which will be in charge of Santiago for the next year. As the newcomers enter the assembled crowd, one by one they are embraced by the members of the old cofradía. What follows is a near poetic interchange between the two cofradías about the meaning and the responsibilities entailed in the fulfillment of the Old Ways. Employing the explicit terminology of Jaloj, each male member of the old cofradía confides that he is soon to die. It is then explained that since time immemorial the Old Ways have served the Atitecos well. Adding the terminology of K'exoj, the cofrades make a final statement that it is the new cofradía's responsibility to carry on with the Old Ways so that the community may continue to regenerate itself and to prosper. With that declaration, the duties of the old cofradía are complete, and in a moment of great emotion, all of its members walk away—symbolically dead. Under the canopy and cacophony of exploding rockets, the new cofradía then takes up the litters, and the procession continues on its way.

The significance of this ceremony was first explained to me in 1987 by Luch Chavajay, a former alcalde of Cofradía Santiago. Luch confided that the Old Ways of Santiago Atitlán are so vital that if they are not performed, the town itself must literally die. Ironically, just weeks after the 1991 procession, this dear old man was himself dead, years of ritual drinking having finally destroyed his liver. During the 1991 procession, I could not keep from recalling Luch's words. Clearly, given the declining significance of the Old Ways, it is doubtful that rituals such as the procession of Santiago (at least in their present form) will be performed for much longer.[15] Watching the "dead" cofradía bid its farewell, while at the same time trying to avoid the international videographers crawling on hands and knees amidst the departing cofradía members in an attempt to get the best camera angle, it struck me that "what is going on" in Santiago Atitlán is the collision of two incompatible worlds. One of those worlds has Santiago Atitlán as its literal center, in fact, its *axis mundi*. In total contrast, the other world would shift Atitlán to an insignificant economic and symbolic periphery. As is evidenced by the explosive growth of antitraditional religiosity in the town, that shift is well underway.

Recalling Luch's caution, I wonder what the full implications of the obsolescence of the Old Ways will be. Will religion continue to play an important role in Atiteco social hierarchies, and will those hierarchies approach the level of past success of the chinamit or cofradía systems? On a quite different level, I wonder if the Atitecos will find some means of subsistence to successfully replace maize agriculture. Clearly, should they fail to do so, Luch's warning about the death of the town may prove to be far more accurate than might otherwise seem possible. Yet, as attested in the eviction of the Army from Santiago Atitlán, the Atitecos' role in determining their own future should not be discounted. These and other questions and uncertainties promise ample territory for future study. For the present, however, the only certainty is that Santiago Atitlán faces an imminent future of most uncertain change.

8

Season of the Witch: The New Millennium in Santiago Atitlán

What Ye Sow Ye Shall Reap.

Banner hung by "social cleansers" in Santiago Atitlán

THE 1997 EDITION OF THIS BOOK concluded by stating, "Santiago Atitlán faces an imminent future of most uncertain change." The ensuing years have in fact ushered in profound change, often in ways that I could not have imagined. This new chapter to the original edition describes and analyzes that change. I pay particular attention to changes in the weaving art and dress patterns, the marginalization of the Old Ways and the corresponding ascendance of Protestantism, and the influx of gang culture.

Where for centuries Atitecos equated their community with a towering cosmic World Tree, a far more poignant symbol of the town today is the huge steel cell phone tower that now dominates Atitlán's skyline. Since that tower was constructed in 2001, it has become normal to see local Mayas walking about chatting on their phones. In stark contrast to the internal orientation of the World Tree that situated the town at the very center of the cosmos, the cell phone tower underscores contemporary Atitlán's integration with a dominant outside world. Reinforcing the centrifugal dynamics at play has been the introduction of the World Wide Web, as evidenced by the Internet cafes scattered throughout the town. I am constantly reminded of Atitlán's new relationship to the outside when Atiteco friends e-mail me in the United States. Further underscoring Atitlán's new relationship with the outside was the 2004 placement of an ATM in the town's central plaza, only yards from the cell phone tower. Atitlán is now directly linked to the world's banking centers. Pivotal to these and other changes affecting the town is globalization—a dynamic which, like the multi-headed serpents depicted in ancient Mayan art, is notable for its complexity, its creativity, its destructiveness, and the incompatibility of many of its basic parts.[1]

ROPA USADA AND THE ATITECO WEAVING ARTS

Handwoven cloth and costume (*traje*) arguably constitute the most salient aspect of post-Conquest highland Mayan culture. One notable characteristic of the Mayan textile tradition is what is commonly referred to as the "village-specific costume," a handwoven garment worn by a community's residents that is unique to their town or region. This tradition has historically functioned to solidify the community and to shield it from outside influences. A type of Atiteco male garment called the *rumuxux ktuon* (lit., umbilical shirt) is particularly illustrative of this tradition. This garment is a backstrap-loomed shirt with a decorative cross-shaped cloth appliqué at the belly level. According to all accounts this odd appendage is a distinct reminder to the wearer of his umbilical connection to the town and to the ancestral past which sustains the living (Carlsen 1997:186). Where some decades ago the use of the *rumuxux ktuon* was common, only a handful of elderly Atitecos still wear them.

In Chapter 2 of this book I wrote about the trend away from male *traje* use in Santiago Atitlán, and argued that one reason for this was the increasing availability of used clothing from the throwaway culture to the distant north. The impact of that clothing, now called *paca* in reference to the large *paquetes* (packages) in which it arrives from the United States, turned out to be profound. *Paca* starts its long journey as items donated to thrift shops in the United States. To raise money, those shops will sell the donated items in bulk to dealers, who then export them to numerous Third World countries, including Guatemala. In Atitlán, at the end of its journey, the used clothing—at times still sporting tags from U.S. thrift shops—is piled high on tarps in the market. The Atiteco consumers of this humble aspect of international commerce jostle each other while scavenging through the T-shirts, sport shirts, sweatshirts, dress shirts, blue jeans, and so on. Transactions are simple: the cost is US$.40 per piece. To the Atiteco consumer whose already low wages do not even keep up with inflation, the wisdom of exchanging locally woven and relatively expensive *traje* for foreign garments that, only months earlier, may have been at the height of fashion in the great north is evident.

Adding to the assault on *traje* is fashionable new clothing available in "boy-boutiques" and from clothes merchants all over town.

These generally maquila-made clothes are more prestigious than *paca* and are particularly popular among young men with ties to the outside; to international soccer culture; to the capital, Guatemala City; and to consumer culture in general. For these young men, this clothing represents the buying power of the social class that they are trying to project. One need only look around to see the impact that maquila-manufactured new clothing and *paca* have had on local dress patterns. Fewer than 10 percent of males now wear *traje*, and most consider it to be unsophisticated and old-fashioned. The availability of Western clothing is also having an impact on female dress patterns. While nearly all women continue to wear *traje*, it is now common to see young girls dressed partly or entirely in *paca*. And as this happens, the frayed warps of ancient traditions become more apparent.

FROM SAINTS TO SINNERS

As is evident in the weaving arts, the incursions of globalization have wrought havoc on customary Atiteco culture. In part, the new information and technology flooding the town have finally overwhelmed lingering religious beliefs that Atitlán somehow constitutes the center of the cosmos, or that the living can rely on their ancestors to sustain them. In the past, those beliefs buttressed the Working People's hegemony as political leaders and also as venerated town elders. As global religions, particularly Roman Catholicism and Protestantism, have become dominant, many Atitecos have come to literally demonize the Old Ways. The few remaining Working People are typically looked upon as, at best, anachronisms, or, at worst, satanic witches. Some Atitecos are willing to act upon a belief that these witches are directly responsible for the numerous problems inflicting the town and must be killed. The resulting murders are part of what is called *limpieza social*, "social cleansing," which has been linked to evangelical elements in town, although some Catholics may also be involved.

Anyone who has spent significant time in Atitlán over the past few decades has certainly known people who have been murdered. In that regard, I am no exception. Though some of the victims were casual acquaintances, I count others among my close friends. None was dearer to me than Pascual Mendoza. It is ironic that in the fall of 2002 when, via e-mail, I learned of Pascual's murder, I was teaching a course on the anthropology of religion at the University of Colorado, and had just begun a series of lectures looking at how, as social power changes, people and things that once had been deemed sacred or holy can be recast as evil. Though the initial subject of the lectures was medieval Europe and that period's "witch craze," my focus soon turned to twentieth-century Guatemala. I don't believe that my students fully understood how personal those lectures had suddenly become.

My first recollections of Pascual are of his leading cofradía processions through the streets of Atitlán in the early 1980s. I recall the Stetson hat—much like the one worn by Maximón—that would be one of his hallmarks until his death. I also recall that, at that time, he was one of the few Working People dressed in long pants and a button-down shirt. I later learned that he had begun wearing Western garb as a disguise when, years earlier, he would sneak into the town of San Pedro la Laguna to court his future wife.

It was not long after I met Pascual that I encountered his characteristic feistiness—for instance, he would tell me, "Wake up your head." Eventually I realized that underlying this type of statement was an element of affection, and also a sharp intellect. One of my most treasured memories of Pascual was of an event that occurred a few years later, when he asked me to join him for a drink at a local cantina. Upon entering, I saw three of Pascual's senior cofradía colleagues (in this case *sacristanes*, who must be literate; theirs is one of only two cofradía offices with this requirement) seated around a table. The *sacristanes*, led by Pascual, immediately began to query me about fine points of the Old Ways, particularly about the significance of the Tree. My explanations pleased Pascual who, along with the other *sacristanes*, commenced to fine-tune and correct my statement. This was the first time that I had experienced such an explicit discussion/ lesson with high-ranking Working People, and I interpreted it as a breakthrough event.

Buoyed by my new status, some weeks later I asked Pascual to join me in the Catholic church and told him that I wanted to discuss a favorite topic of mine, the meaning of the parish's esoteric altar carvings.[2] He agreed to come. In front of the altar, Pascual responded to my questions with the most mundane answers, responses I might have heard years earlier in my Lutheran Sunday preschool. Among his statements were that Jesus was the son of God and also that Jesus's mother was named Mary. The gleam in Pascual's eye let it be known that he operated according to his agenda and not mine.

At the time of his death, Pascual was the de facto leader of the Working People and a steadfast pillar of support for the Old Ways. For years his status in this regard was given a high-profile public display during Atitlán's most important religious event, Semana Santa,

35. *Depicted here is Pascual Mendoza in his cofradía role as* escribano, *or notary, for Cofradía San Juan. He is wearing his* x'kajkoj zut—*not wrapped around his head, as most cofradía members wear it, but draped around his neck, as is typical for* escribanos. *The saint behind and to the left of Pascual is called simply Pastor. (Photograph by the author, 2000.)*

or Holy Week. Despite the changed religious landscape in Atitlán, Semana Santa allows the Working People a stage to temporarily resurrect their former importance, and in some ways Pascual represented the public face of that transition. As head *sacristan*, Pascual had Semana Santa duties that ranged from coordinating the decoration of the church to overseeing the running of San Juan Carajo and ultimately the confrontation between Maximón and Jesus. However, it was during the final major public event of Semana Santa, a massive Good Friday evening procession in which the crucified Christ is carried aloft through the streets surrounding the church, that Pascual's high status was given its most prominent display. Despite the chill air, and usually a steady drizzle, the procession lasted until the wee hours of the following morning. Prior to Good Friday, teams of Catholic Action members had created ornate "carpets" made of multi-colored dyed sawdust on the streets immediately surrounding the church. Those carpets were off-limits to foot traffic until the procession, with Pascual Mendoza at its head, passed through and entirely destroyed them.[3]

It is not surprising that this public display of the Old Ways is an anathema to many in the town. Not only do many Atitecos today resent the front and center role of Maximón, but they also object to the role of Jesus, more precisely the Jesus figure as represented in the Old Ways. In his fascinating book *Rituals of Sacrifice*, which focuses on Atitlán's Semana Santa, Vincent Stanzione explains that, following the Conquest, Atitecos effectively Mayanized the Jesus figure that had been brought to town by their Franciscan overlords. Improvising on the name Immanuel, which was given to Jesus by angels at his birth, and in Latin means "God is amongst us," the Atitecos created a figure called MaNawal de JesuKrista (2003:10). Key to the local Mayas' wordplay was the sacred Tz'utujil word *nawal*, which is a term for a category of ancient deities. According to the Working People's Semana Santa passion play, a deified skull lies buried at the base of MaNawal de JesuKrista's cross, which itself is understood to be the Cosmic World Tree. When the crucified Jesus's blood drips down to the skeletal deity, who, as is explained in Chapter 3, is sometimes called *Tzimai Awa*, the world flowers from the dead. When that happens, the "sacrificed" Jesus is resurrected as a rain deity and maize god (2003: 11). It is significant that Semana Santa takes place during the time of the year when Santiago Atitlán is transitioning from the dry to the wet season.[4]

Whereas Pascual's role as head *sacristan* angered some Atitecos, his embrace of *aj'kuniel* angered even more. As a practioner of *aj'kuniel*, Pascual Mendoza was an *aj'kun*, a professional prayer-maker who provides his services to paying clients—what outsiders sometimes refer to as a shaman. In his *aj'kun* role, Pascual typically spent his days visiting the cofradías San Juan, San Nicolás, and Santa Cruz, where *aj'kuna* with divining bundles in hand are often present. It was also common to see Pascual heading out of town to ply his trade at remote altars or at perhaps the most important of all the ritual sites, the town's mountaintop cemetery.

In that regard, September 14, 2002, was little different from most days for Pascual, though I suspect that, as he headed in the direction of the cemetery late that afternoon, he must have given at least a passing thought to the murder in the mountains only a few weeks before of a fellow *aj'kun* named Xuan. Whoever murdered Xuan performed the act in the Old Testament manner: by stoning. As written in Leviticus 20:27, "a wizard shall surely be put to death: they shall stone them with stones: their blood will be upon their own heads." I wonder if Pascual was followed as he left town, or if his killers encountered him by chance along the way. In any case, Pascual was a tough guy who would have put up a fight, but he was unarmed and they had guns and machetes. Unlike Xuan, Pascual was not murdered by stoning, though his corpse was shrouded in blood. Rather, after shooting Pascual, his killers proceeded to disembowel him, a treatment which is intended to curb the power of a witch.

In a purely dispassionate sense, Pascual Mendoza's murder at the cemetery is explained by the changed social landscape of Santiago Atitlán. It should be recalled from Chapter 3, "The Flowering of the Dead," that for millennia Mayas have associated the underworld, the realm of the dead, with ancestors and the past. They believe that it is from death and the past that life sprouts, and that this is a purely natural process. For *aj'kuna* like Pascual, the cemetery is a logical extension of these beliefs. It is a portal to the realm of the ancestors. Occasionally, rogue spirits of the dead harass the living. As Vincent Stanzione notes, "The cemetery is an important place for *aj'kuna* because it is where they are able to coax the spirits back to their resting place in the Holy Earth. Amongst the traditionalists, the graves and bones are portals to the land of the dead" (e-mail to the author, June 2007). But this view of death is literally the old way of thinking, and there is no place in the new way of thinking for people like Pascual Mendoza. Like many Protestants, Atiteco evangelicals tend to embrace strict Biblical inerrancy—an understanding that the Bible's every word is literally true. As such, had it not been for Satan in the Garden of Eden, we humans would never die. It follows that death is ultimately unnatural, and even tinged with evil. Hanging around cemeteries, especially after dusk, is at least suspect. And in Santiago Atitlán, if the person involved is not an evangelical, he or she is probably in league with the devil. Pascual's death underscores the fact that, in Santiago Atitlán, the confrontation between the Old Ways and the new ways can have a truly hideous outcome.

Far more than the twenty or so other murders of Working People, Pascual's brutal death cast a dark shadow over the traditionalist community. To avoid being targeted themselves, some followed the example of Pascual's widow and converted to Protestantism. As a precaution against attracting unwanted attention, others removed their

Mayan divining talismans, their *q'iijb'al*, from their home altars.[5] Yet some of the Working People, such as the surviving *sacristanes*, refused to be intimidated. Various of the defiant Working People felt armed with a mythology in which the martyred *aj'kuna* join the rain gods, the *achijab*, on their mountaintop thrones (*palibal*), from which they launch lightning or even trigger mudslides.

The Holy Cross Scandals

In Chapter 6 I explained that the Atiteco cofradía system had been in decline for most of the twentieth century. That system is now moribund. In a town whose population exceeds forty thousand inhabitants, there are only thirty to fifty active cofradía members. In contrast to just a few decades ago, when there was considerable demand for the yearlong sponsorship of a cofradía, almost nobody today is willing to take on the obligation. Those Atitecos who currently house cofradías are basically stuck, and what should be a yearlong sponsorship may end up being permanent. The one exception is the Cofradía of the Holy Cross, Santa Cruz. The reason is that Santa Cruz houses Maximón, that cigar-puffing, liquor-chugging "earth god" whose star power among Mayas, ladinos, and foreigners alike guarantees a lucrative cash flow.[6] Put bluntly, it is a sure thing as a business opportunity. In an attempt to channel the pent-up demand to sponsor Santa Cruz into support for the broader cofradía system, in the 1990s the heads of the various cofradías, the *alcaldes*, devised a plan by which, in order to be awarded Santa Cruz for a year, a person had to currently be *alcalde* of one of the other nine public cofradías. For a time this clever incentive plan worked. However, problems began to arise in 2000 when one Pedro Mendoza was *alcalde* of Santa Cruz. Blessed by the proximity of his house to the dock where virtually all tourists land, Alcalde Mendoza made a tidy sum that year. To maximize his take, he even posted a sign written in English at the cofradía listing the prices for entry (two dollars), for taking a photograph (one dollar for each picture), and for shooting a video (ten dollars). The cash flow was too great for Mendoza to give up, so when his sponsorship ended in May, he merely constructed his own Maximón and paid boys at the dock to guide tourists to his fake cofradía rather than to the real Santa Cruz. This move triggered considerable ill will among the *alcaldes*, but it also demonstrated that they were no longer bound by group rules.

A few years later Cofradía Santa Cruz was awarded to the then-*alcalde* of Cofradía Rosario, named MaRuiz. Near the end of his year with Santa Cruz, Alcalde MaRuiz made the shocking announcement that he intended to keep Santa Cruz, and Maximón, for a second year. He justified the action by arguing that, for nineteen years, with little or no remuneration, he had sponsored Cofradía Rosario. The other Working People were immediately up in arms over this development, though down at his fake cofradía, Pedro Mendoza was conspicuous in his silence. Within days MaRuiz was visited in his house by the *cabecera*, the de jure head of the cofradía system and symbolic Trunk of the town. Among the *cabecera*'s jobs was assigning Cofradía Santa Cruz, and he reminded MaRuiz that he had given the cofradía to someone else. In his characteristic bellicose manner, MaRuiz proceeded to shove the *cabecera* out of his house. A short time later, the town's mayor, Diego Esquina, announced that, in an unprecedented move, he would seat a second *cabecera* to rival the town's legitimate cofradía leader. It was not coincidental that the rival *cabecera* authorized MaRuiz's bid to keep Maximón for a second year. Not lost on anyone was the fact that MaRuiz had paid off the mayor, who happened to be a Protestant and, until then, not particularly concerned about the dealings of the Working People.[7] Although the supporters of the legitimate *cabecera* insisted that MaRuiz give up his claim to Cofradía Santa Cruz, they were literally outgunned: in a suspicious turn of events, shortly after one of those supporters was shot, the mayor began providing MaRuiz with on-demand police backup. The police presence was particularly obvious during Holy Week. Far from attempting to be inconspicuous, as might be expected, three heavily armed police planted themselves at the very center of all the high-profile public Maximón rituals. Clearly MaRuiz was more interested in sending a message about his authority than in maintaining any sense of the sacred. At the end of MaRuiz's second year, Santa Cruz was passed to a new *alcalde*, Gaspar Sapalú. MaRuiz also passed Cofradía Rosario to a new *alcalde*, Alux Nawal, to whom we will return shortly.

Alcalde Sapalú was a quick study and, partway into his year of sponsorship, he announced that, following the playbook established by MaRuiz, he too was going to keep the cofradía for a second year. As had been the case during the MaRuiz affair, this situation pitted the existing *alcalde* and his camp against the would-be new *alcalde* and his camp. Again, rival *cabeceras* aligned themselves with the two factions. If anything, the resulting chaos was greater than the first time this scenario played out. At one point, the would-be new *alcalde* attempted to break down the door of the old cofradía and literally seize Maximón.

Both sides hired lawyers to fight for them in the local court. A series of articles on the situation appeared in the national press (*El Periódico* 2007a, 2007b). A web page, created by Alcalde Sapalú with a Spanish domain, was designed to elicit Guatemalan and international support for his cause. Eventually, regional and national government representatives became involved, including Guatemala's ombudsman for human rights, the Procurador de los Derechos Humanos. Despite the rapidly escalating tensions, the various government entities concluded that the situation was outside their jurisdiction and opted to let the aggrieved parties settle things themselves. Predictably, threats of violence became increasingly common and credible. Finally, on an evening in early June 2007, three armed men broke into the Cofradía Rosario, whose *alcalde*, Alux Nawal, was an outspoken supporter of the would-be new *alcalde* of Santa Cruz. Like my friend Pascual Mendoza, Alux Nawal was a *sacristan* and an *aj'kun*, in this case one of the few Atitecos who still used the ancient Mayan calendar for divinations. In front of his wife and children, Alux Nawal was shot. Though gravely wounded, he attempted to escape. In an act that brought to mind social cleansing, the intruders caught Alux Nawal and then proceeded to crush his head with a cinder block.

Because of the largely dysfunctional nature of Guatemalan civil society, particularly its police and judicial systems, violent crimes typically go unsolved. This seems to have been the case with the murder of Alux Nawal, though there was perhaps an extrajudicial resolution to the crime. While the crime may have reflected cofradía fratricide, at least someone was certain that Alux Nawal had been "cleansed," because within hours of his death the reputed leader of the social cleansers, Tomás Susof, and two of his henchmen were themselves dead. It merits mention that Alux Nawal seems to have suspected his own death; I was told that he informed friends that, if killed, he would arrange for retribution from the "other side."[8]

Gang Culture Comes to Santiago Atitlán

Although globalization has had a corrosive impact on Atiteco customary culture, access to the Internet and even to *paca* certainly does offer benefits. Similarly, my Mayan friends adore their cell phones. There is no doubt that, however unevenly distributed, globalization has contributed to the generation of new wealth in Santiago Atitlán. The fact is that some aspects of globalization have been entirely beneficial for the town. For instance, the remarkable expulsion of the army from the town in 1990, described in Chapter 7, would not have been possible without the pressure exerted by the mass media, including national television and the national and international press. Contrasting with positive examples of globalization are others that are entirely negative. The arrival of gang culture, linked to global crime networks, certainly comes to mind.

The origins of the gang problems now having such an impact on Atitlán can be traced back to Guatemala's neighbor El Salvador. In the 1980s, hundreds of thousands of Salvadoran refugees were forced to flee their country's brutal civil war, with many ending up in the impoverished Pico-Union area of Los Angeles.[9] Incubated in poverty and at first intended as a defense against the established Mexican-American gangs, Salvadoran gangs known as *maras* were soon in operation and quickly engaged in unprecedented ruthlessness. Certainly the most violent of these has been Mara Salvatrucha, commonly called simply MS.[10] This gang now operates in at least forty-two states and is the target of an FBI task force, the only such nationwide effort targeting a single street gang (Kraul, Lopez, and Connell 2005). For years it has been U.S. policy to deport Salvadoran gang members convicted of felonies back to their native country. Under a program known as Operation Community Shield, the United States Immigration and Customs Enforcement (ICE) expels foreign-born gang members, particularly MS members, from the United States. A result has been the exportation of U.S. gang culture and increased Central American instability as "suddenly one of the poorest corners of the world, which struggles to meet its people's basic needs, was burdened by a superpower's crime plague" (Thompson and Alder 2004). The damage has not been limited to El Salvador. Reacting to the thousands of repatriated gang members dumped on it, El Salvador enacted a zero-tolerance anti-gang program called Mano Dura (Firm Hand). That program effectively pushed hardcore gang members into neighboring Honduras and Guatemala.[11] Those countries responded in turn with their own versions of Mano Dura, which helped to spread the *maras* north into Mexico. Mexico has since established its own anti-gang program called Operación Acero (Operation Steel). The Operation Community Shield to Mano Dura to Operación Acero dynamic fuels a vicious circle, in which many gang members ultimately end up back in the United States until they are again deported.[12]

In Santiago Atitlán, the impact of gang culture is immediately evident. As is the case in so many other Guatemalan Mayan towns, Atitlán is fertile territory for gang culture. Hundreds of young male Atitecos have grown up orphaned, their fathers generally having been

36. *Gang-related graffiti is so common in Santiago Atitlán today that most Atitecos seem to take little notice of it. This display, which includes tags for Mara Salvatrucha and the rival Eighteenth Street gang, adorned a back wall of the Catholic parish. Parish officials have since painted over the graffiti and closed off the adjoining playground. Notice the boys dressed entirely in* paca. *(Photograph by the author, 2005.)*

killed during *la violencia*. That same *violencia* and all the social disruption that it entailed constituted normalcy for those children of the war during their critical formative years. Already vulnerable, many of these Atitecos have spent considerable time in Guatemala City, where they have witnessed and sometimes participated in the gang-related violence that plagues the capital. Inevitably, the habits learned in that environment get brought back to town, where hardly a block exists without buildings or houses painted with gang graffiti—some, to be sure, coming from so-called gang wannabes. The most common tags are "MS" and "18," the latter referring to the notorious Los Angeles–based 18th Street Gang. Even the town's sixteenth-century Catholic church is not immune to this treatment, as a back wall was covered with the tags of various gangs. Linked to gangs are several crack cocaine houses which operate relatively openly and which, like various *kuxa* (moonshine) outlets, simply pay off the easily corruptible local police.

The ubiquitous graffiti notwithstanding, *maras* do not operate nearly so openly in Atitlán as in other parts of Guatemala, nor are they as roughshod. One reason for this is the shadowy presence of

37. This 1997 banner may be the first hung in Santiago Atitlán by vigilantes, who at that time had yet to start identifying themselves as "social cleansers." However, the ultimate mission of the "social cleansers" was already identifiable. This particular banner, written in poor Spanish, claims responsibility for a recent killing and boasts that more will be coming. The targeted groups are thieves and muggers. The vigilantes claim that they know who the culprits are and that they will be attacked in the houses where they live. (Photograph by the author, 1997.)

vigilantes with no aversion to extrajudicial killing. In 1997, crudely crafted banners painted on white sheets began to appear draped over streets. These mysterious banners, hung in the obscurity of night, announce the coming of the vigilantes, the "social cleansers." The banners typically claim responsibility for a killing and boast that more are to come, sometimes identifying the future victims by name. In addition to naming gang members, the banners, like paper fliers left by the cleansers, boast that drug traffickers, adulterers, and witches will be targeted. To fund their activities, the social cleansers extort a "security service tax" from drivers at checkpoints outside the town. In return for paying the "tax," drivers are given a receipt printed "The People's Social Cleansing Group" (Aizenman 2006). Few Atitecos feel more secure because of the cleansers; rather, most are scared to death. The social cleansers, who often dress in olive green with red bandannas around their necks and have their faces hidden under knit masks, are heavily armed. The defined mission of the social cleansers entails far more than simply purging criminals from the streets of one Mayan town; they believe that they are central figures in an epic battle against Satan, whose devotees lurk among holdout followers of the Old Ways. Hence, along with other undesirables, those followers are candidates for "cleansing" at the hands of the holy death squads.[13]

THE NEW WAYS IN TWENTY-FIRST-CENTURY SANTIAGO ATITLÁN

The appearance of the social cleansers, and particularly their targeting of the Working People, underscores the changed social landscape in Santiago Atitlán. Coinciding with the marginalization of the traditional religion has been the creation of new power loci centered in the orthodox Catholic and Protestant communities. The coalescence of Catholic authority can be traced back to the introduction of Catholic Action, as well as to the staffing of the parish in 1964 with Oklahoma priests. It should be recalled, however, that the Oklahoma priests (particularly Stan Rother and Tom McSherry) tended to favor accommodation with the Working People, sometimes to the consternation of Catholic Action. This is no longer the case. In 2001, Micatokla (the Catholic Mission of Oklahoma) dissolved itself and turned the parish over to the local diocese of Sololá. Although himself a Kaqchikel Maya, the incoming priest, Father Pedro Chachal Mus, was a follower of the rigidly conservative Catholic organization Opus Dei and had no tolerance for the Working People and the Old Ways. Father Pedro made this clear when, in one of his early actions, he removed the lectern and the priest's chair from the parish altar. Those two pieces were designed by Father McSherry and included Mayan and Christian symbols. As McSherry noted, "My thought was to integrate and complement symbols, not to replace/supplant/correct or judge the superiority of either Catholic (Christian) or Mayan symbols" (e-mail to the author, November 2002). With Micatokla gone, the parish and the members of Catholic Action were allied against the Old Ways.

In Chapter 6 I demonstrated that, while over the last few decades both Catholics and Protestants experienced remarkable growth in membership at the expense of the Working People, the greater increase was in the number of Catholics. Although there are probably still more Atiteco Catholics than Protestants, in terms of overall power the differential in recent years has shifted noticeably toward the Protestant camp. This trend is particularly evident as regards the previously mentioned church, ELIM, now called Iglesia Palabra MIEL, or simply MIEL.[14] The theological outreach of that church, located in seemingly insignificant Santiago Atitlán, extends far beyond the boundaries of the town. MIEL churches are located throughout the Americas and even in Europe. The United States alone has nearly a hundred, one located only miles from my Denver home. Remarkably, all the MIEL congregations recognize that the "mother church" is in Atitlán and that its head pastor, Gaspar Sapalú, is their spiritual leader, whom they refer to as "the Apostle."

Fueling this most unlikely scenario is Sapalú's charisma; a sophisticated use of the Internet, particularly YouTube; and an underlying millenarian fervor that anticipates the imminent return of Jesus Christ. In all cases, whether the MIEL church be in Italy, Sweden, or the United States, services are conducted in Spanish. While the theology of the satellite churches is much like that of any number of charismatic evangelical organizations, the message conveyed in the mother church is somewhat different. No doubt inspired by the remarkable global expansion of MIEL and their central role in that growth, church members in Atitlán believe that their congregation, and indeed their town, is pivotal in the defining cosmic drama of the ages, Christ's return. The Apostle Sapalú teaches that, while Christ's return is certainly imminent, the Savior will not return as long as evil and the unrighteous hold sway in the town. That message is not lost on the social cleansers.

I should be clear that I am not aware of any formal links between the social cleansers and MIEL. To be sure, some cleansers are members of other Protestant churches—including Alux Nawal's alleged murderer Tomas Susof, who attended the Alianza Cristiana church. However, according to numerous accounts, including conclusive statements given to me by congregation members, the cleansers are disproportionately represented in MIEL. In any case, there is no need for a direct link between the social cleansers and MIEL, as there exists a natural symbiosis. The attraction that binds is the aforementioned activist millenarian fervor.

In a general sense, millenarianism is a belief that the world in its present form is short-lived, and that it will be replaced by one in which harmony, justice, and holiness will reign. Underlying these beliefs is an understanding that the present world is not simply corrupt but is controlled by great evil. In his classic study *The Pursuit of the Millennium*, Norman Cohn observes that millenarians are enthralled by "the prospect of carrying out a divinely ordained mission of stupendous and unique importance." He adds that those attracted to millenarian movements are typically "the populations of certain technologically backward societies which are not only overpopulated and desperately poor but also involved in a problematic transition to the modern world, and are correspondingly dislocated and disoriented." They are drawn to a prophet who possesses a personal magnetism that enables him to "claim with some show of plausibility, a special role in bringing history to its appointed consummation" (Cohn 1970:285). A primary characteristic of millenarian movements is the passion for the end of the world that the prophet is able to ignite in his followers. Pascual Mendoza's disemboweling, along with other "cleansings," demonstrates that this passion can be played out in what Cohn describes as "a bloody vengeance on the unrighteous," all designed to give rise to a new world.

Contemplating the Umbilicus of the World

It is ironic that the Spanish word *miel* denotes something sweet, particularly honey. When pondering Atitlán's Iglesia Palabra MIEL, sweetness is hardly a term that leaps to mind. This is certainly not the only irony involving MIEL. Given that a primary goal of MIEL is to completely exorcise the Old Ways from Santiago Atitlán, it is ironic that, while outer forms may have changed, significant aspects of that church's religious beliefs are strikingly similar to those of the Working People. One example is the view that the Working People and MIEL have of their own positions in the great cosmic scheme of things. Both place themselves directly at the center and believe that it is only from that position, from Santiago Atitlán, that the world can be renewed. From the point of view of the Working People, that renewal is periodic and circular. In the case of MIEL, it is a one-time event, which is to say that it is linear. In both cases, an element of sacrifice is necessary to fuel the desired transition. While the Working People seldom engage in actual blood sacrifice, and then only using poultry, their broader tradition of cofradía sacrifice was handed down to them by the ancient Mayas, who did practice human sacrifice. It is the Protestant social cleansers who are more directly aligned with the ancients in this regard, as they believe that the world's renewal is dependent on ridding it of sinful behavior—and their means of accomplishing this include murder.

The fact is that Santiago Atitlán is a place of great ironies and similarly great contradictions. I have described examples of hideous cruelty, such as Alux Nawal's murder in front of his family. The fanatical religiosity of the town, like the "scandals" that seem always to engulf the Maximón cult, can easily cause one to wonder, "What in the world is going on in Santiago Atitlán?" At the same time, Atitlán is a place of incredible beauty, both human and geographic. It is hard not to be moved by the exquisite beauty of the "mothers"—the *tixeli*, as female cofradía members are called—as they walk in processions dressed in their finest handwoven garments, with their heads wrapped around with *xk'ap*, the hair ribbons that resemble halos. And, from a personal point of view, I am reminded of the numerous occasions on which I have experienced the compassion and warmth of the Atitecos, including the times when they shielded me from possible violence at the hands of the army.

I have often sensed a near-otherworldly beauty when taking in the town of Santiago Atitlán, nestled as it is between Lake Atitlán and the three volcanoes towering above. During the rainy season, a violent and beautiful play is staged most days when afternoon thunderstorms roll in from the coast. In an awesome display of nature's might, lightning crashes in on the town and the mountains while, high above, clouds swirl around the volcano tops, forming delicate rings. Atitecos liken the cloud rings to the halos worn by the *tixeli*. According to some accounts, specifically from the dwindling community of Working People, this drama is orchestrated by the rain gods and the martyred shamans who shoot lightning from their mountaintop thrones. To paraphrase the great nineteenth-century explorer John Lloyd Stephens's reaction when he first gazed at Lake Atitlán, it is the most remarkable spectacle that one has ever seen. This is what it is like at the center, in "the Umbilicus of the World."

Notes

1. What in the World Is Going On in Santiago Atitlán?

1. The protection of indigenous subjects is basic to the presentation of anthropological information. This demand is only amplified when writing about volatile locales such as Guatemala. Accordingly, the present volume employs various levels of caution. Except for citing the names of deceased individuals or such common information as the name of a mayor, little attention is accorded individual persons. In the few exceptions, pseudonyms are used and the individual's permission has been received. In no case has information been presented which might conceivably jeopardize an individual's security.

2. See Carlsen and Prechtel (1994) for a comprehensive description and analysis of Atiteco shamanism.

3. The name ELIM is taken from Exodus 15:27, and means "rest."

4. There are currently three Assemblies of God missions in Santiago Atitlán. There had been a fourth. However, in what is spoken of in local A.G. circles as near-heresy, in the early 1980s one mission broke away and joined with the ELIM denomination, which is centered in Guatemala City. That Protestant sect is now Atitlán's largest. In fact, contributing to the scandal, the upstart ELIM group has lured numerous members from the remaining A.G. missions, an action known in evangelical parlance as "sheep raiding."

5. My own investigations lead me to believe that this figure is too high. The number killed must be far closer to five hundred than to the figure cited by CUC.

6. The designation Working People refers to participation in the grueling rituals which followers of the Old Ways (*costumbres*) believe are absolutely essential for the continuity of the world's vital cycles of existence. While I am not aware that followers of the Old Ways anywhere in Guatemala have a formal name for their religion (nor that any of the numerous Mayan languages even have a word for "religion"), in Santiago Atitlán the name R'kan Sak R'kan Q'ij (lit. "Footpath of the Dawn, Footpath of the Sun") comes close. Technically, however, that name specifies not who the Working People are but what they do, which is perform rituals to help move the sun across the sky. A distinction between performance and identity as a defining aspect of religiosity constitutes a fundamental difference between the Old Ways and both Guatemalan Catholicism and Protestantism.

7. An intermix of misguided theology and politics is exemplified in the persona of Guatemala's former dictator, General Efraín Ríos Montt. After taking power in a

1982 military coup, Ríos Montt engaged in an Old Testament–like campaign of terror which, according to Amnesty International, led to the total destruction of more than 400 Mayan communities. In sanctioning this campaign, the "born again" general time and again noted Guatemala's central role in divine providence. "We are the chosen people of the New Testament," Ríos Montt said. "We are the new Israelites of Central America" (Annis 1987:4).

8. In a sensitive and theoretically elegant alternative interpretation, Kay Warren writes that ethnicity and world view in the Lake Atitlán town of San Andrés Semetebaj centers around "a concern with ethics, specifically with the relation of the individual to community in a world of injustice" (1989:27). Key to her argument is that such injustice deals expressly with Mayan and Ladino social relations and that the local Mayan world view and culture must ultimately be understood within the larger context of the dominant Ladino society. Accordingly, it is definitively post-Columbian in essence.

9. In making this claim, I am certainly not suggesting that in thwarting the advances of the world system the Mayas relied solely on cognitive aspects of their culture. Carol Smith (1984), for instance, demonstrates that the highland Mayas' control of the regional market system in Guatemala has exerted such a function as well.

10. The religious interpretation of nonreligious problems is exemplified in a movie shown in one of Atitlán's Assemblies of God missions. That movie was about the religious conversion of a young fisherboy whose daily catch was only a few scrawny fish. Yet after his conversion, the boy regularly caught numerous huge fish. As explained in Chapter 2, Lake Atitlán fishery was devastated several decades ago after Pan American Airlines, wanting to develop a sport-fishing industry, introduced bass into the lake. The bass quickly vacuumed the lake of its native fish population.

11. Guiteras-Holmes (1961:77–78) describes how ideology and agricultural production influence political authority among the Tzotzil Mayas of Chiapas, Mexico. "Authorities are in charge of the welfare of the community; that is, they are responsible for the preservation of life and the perpetuation of the group through its institutions. By the preservation of life is understood the well-being of body and soul; this implies control over the powers of nature that will insure the regular succession of the days and the seasons, and the fertility of the soil; that will protect man against the evil powers in the world and in his fellow men, and ward off violence and envy, illness and death. Ritual prayers and ceremonies held for this end fall in with the duties of government. To govern is to care for and to protect; therefore, he who governs wrestles with evil and through his sacrifice and efforts draws upon the people the blessings of the ever-reluctant gods. Continuity is stressed: the bodies politic and religious should function uninterruptedly 'as they have since the beginning' so that life may continue to be lived. Those authorities do not act in their own name: each one represents or is the personification of all those who preceded him back to the 'beginning of the world': they personify the gods, they are sacred. Their authority is supported by the belief in their supernatural power."

12. The name "Maximón" requires clarification. First, it should be noted that, except when conversing with inquisitive tourists, Working People seldom, if ever, use the name. Most commonly, they use the name Rilaj Mam (Venerable Grandfather/Grandchild). Second, I contend that the name Maximón is invariably mistranslated in the literature. Following Mendelson's seminal work on the cult

(1956, 1959, 1965), scholars have argued that the name represents a conflation of two of the deity's other names, Mam and Simón (e.g., see Canby 1992; D. Tedlock 1993). It is my argument that the name Maximón is derived from two Tz'utujil words, *ma* (mister) and *xim* (knot), and means "Mr. Knotted," this in reference to his manner of construction.

13. In her marvelous dissertation on the traditional songs of Santiago Atitlán, O'Brien identifies Maximón as "Lord of Dualities" (1975:173). O'Brien correctly notes a relationship to time, particularly the vernal equinox. In fact, this relationship is directly related to Maximón's dimension as Lord of the Middle (R'jawal R'kux Ruchiliew), in this case the middle of the solar year and hence the opposite halves of that time period.

14. Jerónimo subsequently accused one of his neighbors, a rival shaman, of having been behind the murder attempt.

2. The Atiteco Mayas at the End of the Twentieth Century

1. Paul and Paul (1952; 1962; 1963; 1975) discuss San Pedro la Laguna. For anthropological studies of the Tz'utujil-speaking community of San Juan la Laguna, see Sexton (1978; 1981; 1985) and Loucky (1988).

2. During two one-week periods, in March and May 1990, I directed a survey of 150 tourists in Atitlán. In each case, visitors filled out questionnaires while waiting for the boat to leave. The average tourist questioned reported spending $7.73 in Atitlán. In a separate survey, I estimated that an average of 63 tourists visit the town daily. Based on this, it can be roughly estimated that tourism brings in around $175,000 annually. However, given the intense competition amongst Atiteco "penny capitalists," the actual profit margin for goods sold to the tourists is quite low. Incidentally, a common complaint cited in the questionnaires dealt with the aggressive nature of the local penny capitalists.

3. See Gross and Kendall (1983) for analysis of Atiteco domestic organization.

4. Hill and Monaghan (1987) include a current and perhaps the best analysis of highland Mayan social organization. Hunt and Nash's pioneering 1967 article includes a helpful discussion of the topic.

5. As problematic as the construct "traditional" may be, its facility certainly guarantees its survival. I suggest approaching the construct by utilizing Nadel's (1953:266) definition of "traditional" as meaning "in accordance with old inherited models." By identifying those models, what I would choose to call variables, for the considered cultural context, traditionality is given useful operational value.

6. Certainly the single best study of the language is Dayley's 1985 Tz'utujil grammar. Other studies on Tz'utujil language include Andrade 1946; Grimes 1968; Carlin 1970; Kieffer 1974; Butler and Butler 1977; Dayley 1978; Butler and Peck 1980; Ximénez [c. 1710] 1985; Ixmatá 1993.

3. The Flowering of the Dead

A version of this chapter appeared as an article in *Man* (new series volume 26, number 1) in 1991 under the title "The Flowering of the Dead: An Interpretation of Highland Maya Culture." Appreciation is extended to *Man* for allowing the article to appear in the present context.

1. Subsequent to the publication of the original version of this chapter, Karl Taube wrote an article which discusses aspects of *k'ex* as depicted on Classic-period ceramics. In a fascinating flipside to arguments presented by me and Martín Prechtel about *k'ex* in the world of the living, Taube writes that it has an important counter-role in the world of the dead as well. According to Taube (1994:673), "Whereas Carlsen and Prechtel focus upon the concept of the child being the *k'ex* [what in Tz'utujil is called the *k'exel*] of the parent or ancestor, this is in terms of the world of the living. Bringing the newborn into this world also requires a replacement in the world of the dead; in this case, the deceased ancestor destined for the underworld is the *k'ex* for the newborn child."

2. Since at least the Classic period, Mayan cosmology has included a conception of the world as a house, with a tree at its center.

3. In her study of religious symbolism in the Kaqchikel-speaking Mayan community of San Andrés Semetebaj, Warren describes the salience of agricultural metaphor. She states (1989:34) that this metaphor "likens the planting and harvesting of the agricultural cycle to creation and destruction as well as to birth and death."

4. The circa A.D. 1650 Coto dictionary (Kaqchikel) describes a relationship between roots and human ancestors (Coto 1983:559).

5. The *Popol Vuh* is often regarded as the most important native-language New World text. The manuscript from which all existing translations of this text come is a K'iche' version dating from shortly after the Conquest. Tedlock's 1985 translation of this version is used here.

6. In his commentary on the spitting into the hand of Blood Woman, Tedlock (1985:274) mentions that the hand is significant in that it unites the fingers, which are symbolic of the living members of one's family. This belief is certainly related to those of the contemporary Atitecos.

7. Based on glyphic evidence, a Mayan use of the *k'ex* naming tradition can be established for the Classic period. However, in that epoch, its use was not as uniform as in the present. According to Linda Schele (pers. comm. 1990), *k'ex* may have been voluntary. Professor Schele adds that in the epigraphic record, evidence for "skip generation naming" is associated with "successor glyphs," and includes connotations of "sameness and replacingness." Also see Taube (1994).

8. "Grinding Bones under Grandmother's House" was the title of an essay coauthored by Robert Carlsen and Davíd Carrasco and presented at the 1987 American Academy of Religions Western Annual Meeting in Boulder, Colorado. Appreciation is extended to Professor Carrasco for agreeing to the use of this title in its present context.

9. Reina (1966), Warren (1989), and Watanabe (1992) offer alternative and generally fascinating interpretations of Catholic saints in other Mayan communities.

4. CONQUEST AND ADAPTATION IN SANTIAGO ATITLÁN

1. Although the designation "Atiteco" is certainly post-Columbian, for reasons of ethnographic facility, in this volume it sometimes designates the pre-Columbian Tz'utujil speakers that inhabited the region in and around contemporary Santiago Atitlán. Any specific name or names by which those people called themselves is not known, though other Mayan groups sometimes referred to them by their *chinamit*

or *amak* affiliations, e.g., Ajtz'iquinajay. On a generic level, it is likely that they referred to themselves as *winuk*, which can be glossed to mean "the people."

2. I find it interesting that scholars who base their arguments on discontinuity between pre-Columbian and post-Columbian Mayan culture almost invariably offer, at best, superficial analysis of the earlier component. For instance, in his study of the post-Columbian "fiesta system" (a rubric which includes the cofradía system), Marvin Harris merely writes that "talk about aboriginal survivals in this context is clearly out of the question," and halts his analysis of continuity at that (1964: 27). In fact, I can think of no scholars taking this position who are also well versed in ancient Mayan culture. In marked contrast, it is revealing that scholars whose focus includes both the pre-Columbian and the post-Columbian almost invariably find significant continuities.

3. It seems that only regional, linguistic, or micro-variation existed in the pre-Columbian Mayas' use of the terms *chinamit, calpul,* and/or *molab* (P. Carrasco 1971:364; MacLeod 1973:29; Hill and Monaghan 1987). Following the Conquest, the Spanish word *parcialidad* was added to the lexicon. For reasons of ethnographic facility, I use *chinamit* throughout this volume.

4. Regardless of the outcome of this debate, in a masterful recent book, Robert Carmack, a leading proponent of the idea that language groupings corresponded to the ancient political groupings, notes that in the K'iche' area around contemporary Momostenango the "picture that emerges [for the pre-Columbian epoch] is one of a series of cantons and their respective hamlets, similar to those found in rural Momostenango today" (1995:31).

5. Carrasco's essay first appeared in *Estudios de Cultura Maya* (1964 4:323–334).

6. Nearly thirty years ago, Aguirre Beltrán argued similarly for the ancient Aztecs, writing that the Aztec monarchy "only existed in the imagination of the Spanish" (1952:275). According to Aguirre Beltrán, Aztec social organization was based on a confederation of *calpullis* (*chinamits*). But Aguirre Beltrán was not the first to come to this conclusion. In 1879 Bandelier (1975:145) wrote of the Aztecs that "there was no form of society other than that based on kin, and of this, the tribe, characterized by independent territory, a dialect of its own and a common name and worship, formed the highest governmental expression." While both Aguirre Beltrán's and Bandelier's positions are overstated, they should not be entirely dismissed.

7. This is certainly not to say that there are no more Indians in the region. In fact, some of the most traditional Tz'utujil speakers live in that area. During any given week, numerous coastal Tz'utujils come to the cofradías in Santiago Atitlán to do their *costumbres*. Moreover, it is common knowledge in Atitlán that the best Tz'utujil-speaking calendar shamans (*aj'q'ij*) live in the lowlands.

8. The contemporary Atiteco bundle cult was first discussed by E. Michael Mendelson (1958). In Santiago Atitlán, bundles are currently housed in Cofradías San Antonio, San Gregorio, San Juan, San Nicolás, San Martín and Ch'eep San Juan.

9. Though a revisionist attempt to deny pre-Columbian Mayan human sacrifice (Montejo 1991) has surfaced recently, the evidence for such sacrifice is conclusive. By way of example, the *Popol Vuh* describes sacrificial victims whose "hearts were cut out" and acts of autosacrifice in which elbows and ears were bled. Moreover, human sacrifice is given graphic representation on pre-Columbian Mayan ceramics (e.g., Coe 1982:17).

10. This no doubt reflected in part the initial epidemics of European-introduced diseases that had reached the Guatemalan highlands in 1519, several years before the first Spaniards even set foot in the area (e.g., MacLeod 1973:98). As a result, when the invaders finally did arrive, disease, their "shock troops," had already impaired the Mayas' capacity to resist military intrusion (MacLeod 1973:20; also see Lovell 1988).

11. As had been true before contact, throughout most of the Colonial period cacao was used by the highland Mayas as a primary form of currency. While this might at first seem to be indicative of separate Indian and Spanish economies, the fact is that during stretches of Central American history, cacao was also used as currency by the Spanish sector. In fact, at one point in Costa Rica, cacao was declared the official coinage of the province (MacLeod 1973:386). Rather than indicating social plurality between ethnic sectors, the use of cacao as money reflects the economic peripherality of the region as a whole and the difficulty in procuring enough precious metal to serve as coinage.

12. Importantly, both the "New Laws" and the "Laws of the Indies" mandated separate Indian and Spanish societies, buttressing social "pluralism." According to the "Laws of the Indies," for instance, Spaniards were prohibited from residing in Indian towns (García Añoveros 1987:104–105). The demands that Spaniards could place on Indian labor were restricted as well. Although such mandates were often violated, for many rural Guatemalan communities they did provide a buffer between Mayan and Spanish interaction. It is hardly coincidental that these laws were fostered by the clergy, the only non-Indians allowed to reside in the Indian towns.

13. In an interesting revival, the term "New Jerusalem" has been picked up within the largely pre-Millennial circles of contemporary Guatemalan Protestantism. As was the case 500 years ago, it is believed that the New Jerusalem being created in Guatemala prefigures Christ's imminent return. The term itself comes from Revelation 21:2.

14. Madigan (1976:58) writes that the "spiritual conquest" of Atitlán had begun with the arrival of the Franciscan Gonzalo Méndez in 1524, adding that "Méndez appears to have been a capable man who distinguished himself as one of the founders of the Franciscan Order in Guatemala." In fact, the first Franciscans did not come to Guatemala until the early 1540s, and Méndez apparently arrived in Atitlán after other clerics had arrived, including Francisco de la Parra and Pedro de Betanzos.

15. Although Gage does not specify this as being cofradía ritual, his observations certainly refer to those sodalities. Gage writes of the *octave* ritual. This is a fiesta which takes place eight days after the titular fiesta and prefigures the transfer of a cofradía to a new caretaker (*mayordomo* or *alcalde*).

16. The *Larousse Diccionario Usual* (1985) defines *zarabanda* as "a sixteenth and seventeenth century vagabond dance of Spain." The term is still used in some highland Mayan towns (e.g., see Falla 1980:115). I am not sure of the derivation of the term *fune*.

5. On Enlightenment, Liberalism, and Ladinos

1. I am very aware of the scholarly debate about social "pluralism," the purported coexistence of autonomous indigenous and Hispanic social spheres. One

leading voice in this debate, my former professor Waldemar Smith, challenges pluralist interpretations because of their emphasis on "cultural differences and institutional duplication much more than economic competition, conflict, and the political domination of one ethnic group by another" (1975:226). In his essay "Beyond the Plural Society" Smith adds that it is only in largely epiphenomenal noneconomic institutions and cultural beliefs that the highland Mayan area might in any way be autonomous, hence that pluralism is of negligible analytic value. In contrast, I contend the existing data make clear that defining aspects of Mayan society and culture, including integrating beliefs and economic and noneconomic institutions, survived the Conquest and remained vital long after. That is certainly not to say that the surviving indigenous societies somehow remained pristine forms of their earlier selves but rather that they were resilient enough to adapt.

2. This contrasts with other Guatemalan towns. In Sacapulas, for instance, residents attach more value to *cantón* affiliation than town affiliation. Such *cantón* affiliations can be directly linked to pre-Conquest *chinamits* and *amaks*. Accordingly, in Sacapulas individual cofradías are permanently associated with particular *cantones* (Hill and Monaghan 1987).

3. In its contemporary Guatemalan usage, the term *Ladino* is based not on phenotype but on ethnicity. In short, a Guatemalan is Ladino if he or she identifies himself or herself as such. The term, however, has gone through a rather significant evolution. In Spain, at the time of the Conquest, *Ladino* signified a Spanish Jew and was the name of the dialect of Sephardic Jews. Reflecting Spanish anti-Semitism, the term had a connotation of cunning and shiftiness. In Guatemala, *Ladino* quickly came to mean an Indian who could speak Spanish. The cunning and shifty connotations were included. By the beginning of the seventeenth century, however, the term had come to apply not to a subcategory of Indians but to ethnic *mestizos*, where "ethnicity" is defined as a real or imagined self-identification. (See Adams 1964 for a comprehensive, albeit somewhat dated account of Ladinos in Guatemala.)

4. As it goes beyond my purpose to address the Carrera revolution in detail, interested readers are directed to the extensive writings about that event. Included in that corpus of work are Tobar Cruz 1958; Marroquín Rojas 1971; Woodward 1972; Ingersoll 1972; Miceli 1974; and Pinto Soria 1986. Woodward's impressive 1993 volume on the topic is certainly the most comprehensive.

5. Rural Catholic priests argued that the arrival of cholera in 1837 was due to the government's poisoning of the water. The purported reason was a desire to exterminate the Indian population so that their land could be colonized by immigrating Protestant heretics (Stephens [1841] 1969 1:225; Miceli 1974:75).

6. Ebel (1964:94) and Carmack (1981:360) discuss exploitative aspects of the forced implementation in 1945 of open elections in Mayan communities.

6. UNDER THE GUN IN SANTIAGO ATITLÁN

1. About a pioneering venture to Lake Atitlán, Townsend wrote, "[W]e had a regular riot before the evening service, but God kept the angry crowd from doing us injury and we had a great time giving out the old, old story" (in Stoll 1982:34). Townsend's establishment of the Wycliffe organization was perhaps prefigured when, prior to moving back to the United States, he involved himself in the translation into Kaqchikel of the New Testament.

2. After his work in Guatemala, Mendelson went on to pursue anthropological research in Burma. Soon thereafter, he began to publish poetry under the heteronym Nathaniel Tarn. Eventually Tarn's poetic and literary endeavors took precedence over Mendelson's anthropological work. In fact, Tarn went on to become a professor of literature at Rutgers University. In 1979 he returned for a year of research in Atitlán. That stay resulted in several publications (Tarn and Prechtel 1981, 1986, 1990).

3. As is widely known among Atitecos, Maximón's "real" face (mask) is not the one given public display but is hidden, facing backward, under scarves and faces. One of the stolen masks eventually found its way to the Musée de l'Homme in Paris. Through the joint efforts of Nathaniel Tarn and Martín Prechtel, that mask was returned to Atitlán in 1979. The other mask remains lost, although it is rumored to be in a private collection in Guatemala City.

4. According to my primary assistant, the deteriorating state of community existence, when compared to 1966, was reflected in an increased difficulty in persuading Atitecos to cooperate with the survey. Stated simply, given the town's increased factionalism, compounded by the suspicion born of a decade of tremendous violence, and an underlying fear that our project included a covert political agenda, some Atitecos refused to be interviewed. Nonetheless, a strength of employing residents of the blocks as assistants was that we were able to complete the data in most cases by using indirect methods.

5. Douglas' 1966 figures for Atiteco Catholics actually exceed those gathered by the Church in 1967. According to the Church (*Guía de la Iglesia* 1967:343), 7.14 percent of the total population was Catholic, a figure which included 221 (1.56 percent of the total Atiteco population) members of the Catequista group called Catholic Action.

6. A full cofradía includes an *alcalde* (male leader), a *xua'* (*alcalde*'s wife), a *juez* (second ranking male member), plus up to six *cofrades* (male members), and an equal number of *tixeli* (female members). At the time of this writing, the membership of the cofradías in Atitlán is as follows: Concepción has an *alcalde* and a *xua'*. San Felipe has the same, plus one *tixel*, San Francisco has an *alcalde* and a *xua*. San Gregorio has an *alcalde*, a *xua'* and a *cofrade*. San Nicolás has an *alcalde*, a *xua'* and a *juez*. Two of the cofradías, San Antonio and San Juan, are without *alcaldes*, those men having died during the past year. While attempts are being made to find individuals willing to take the cofradías, they are presently under the charge of their respective *xua's*. Because of the dearth of Atitecos willing to assume formal cofradía membership, most cofradías are now forced to rely on "helpers" during fiestas. Further illustrating the crisis nature of this situation is that only the two primary cofradías, Santiago and Santa Cruz, regularly change hands on a yearly basis. There is scant enthusiasm for the personal sponsorship of the lesser cofradías.

7. The Association of Pastors comprises some fifteen pastors from Atitlán's Protestant missions and churches. Notably absent from membership is the pastor of the megachurch ELIM. In fact, while stopping short of satanizing the town's other Protestant churches, the intelligentsia at ELIM consider those churches to be only marginally better than the Catholic Church, or even the cofradías.

8. The *cuerda* is a pre-Conquest Mayan unit of measurement (mentioned in the *Popol Vuh*) that remains widely used throughout the Guatemalan highlands. The term comes from the Mayan word *k'aam*, which means "cord." Like other native

units of measurement, for instance the "stick," the *cuerda* is not a standard unit. While at one time the measurement no doubt depended on how much cord one happened to have balled, in its present usage the *cuerda* most often refers to 24, 28, and 32 yards squared. I have used the 28-yard measurement, the most common among Atitecos.

9. To arrive at this figure, I calculated the daily amount of maize needed for the average Atiteco to be 1.1 pounds, which if anything may be slightly low. Multiplied by the average family size, which my calculations show to be 5.15, this equals 5.67 pounds per day per family, or approximately 2,068 pounds per year. Estimating an average of 200 pounds of maize produced per *cuerda* per year, I arrive at a figure of 10.34 *cuerdas* needed per year, a figure which I have rounded to 10.5.

10. In a 1987 study of the Kaqchikel town San Antonio Aguascalientes, Sheldon Annis addressed certain of these same issues. Annis argued that the adoption of novel petty means of subsistence actually conforms to a traditional indigenous survival strategy, what he calls "milpa logic." He argues that this minimizing economic strategy acts to transfer local labor into the production of small quantities of a large number of products. Annis stresses that by optimizing inputs rather than maximizing outputs and hence working against the accumulation of capital, milpa logic is antithetical to entrepreneurship. It is his contention that historically this system has reinforced the egalitarian nature of the community and has been socially stabilizing. According to Annis, while Catholics (under which he lumps cofradía members) tend to adhere to milpa logic, Protestants tend to break from the traditional pattern. That break is evident in the Protestants' greater tendency toward mercantilism, particularly in their selling of hand-woven textiles.

I have shown elsewhere that a different set of dynamics apply to Santiago Atitlán (Carlsen 1993). Specifically, a survey of Calle Gringo indicates that the representation of both Atiteco Catholic and Working People textile merchants is disproportionately high, while Protestants are underrepresented. Moreover, as I show in the present study, Atiteco mercantilism tends to be a petty enterprise, and in that sense might conform to Annis' description of milpa logic.

11. In 1991, the Protestant church ELIM also opened its own school. Although ELIM religiously avoids any communication with nonmembers, I hope to gather data on its school in the future.

12. It is quite possible that in the not too distant past there may have existed correlations between Atiteco Protestantism and increased economic performance. More specifically, it is reasonable to assume that by severing their ties with traditional modes of belief and behavior, earlier converts to Protestantism might have been exposed to unexploited avenues and niches of potential prosperity. Sexton (1978), for instance, found that to be true in the west Lake Atitlán area. In any case, as those niches were exploited and as the Atiteco Protestant population mushroomed, such opportunities would have been fully overwhelmed by would-be wealth seekers. Sexton (pers. comm. 1988) acknowledges that similar dynamics may have occurred in the west Lake Atitlán area since the time of his earlier observations.

13. My conclusion contrasts with those reached in several earlier studies, as perhaps best exemplified by Ricardo Falla's *Quiché Rebelde*. Based on research in San Antonio Ilotenango, Falla attempted to identify patterns in the abandonment of the *costumbres* (the Old Ways) and in the rise of the Catequista movement. (To

his credit, Falla is one of few researchers who has systematically treated *costumbristas* as being different from Catequistas.) At the basis of Falla's study is the assumption that the *costumbres* functioned to level wealth within a closed and corporate Ilotenango. He argues that in the decades leading up to his research, several factors, particularly a relaxing of forced indigenous labor as well as the Mayas' utilization of chemical fertilizers and hence increased crop yields, have led to the increased capitalization of the local peasantry. Falla argues that with money in hand, various members of the community actively began to engage in mercantilism. He describes a process in which one burro would be purchased for use in hauling goods, the profits of which were reinvested in more burros, and finally in buying buses (1980: 148–150). In turn, competition among bus owners resulted in lower fares so that even more local residents were able to engage in mercantilism outside of the community. In other words, an increase of integration with the outside was part and parcel of a significant rise in the quality of life. A most important claim of the study is that within Ilotenango this process of indigenous capitalism correlated with conversion to Catholicism, and hence that such conversion is a moment in the process of adaptation. An underlying assumption then, one which is in opposition to my arguments for Atitlán, is that the driving force behind the abandonment of the *costumbres* was the opening of avenues for significant wealth accumulation. In assessing Falla's argument, it need be realized that of a total Ilotenango Catholic population of approximately 2,000 (out of a total population of about 6,000), only 38 were merchants.

14. The Atitecos' actions concerning the civil patrols offer an alternative to that of Guatemala's Ixil-speaking Mayas, as described by Stoll (1993). Where the Atitecos conclusively rejected the civil patrols, the Ixils have employed them as an adaptive buffer between themselves and both the warring EGP (Guerrilla Army of the Poor) guerrillas and the Guatemalan Army.

7. When Immortals Die

1. The description of this episode is based on my 1990 personal communication with the driver of the car.

2. In part because there is no direct remuneration for the grueling job, very few shamans agree to serve more than a single one-year term. At the time of his shooting, Jerónimo was only the second *aj'kun* in many years to have done so.

3. Jerónimo's recovery from his bullet wound was hampered by exploratory surgery received in the hospital. Skeptical that a bullet could have passed entirely through his midsection and not have hit vital organs, his doctor decided to operate. When I talked to the doctor afterward, he confessed that the bullet had hit "only meat."

4. The Working People include the various songs to Maximón in the general category *r'xin bix ruchiliew*, which means "songs to the face of the earth." These sacred songs are most commonly played on a five-string guitar, although they may be played on other instruments such as the marimba. Because of the association with the Old Ways, according to pastoral mandate Protestant Atitecos are not allowed to play, or even to listen to, five-string guitars or marimbas. The instrument of choice among Protestants is the electric guitar.

5. See O'Brien (1975) for a fine account of Semana Santa and of the associated ritual music.

6. Jerónimo subsequently accused a rival shaman of having been behind his own attempted murder. In the case of Martín Kik, it was common knowledge that he fell victim to the wrath of a jealous lover. In both cases a most interesting change would eventually affect the interpretation. Following the 2 December 1990 massacre, virtually all modern violence in the community came to be attributed to the Army, including that which targeted the two *telinels*. As such, the legacies of Jerónimo Quieju Pop and Martín Kik are now informed by the marriage of historical revisionism with myth. As has been demonstrated countless times, in Santiago Atitlán, myth can take root very quickly.

7. In April 1995, it was made public that the CIA continued to covertly channel the military aid to the Army, hence undermining State Department intentions.

8. During a meeting that I had in the United States embassy in Guatemala City ten days after the Atitlán massacre, a ranking embassy official confided the particulars of the Guatemalan Army's decision to vacate its Atitlán garrison. In a meeting between U.S. Ambassador Thomas Strook, then Guatemalan President Cerezo, and the head of the Guatemalan Army, Leonel Bolanos, Strook informed the two Guatemalans that anything less than a total Army withdrawal from Atitlán would be unacceptable to the U.S. State Department. After considerable foot-dragging on the part of the Guatemalans, the Army agreed to leave Atitlán. Although a discussion of the actions of the United States lies far outside the scope of the present study, it should be noted these actions varied tremendously from U.S. policy of even a few years earlier. Suffice it to say that the change reflected the evolution of the United States' strategic interests in the region.

9. Interested readers are directed to Ricardo Falla's 1994 treatise on Army massacres in Guatemala's Ixcán region. Testifying to the accuracy of Falla's account, forensic specialists have been successfully using this book to locate mass-burial sites.

10. Not knowing exactly what to do with such captives, the vigilantes eventually opted to turn them over to the Army garrison in San Lucas Tolimán. The following day, the captors were visited by military authorities who promised that if they remained quiet about the whole affair the Army "would do good things" for them. Realizing from past history what "good things" could be expected, the group hired a lawyer to write up an *acta*. In this case, an *acta* is a legal document which describes an incident and then lists prime suspects should stated negative consequences occur because of the original incident. If the suspected party knows that this instrument exists, that offers a level of protection.

11. Although the Guatemalan constitution specifies that military recruitment must either be voluntary or by public draft, it is far more common that eligible-looking young men are seized off the streets or off public buses. As a rule, only Indians and poor Ladinos are taken. During the Army's occupation of Atitlán the families of young men conscripted in this manner would commonly receive bribe offers from the local garrison. For the equivalent of around one hundred dollars, they could have their sons and brothers back.

12. All of the mayor's encounters with the Army have been witnessed by other Atitecos and therefore cannot be dismissed as mere bravado, as mayor Ramírez never traveled alone outside town.

13. Distressed that suspected criminals seized by the *rondos* tended to be released almost immediately by the authorities in Sololá, in 1992 the Atitecos took it upon themselves to incarcerate local criminals. By order of the government, however, that practice had to be halted. Due in part to frustration, Atiteco authorities have at times opted for public humiliation of suspected petty criminals. Certainly the most dramatic display was the hanging of several thieves by their wrists in front of the town hall.

14. See Annis (1991) for an interesting discussion of the role of global electronic integration in peasant movements.

15. The rapid decline of the Old Ways was thrown into high profile in July 1994, when for the first time in memory nobody was found who was willing to assume the year's sponsorship of Cofradía Santiago and the town's patron saint.

8. Season of the Witch: The New Millennium in Santiago Atitlán

1. Globalization is defined as the process leading to an increasingly interdependent world, facilitated largely by electronic integration and by global systems of production and consumption. Globalization stems from the consolidation of the world economic system, but entails diverse corollary features including the Internet, aspects of transnational crime, and the transmission of diseases.

2. In the first edition of this book I erroneously wrote that the altar was "constructed when the church was without a resident priest and under full cofradía control." In fact, the altar was constructed during the tenure of Father Stanley Rother. Prior to its present form, the altar featured a large painting of a mountain. To my eye, that painting appears to have been the work of the famous Atiteco primitivist painter Juan Sisay, and probably dates to the 1940s. I do not know what the altar looked like before.

3. The Easter Week sawdust carpets, "*alfombras*," have long been popular in the Guatemalan city of Antigua. While most Easter week visitors to Santiago Atitlán assume that the town's *alfombras* represent a similarly lengthy tradition, the fact is that Atitecos only began creating them twenty or so years ago. A primary motivation for this new "tradition" is the considerable sum of money that the Guatemalan Tourism Board INGUAT contributes for the creation of the *alfombras*.

4. The Atitecos' creation of MaNawal de JesuKrista represents a fine example of "transculturation," a process in which "subordinated or marginal groups select and invent from materials transmitted to them by a dominant or metropolitan culture" (Pratt 1992:6). Also see Carlsen (2001).

5. Linda Brown (2000) offers a superb overview of the Mayas' utilization of *q'iijb'al* from the ancient past to the present.

6. The first comprehensive study of the Maximón cult was conducted in the early 1950s by E. Michael Mendelson. That research led to his masterful 1956 University of Chicago doctoral dissertation, eventually published in modified form as *Los Escándalos de Maximón* (The Maximón Scandals). In the late 1970s the author returned to Atitlán for a year of research. The results of that work form the basis of his 1998 book *Scandals in the House of Birds*, which was published using the heteronym Nathaniel Tarn—which had long since marked his move from anthropology to poetry—and to whom this volume is dedicated. My debt to Mendelson/Tarn is

evident in the present Maximón material, which I have accordingly included under the subheading "The Holy Cross Scandals."

7. The primary reason for Mayor Esquina's creation of a rival *cabecera* seems to have been his interest in getting a box of colonial-period municipal charter documents, known as the *caja real*, from the Working People.

8. See Francisco Goldman's *The Art of Political Murder*, about the murder of Catholic bishop Juan Gerardi, for a sobering account of the state of the Guatemalan "justice system." Goldman demonstrates that, while sometimes that system is simply inept, at other times, behind what appears to be ineptness is calculated manipulation by shadowy figures capable of monstrous violence. That violence was given full display in Bishop Gerardi's murder by cinder block. I must assume that the similarity to Alux Nawal's death is coincidental. The corrupt nature of the system is evident in the case of Tomás Susof, who, along with six other social cleansers, was caught redhanded extorting money from motorists but was quickly released for "lack of evidence."

9. From 1980 to 1990, the number of Salvadorans reportedly living in the United States increased from 94,447 to 465,433. By 2000, an estimated 600,000 to 900,000 were living in the United States (U.S. Bureau of the Census and U.S. Department of Commerce 2001:12).

10. The name Mara Salvatrucha comes from the word *mara*, which is a type of stinging ant found in El Salvador; the word *salva*, which in Salvatrucha refers to El Salvador; and the word *trucha*, the Spanish word for trout (but also slang for shrewdness).

11. Underscoring the global nature of *maras* are their linkages to Mexican and Colombian drug cartels. Bruce Bagley writes that these linkages "have allowed the Central American gangs to upgrade their arsenals and build more sophisticated criminal organizations than ever before" (2001). He adds that "violent local Central American gangs with international connections, financed by drug money, and equipped with Russian AK-47 assault weapons and rocket-propelled grenades, are currently challenging—and sometimes overwhelming—civilian law-enforcement agencies throughout the Isthmus."

12. Aníbal Rivera-Paz, the leader of MS in Honduras, offers a case in point regarding this vicious circle. Rivera-Paz, who goes by the alias El Culiche (The Tapeworm), is infamous for masterminding a bus attack in Honduras in 2005. This "exemplary attack" on a randomly selected bus was designed to demonstrate to authorities the consequences of crossing MS, and resulted in the deaths of twenty-eight people, including six children. The United States has deported Rivera-Paz four times.

13. Social cleansers are now found throughout Guatemala, although there is no central organization. The country's social cleansers originally seem to have come largely from Santiago Atitlán (Prensa Libre 2008).

14. Several years ago ELIM renamed itself MIEL, though a small splinter congregation in Atitlán retains the original name.

Glossary

amak	An originally pre-Columbian unit of social organization, made up of a group of confederated *chinamits*.
Asamaj Achi	Literally, "working people." A title used by *cofradía* members in Santiago Atitlán to define themselves.
Atitecos	The common name for the Mayas of Santiago Atitlán.
bokunab	Derived from the word *bokul* ("so many"), this archaic term refers to a category of fertility deity noted for the capacity to create multiple replacements of an original entity.
calpul	An originally pre-Columbian unit of political organization and social identification largely equivalent to the *chinamit*. From the Nahuatl *calpulli*.
chinamit	An originally pre-Columbian unit of political organization and social identification. In many highland Mayan communities these units continued to be of central importance until long after the Conquest. *Chinamits* were corporate landholding units, in which membership entailed variable rights and responsibilities. Though *chinamits* were not strictly lineage-based, identification with the chinamit leader was an important feature and group membership included the adoption of the leader's surname.
cofrade	A member, male or female, of a *cofradía*.
cofradia	A religious sodality charged with the maintenance of a particular Catholic saint. The institution was brought from Spain in the sixteenth century for the purpose of helping to integrate the native population into the Church, as well as to facilitate the Spaniards' collection of revenues. The Indian population, however, quickly refabricated the *cofradías* into syncretistic, though distinctly native, institutions.
costumbres	Old inherited models for Mayan behavior and knowledge. The "Old Ways."
Creole	A person born in Latin America who is of pure or almost pure Spanish descent.

encomienda	A grant of the right to Indian tribute awarded by the Crown after the Conquest. Though some families managed to hold *encomienda* rights over an area for several generations, those rights were not permanent and did not entail ownership of land.
Ladino	An ethnic mestizo in Guatemala, where ethnicity is defined as group identity based on a real or imagined cultural, social, and/or racial past. While Ladinos tend to be genetically mostly Mayan, they do not recognize themselves as such.
Maximón	Literally, "Mr. Knotted." A central deity in the Atiteco pantheon. Related to multiple aspects, including calendrical, geographical, vegetational, and fertility phenomena. Contains scores of names, including San Simón and Rilaj Mam (Venerable Grandchild).
milpa	A maize field. Typically farmed using swidden agriculture.
nabeysil	Bundle priests in the *cofradía* system of Santiago Atitlán.
ORPA	Organización de Pueblos en Armas. The guerrilla organization which operates in the Lake Atitlán area.
repartimiento	A forced draft of Indian labor; also a forced sale or payment to Indians for unjustly priced commodities.
telinel	A position in the Atiteco cofradia system. The position is typically held for one year at a time and must be filled by a shaman (*aj'kun*). The primary task of a *telinel* is to perform ceremonies to the deity Maximón, particularly during Holy Week.
uayeb	The five days remaining in a Mayan calendrical year composed of eighteen months of twenty days each. Because specific rituals must be properly performed during this time to avert cosmic calamity, these five days are held to be "delicate."

Bibliography

ADAMS, RICHARD N.
1964 *Encuesta sobre la cultura de los ladinos en Guatemala.* 2d ed. Guatemala City: Seminario de Integración Social Guatemalteca.

AGUIRRE BELTRÁN, GONZALO
1952 El gobierno indígena en México y el proceso de aculturación. *América Indígena* 12:271–297.

AIZENMAN, N. C.
2006 Self-Styled Justice in Guatemala: "Social Cleansing" Squads, Though Welcomed by Some, Evoke Horrors of Long Civil War. *Washington Post,* February 24.

AMERICAS WATCH, PHYSICIANS FOR HUMAN RIGHTS
1991 *Guatemala: Getting Away with Murder.* New York: Human Rights Watch.

ANDERSON, ARTHUR J. O.
1960 Sahagun's Nahuatl Texts as Indigenist Documents. *Estudios de Cultura Nahuatl* 2:33.

ANDRADE, M. J.
1946 Materials on the Quiché, Cakchiquel and Tzutujil Languages. Microfilm Collection of Manuscripts on Middle American Cultural Archaeology, no. 11. University of Chicago Library.

ANNIS, SHELDON
1987 *God and Production in a Guatemalan Town.* Austin: University of Texas Press.
1991 Giving Voice to the Poor. *Foreign Policy* 84:93–106.

BAGLEY, BRUCE MICHAEL
2001 Globalization and Transnational Organized Crime: The Russian Mafia in Latin America and the Caribbean. Electronic document. http://www.mamacoca.org/feb2002/art_bagley_globalization_organized_crime_en.html. Accessed December 5, 2008.

BANDELIER, ADOLPH F.
[1879] 1975 *On the Social Organization and Mode of Government of the Ancient Mexicans.* New York: Cooper Square.

BATESON, GREGORY
1972 *Steps to an Ecology of Mind.* New York: Ballantine.

BERRYMAN, PHILLIP
1984 *The Religious Roots of Rebellion: Christians in Central America.* Maryknoll, N.Y.: Orbis Books.

BETANCOR, ALONSO PAEZ, AND FRAY PEDRO DE ARBOLEDA
1964 Relación de Santiago Atitlán, año de 1585. *Anales de la Sociedad de Geografía e Historia de Guatemala* 37:87–106.
1965 Descripción de San Bartolomé, del Partido de Atitlán, año 1585. *Anales de la Sociedad de Geografía e Historia de Guatemala* 38:262–276.

BRINTNALL, DOUGLAS E.
1979 *Revolt against the Dead: The Modernization of a Mayan Community in the Highlands of Guatemala.* New York: Gordon and Breach.

BROWN, LINDA A.
2000 From Discard to Divination: Demarcating the Sacred through the Collection and Curation of Discarded Objects. *Latin American Antiquity* 11:319–333.

BURGESS, PAUL
1926 *Justo Rufino Barrios.* Philadelphia: Dorrance and Company.

BURNETT, VIRGINIA GARRARD
1989 Protestantism in Rural Guatemala, 1872–1954. *Latin American Research Review* 24:127–142.

BUTLER, JAMES H., AND JUDY GARLAND BUTLER
1977 *The Tzutujil Verbs.* Guatemala City: Summer Institute of Linguistics.

BUTLER, J. H., J. G. BUTLER, AND C. PECK
1980 The Uses of Passive, Antipassive, and Absolute Verbs in Tzutujil of San Pedro la Laguna. *Journal of Mayan Linguistics* 2:40–52.

CAMBRANES, JULIO CASTELLANOS
1985 *Coffee and Peasants: The Origins of the Modern Plantation Economy in Guatemala, 1853–1897.* South Woodstock, Vt.: CIRMA.

CANBY, PETER
1992 *The Heart of the Sky: Travels among the Maya.* New York: Harper Collins.

CARLIN, RAMON A.
1970 Tzutujil (Mayan) Clause Nuclei. *Anthropological Linguistics* 12 (4):103–111.

CARLSEN, ROBERT S.
1990 Report from Santiago. *Report on Guatemala* 11:4–5.
1993 Discontinuous Warps: Textile Production and Ethnicity in Contemporary Highland Guatemala. In June Nash, ed., *Crafts in the World Market: The Impact of Global Exchange on Middle American Artisans.* Albany: State University of New York Press.
1994 After the Bloodshed: Reexamining the Peace in Santiago Atitlán. *Report on Guatemala* 15: 6–11.
1997 Ceremony and Ritual in the Maya World. In Jeffrey J. Foxx and Margot Blum Schevill, eds., *The Maya Textile Tradition.* New York: Harry N. Abrams, Inc.
2001 Transculturation. In *Oxford Encyclopedia of Mesoamerican Cultures*, Vol. 3, edited by Davíd Carrasco, 257–260. New York: Oxford University Press.

CARLSEN, ROBERT S., AND JUAN KIK IXBALAM
1992 Death of Community, Rebirth of Hierarchy in Santiago Atitlán. Paper presented at the Latin American Studies Association XVII International Congress. Los Angeles, 24–27 September 1992.

CARLSEN, ROBERT S., AND MARTÍN PRECHTEL
1991 The Flowering of the Dead: An Interpretation of Highland Maya Culture. *Man* (n.s.) 26:23–42.

1994 Walking on Two Legs: Shamanism in Santiago Atitlán, Guatemala. In Gary Seaman and Jane Day, eds., *Ancient Traditions: Culture and Shamanism in Central Asia and the Americas.* Niwot: University Press of Colorado.

CARLSEN, ROBERT S., AND DAVID A. WENGER

1991 The Dyes Used in Guatemalan Textiles: A Diachronic Approach. In Margot Blum Schevill, Janet Catherine Berlo, and Edward C. Dwyer, eds., *Textile Traditions in Mesoamerica and the Andes: An Anthology.* New York: Garland Press.

CARMACK, ROBERT M.

1966 La perpetuación del clan patrilineal en Totonicapán. *Antropología e Historia de Guatemala* 18:43–60.

1979 *Historia social de los Quichés.* Publication no. 38. Guatemala City: Seminario de Integración Social Guatemalteca.

1981 *The Quiché Mayas of Utatlán: The Evolution of a Highland Guatemala Kingdom.* Norman: University of Oklahoma Press.

1983 Spanish-Indian Relations in Highland Guatemala, 1800–1944. In Murdo J. MacLeod and Robert Wasserstrom, eds., *Spaniards and Indians in Southeastern Mesoamerica.* Lincoln: University of Nebraska Press.

1990 State and Community in Nineteenth-Century Guatemala City: The Momostenango Case. In Carol A. Smith, ed., *Guatemalan Indians and the State: 1540 to 1988.* Austin: University of Texas Press.

1995 *Rebels of Highland Guatemala: The Quiché-Mayas of Momostenango.* Norman: University of Oklahoma Press.

CARMACK, ROBERT M., ED.

1988 *Harvest of Violence: The Maya Indians and the Guatemalan Crisis.* Norman: University of Oklahoma Press.

CARMACK, ROBERT M., AND JAMES L. MONDLOCH

1983 *El Título de Totonicapán.* Mexico City: Universidad Nacional Autónoma de México.

CARRASCO, DAVÍD

1982 *Quetzalcoatl and the Irony of Empire: Myths and Prophecies in the Aztec Tradition.* Chicago: University of Chicago Press.

1993 Religions of Mesoamerica. In H. Byron Earhart, ed., *Religious Traditions of the World.* New York: Harper and Row.

CARRASCO, PEDRO

1961 The Civil-Religious Hierarchy in Mesoamerican Communities: Pre-Spanish Background and Colonial Development. *American Anthropologist* 63:483–497.

1971 Social Organization of Ancient Mexico. In Gordon F. Eckholm and Ignacio Bernal, eds., *Handbook of Middle American Indians* 10:349–375. Austin: University of Texas Press.

1982 *Sobre los indios de Guatemala.* Guatemala City: Editorial "Jose de Pineda Ibarra."

1982a Los nombres de persona en la Guatemala antigua. In *Sobre los indios de Guatemala.* Guatemala City: Editorial "Jose de Pineda Ibarra."

1982b El Señorio Tz'utuhil de Atitlán en el siglo XVI. In *Sobre los indios de Guatemala.* Guatemala City: Editorial "Jose de Pineda Ibarra."

1982c Don Juan Cortés, cacique de Santa Cruz del Quiché. In *Sobre los indios de Guatemala.* Guatemala City: Editorial "Jose de Pineda Ibarra."

CEPAL
1982 *Notas sobre la evolución del desarrollo social del istmo centroamericano hasta 1980.* Mexico City: CEPAL.
CHADOURNE, MARC
1954 *Anahuac: Tale of a Mexican Journey.* London: Elek Books.
CHANCE, JOHN K., AND WILLIAM TAYLOR
1985 Cofradías and Cargos: An Historical Perspective on the Mesoamerican Civil-Religious Hierarchy. *American Ethnologist* 12:1–26.
COCKRELL, CATHY
1991 Santiago Atitlán: Popular Pressure Forces the Army Out. *Report on Guatemala* 11(5):4–13.
COE, MICHAEL D.
1982 *Old Gods and Young Heroes: The Pearlman Collection of Maya Ceramics.* Jerusalem: The Israeli Museum.
1984 *The Maya.* New York: Thames and Hudson.
COGGINS, CLEMENCY
1989 Classic Maya Metaphors of Death and Life. *Res* 16:65–84.
COHN, NORMAN
1970 *The Pursuit of the Millennium: Revolutionary Millenarians and Mystical Anarchists of the Middle Ages.* 2nd ed. New York: Oxford University Press.
COHODAS, MARVIN
1976 The Iconography of the Panels of the Sun, Cross and Foliated Cross at Palenque: Part III. In Merle Greene Robertson, ed., *The Art, Iconography and Dynastic History of Palenque, Part III.* Pebble Beach: Robert Louis Stevenson School.
COLBY, BENJAMIN N.
1976 The Anomalous Ixil—Bypassed by the Post Classic? *American Antiquity* 41: 74–80.
COLBY, BENJAMIN N., AND PIERRE L. VAN DEN BERGHE
1969 *Ixil Country: A Plural Society in Highland Guatemala.* Berkeley: University of California Press.
COMAROFF, JEAN, AND JOHN COMAROFF
1991 *Of Revelation and Revolution: Christianity, Colonialism, and Consciousness in South Africa.* Chicago: University of Chicago Press.
CORTÉS Y LARRAZ, PEDRO
[1770] 1958 *Descripción Geográfico-Moral de la Diócesis de Goathemala.* 2 vols. Guatemala City: Biblioteca de la Sociedad de Geografía e Historia de Guatemala.
COTO, FRAY THOMAS DE
[c. 1650] 1983 *Thesavrvs Verborv: Vocabvlario de la Lengua Cakchiquel V[El] Guatemalteca, Nueuamente Hecho y Recopilado con Summo Estudio, Trauajo y Erudicion.* Mexico City: Universidad Autónoma de México.
CRAPANZANO, VINCENT
1980 *Tuhami: Portrait of a Moroccan.* Chicago: University of Chicago Press.
CULTURAL SURVIVAL QUARTERLY (RESEARCH REPORT)
1988 Counterinsurgency and the Development Pole Strategy in Guatemala. *Cultural Survival Quarterly* 12:11–17.
DAYLEY, JON P.
1978 Voice in Tzutujil. *Journal of Mayan Linguistics* 1:20–52.

1985 *Tzutujil Grammar.* University of California Publications in Linguistics, vol. 107. Berkeley: University of California Press.

DEWALT, BILLIE R.
1975 Changes in the Cargo Systems of Mesoamerica. *Anthropological Quarterly* 48: 87–105.

DÍAZ DEL CASTILLO, BERNAL
[1568] 1968 *Verdadera historia de la conquista de la Nueva España.* 2 vols. Edited by Joaquín Ramiro Cabañas. Mexico City: Editorial Porrúa.

DOUGLAS, WILLIAM
1969 Illness and Curing in Santiago Atitlán. Ph.D. dissertation, Stanford University.

EARLE, DUNCAN, AND D. SNOW
1985 The Origin of the 260-day Calendar: The Gestation Hypothesis Reconsidered in Light of Its Use among the Quiché Maya. In Merle Greene Robertson and Virginia Fields, eds., *Fifth Palenque Roundtable, 1983,* vol. 7. San Francisco: Pre-Columbian Art Research Center.

EARLY, JOHN
1970a The Structure and Change of Mortality in a Maya Community. *Milbank Memorial Fund Quarterly* 48:179–201.
1970b Demographic Profile of a Maya Community. *Milbank Memorial Fund Quarterly* 48:167–178.
1975 Population Increase and Family Planning in Guatemala. *Human Organization* 34(3):275–287.
1983 Some Ethnographic Implications of an Ethnohistorical Perspective on the Civil-Religious Hierarchy among the Highland Maya. *Ethnohistory* 30:185–202.

EBEL, R. H.
1964 Political Change in Guatemalan Indian Communities. *Journal of Inter-American Studies* 6:91–104.

EDMONSON, MUNRO
1971 *The Book of Counsel: The Popol Vuh of the Quiché Maya of Guatemala.* Publication no. 35. Middle American Research Institute. New Orleans: Tulane University.

EHLERS, TRACY BACHRACH
1990 *Silent Looms: Women and Production in a Guatemalan Town.* Boulder, Col.: Westview Press.

ELIADE, MIRCEA
1969 *The Quest: History and Meaning in Religion.* Chicago: University of Chicago Press.
1971 *The Myth of the Eternal Return.* Princeton: Princeton University Press.

El Periódico
2007a Donde Maximón también está en la campaña política Maya. May 8.
2007b La paz no llega a Maximón: crece la disputa en Santiago. May 17.

EVANS-PRITCHARD, EDWARD E.
1940 *The Nuer.* Oxford: Clarendon Press.

FALLA, RICARDO
1980 *Quiché Rebelde: Estudio de un movimiento de conversión religiosa, rebelde a las creencias tradicionales, en San Antonio Ilotenango, Quiché (1948–1970).* Guatemala City: Editorial Universitaria de Guatemala.

1994 *Massacres in the Jungle: Ixcán, Guatemala 1975–1982.* Boulder, Col.: Westview Press.

FARRISS, NANCY M.
1984 *Maya Society under Colonial Rule: The Collective Enterprise of Survival.* Princeton: Princeton University Press.

FOSTER, GEORGE M.
1953 Cofradía and Compadrazgo in Spain and Spanish America. *Southwestern Journal of Anthropology* 9:1–28.

FOX, JOHN W.
1987 *Maya Postclassic State Formation.* Cambridge: Cambridge University Press.

FREIDEL, DAVID A.
n.d. Children of First Father's Skull. Paper presented at the 68th Annual Meeting of the American Anthropological Association. Chicago, 19 November 1987.

FREIDEL, DAVID, LINDA SCHELE, AND JOY PARKER
1993 *Maya Cosmos: Three Thousand Years on the Shaman's Path.* New York: William Morrow and Co.

FRIED, JONATHAN L., ET AL.
1983 *Guatemala in Rebellion.* New York: Grove Press.

FRIEDLANDER, JUDITH
1981 The Secularization of the Cargo System: An Example from Post-Revolutionary Central Mexico. *Latin American Research Review* 16:132–143.

FUENTES Y GUZMAN, FRANCISCO ANTONIO DE
[1690] 1932–1933 *Recordación Florida: discurso historial y demostración natural material, militar política del Reyno de Guatemala.* 3 vols. Guatemala City: Sociedad de Geografía e Historia de Guatemala.

GAGE, THOMAS
[1648] 1958 *Thomas Gage's Travels in the New World.* Edited by J. Eric S. Thompson. Norman: University of Oklahoma Press.

GARRARD-BURNETT, VIRGINIA
1998 Protestantism in Guatemala: Living in the New Jerusalem. Austin: University of Texas Press.

GARCÍA AÑOVEROS, JESÚS MARÍA
1987 *Población y estado sociorreligioso de la diócesis de Guatemala en el último tercio del siglo XVIII.* Guatemala City: Editorial Universitaria.

GEERTZ, CLIFFORD
1973 *The Interpretation of Cultures.* New York: Basic Books.

GOLDMAN, FRANCISCO
2007 *The Art of Political Murder: Who Killed the Bishop?* New York: Grove Press.

GOSSEN, GARY H.
1974a A Chamula Solar Calendar Board from Chiapas, Mexico. In Norman Hammond, ed., *Mesoamerican Archaeology: New Approaches.* London: Duckworth.
1974b *Chamulas in the World of the Sun.* Cambridge: Harvard University Press.

GRIMES, JAMES LARRY
1968 *Cakchiquel-Tzutujil: Estudio sobre su unidad lingüística.* Estudios Centroamericanos, no. 4. Guatemala City: Seminario de Integración Social Guatemalteca.

GROSS, JOSEPH, AND CARL KENDALL
1983 The Analysis of Domestic Organization in Mesoamerica: The Case of Postmarital Residence in Santiago Atitlán, Guatemala. In Carl Kendall, John Hawkins, and Laurel Bossen, eds., *Heritage of Conquest: Thirty Years Later*. Albuquerque: University of New Mexico Press.

GUÍA DE LA IGLESIA EN GUATEMALA
1967 Guatemala City: Santa Isabel.

GUITERAS-HOLMES, CALIXTA
1961 *Perils of the Soul: The World View of a Tzotzil Indian*. New York: The Free Press of Glencoe.

HANDY, JIM
1990 The Corporate Community, Campesino Organizations, and Agrarian Reform: 1950–1954. In Carol A. Smith, ed., *Guatemalan Indians and the State: 1540 to 1988*. Austin: University of Texas Press.

HARRIS, MARVIN
1964 *Patterns of Race in the Americas*. New York: W. W. Norton.
1980 *Cultural Materialism: The Struggle for a Science of Culture*. New York: Vintage.

HAWKINS, JOHN
1984 *Inverse Images: The Meaning of Culture, Ethnicity and Family in Postcolonial Guatemala*. Albuquerque: University of New Mexico Press.

HILL, ROBERT M.
1984 Chinamit and Molab: Late Post-Classic Precursors of the Closed Corporate Community. *Estudios de Cultura Maya* 15:301–327.
1989 Social Organization by Decree in Colonial Highland Guatemala. *Ethnohistory* 36:170–198.
1992 *Colonial Cakchiquels: Highland Maya Adaptation to Spanish Rule, 1600–1700*. Fort Worth: Harcourt Brace Jovanovich.

HILL, ROBERT M. II, AND JOHN MONAGHAN
1987 *Continuities in Highland Maya Social Organization: Ethnohistory in Sacapulas, Guatemala*. Philadelphia: University of Pennsylvania Press.

HUNT, EVA, AND JUNE NASH
1967 Local and Territorial Units. In Robert Wauchope, ed., *Handbook of Middle American Indians* 6:253–282. Austin: University of Texas Press.

HUXLEY, ALDOUS
1934 *Beyond the Mexique Bay*. New York: Harper and Brothers.

INGERSOLL, HAZEL
1972 The War of the Mountains: A Study of Reactionary Peasant Insurgency in Guatemala, 1837–1873. Ph.D. dissertation, University of Maryland.

IXMATÁ, PABLO GARCÍA
1993 *Gramática Pedagógica Tz'utujil*. Guatemala City: Universidad Rafael Landívar.

JONAS, SUZANNE
1991 *The Battle for Guatemala: Rebels, Death Squads, and U.S. Power*. Boulder, Col.: Westview Press.

JONES, GRANT D.
1989 *Maya Resistance to Spanish Rule: Time and History on a Colonial Frontier*. Albuquerque: University of New Mexico Press.

KAUFMAN, TERRENCE
1976 Archaeological and Linguistic Correlations in Mayaland and Associated Areas of Mesoamerica. *World Archaeology* 8:101–118.
KIEFFER, MARGARET
1974 *Color and Emotion: Synesthesia in Tzutujil Mayan and Spanish.* Ph.D. dissertation, University of California at Irvine.
KRAUL, CHRIS, WITH ROBERT J. LOPEZ AND RICH CONNELL
2005 L.A. Violence Crosses the Line. *Los Angeles Times,* May 15.
LABASTILLE, ANNE
1990a And Now They Are Gone. *International Wildlife* 20:18–23.
1990b *Mama Poc. An Ecologist's Account of the Extinction of a Species.* New York: W. W. Norton.
LA FARGE, OLIVER
1940 Maya Ethnology: The Sequence of Cultures. In Clarence L. Hay, ed., *The Maya and Their Neighbors.* New York: D. Appleton Century.
1947 *Santa Eulalia: The Religion of a Cuchumatan Indian Town.* Chicago: University of Chicago Press.
LA FARGE, OLIVER, AND DOUGLAS BYERS
1931 *The Year Bearer's People.* Publication no. 3. Middle American Research Institute. New Orleans: Tulane University.
LEÓN-PORTILLA, MIGUEL
1988 *Time and Reality in Mayan Thought.* 2d ed. Norman: University of Oklahoma Press.
LIENZO DE TLAXCALA
1892 *Homenaje a Cristóbal Colón: Antigüedades mexicanas publicadas por la Junta Colombina de México en el cuarto centenario del descubrimiento de América.* Mexico City: Oficina Tipográfica de la Secretaría de Fomento.
LOEB, DAVID, AND DANA STOLZMAN
1992 "Serrano's 'Economic Miracle'?" *Report on Guatemala* 13:10–14.
LÓPEZ AUSTIN, ALFREDO
1980 *Cuerpo humano e ideología: Las concepciones de los antiguos Nahuas.* 2 vols. Mexico City: Universidad Autónoma de México.
LOTHROP, ELEANOR
[1932] 1948 *Throw Me a Bone: What Happens when You Marry an Archaeologist.* New York: Whittlesey House.
LOTHROP, SAMUEL K.
1928 Santiago Atitlán, Guatemala. *Indian Notes* 5:370–395. New York: Museum of the American Indian.
1929 Canoes of Lake Atitlán, Guatemala. *Indian Notes* 6:216–221.
1933 *Atitlán: An Archaeological Study of the Ancient Remains on the Borders of Lake Atitlán, Guatemala.* Publication no. 44. Washington, D.C.: Carnegie Institution of Washington.
LOUCKY, JAMES
1988 Children's Work and Family Survival in Highland Guatemala. Ph.D. dissertation, University of California at Los Angeles.
LOUCKY, JAMES, AND ROBERT S. CARLSEN
1991 Massacre in Santiago Atitlán: Turning Point in the Mayan Struggle? *Cultural Survival Quarterly* 15:65–70.

LOUNSBURY, FLOYD G.

1985 The Identities of the Mythological Figures in the Cross Group Inscriptions of Palenque. In Merle Greene Robertson and Elizabeth P. Benson, eds., *Fourth Palenque Roundtable, 1980,* vol. 6. San Francisco: Pre-Columbian Art Research Institute.

LOVELL, W. GEORGE

1985 *Conquest and Survival in Colonial Guatemala: A Historical Geography of the Cuchumatán Highlands, 1500–1821.* Kingston: McGill-Queen's University Press.

1988 Surviving Conquest: The Maya of Guatemala in Historical Perspective. *Latin American Research Review* 23:25–58.

LUTZ, CHRISTOPHER H.

n.d.a Guatemala: The Demography of the Non-Indian Population 1524–1700. In Jorge Lujan Muñoz, ed., *Historia General de Guatemala II* (forthcoming).

n.d.b Guatemala's Non-Spanish and Non-Indian Population: Its Spread and Demographic Evolution, 1700–1821. In Jorge Lujan Muñoz, ed., *Historia General de Guatemala III* (forthcoming).

LUTZ, CHRISTOPHER H., AND W. GEORGE LOVELL

1990 Core and Periphery in Colonial Guatemala. In Carol A. Smith, ed., *Guatemalan Indians and the State: 1540 to 1988.* Austin: University of Texas Press.

MACLEOD, MURDO J.

1973 *Spanish Central America: A Socioeconomic History, 1520–1720.* Berkeley: University of California Press.

1983 Ethnic Relations and Indian Society in the Province of Guatemala ca. 1620–ca. 1800. In Murdo J. MacLeod and Robert Wasserstrom, eds., *Spaniards and Indians in Southeastern Mesoamerica: Essays on the History of Ethnic Relations.* Lincoln: University of Nebraska Press.

MADIGAN, D.

1976 Santiago Atitlán: A Socioeconomic and Demographic History. Ph.D. Thesis, University of Pittsburgh.

MANZ, BEATRIZ

1988 *Refugees of a Hidden War: The Aftermath of Counterinsurgency in Guatemala.* Albany: State University of New York Press.

MARROQUÍN ROJAS, CLEMENTE

1971 *Francisco Morazán y Rafael Carrera.* Guatemala City: Editorial "Jose de Pineda Ibarra."

MARTÍNEZ PELÁEZ, SEVERO

1971 *La patria del criollo.* Guatemala City: Editorial Universitaria.

MARX, KARL

[1859] 1970 *A Contribution to the Critique of Political-Economy.* New York: International Publishers.

McBRYDE, FELIX W.

1947 *Cultural and Historical Geography of Southwest Guatemala.* Publication no. 4. Smithsonian Institution, Institute of Social Anthropology. Washington, D.C.: Smithsonian Institution.

McCREERY, DAVID

1976 Coffee and Class: The Structure of Development in Liberal Guatemala. *Hispanic American Historical Review* 56:438–460.

1983 Debt Servitude in Rural Guatemala, 1876–1936. *Hispanic American Historical Review* 63:735–759.

1986 An Odious Feudalism: Mandamiento Labor and Commercial Agriculture in Guatemala, 1858–1920. *Latin American Perspectives* 48:99–117.

1990 State Power, Indigenous Communities, and Land in Nineteenth-Century Guatemala, 1820–1920. In Carol A. Smith, ed., *Guatemalan Indians and the State: 1540 to 1988*. Austin: University of Texas Press.

1994 *Rural Guatemala: 1760–1940*. Stanford: Stanford University Press.

McDOUGALL, ELSIE

1955 Easter Ceremonies at Santiago Atitlán in 1930. *Notes on Middle American Archaeology and Ethnology* 123:63–74. Washington, D.C.: Carnegie Institution of Washington.

McDOWELL, PAUL, AND CAROL A. SMITH

1976 Guatemalan Stratification and Peasant Marketing Arrangements: A Different View. *Man* (n.s.) 11:273–278.

MENDELSON, E. MICHAEL

1956 Religion and World-View in Santiago Atitlán. Ph.D. dissertation, University of Chicago.

1957 Religion and World View in a Guatemalan Village. Microfilm Collection of Manuscripts on Middle American Cultural Anthropology, no. 52. Chicago: University of Chicago Library.

1958 A Guatemalan Sacred Bundle. *Man* 58:121–126.

1959 Maximón: An Iconographical Introduction. *Man* 59:57–60.

1962 Dos oraciones indígenas. *Guatemala Indígena* 2:47–71.

1965 *Los escándalos de Maximón*. Publication no. 19. Guatemala City: Seminario de Integración Social Guatemalteca.

MICELI, KEITH

1974 Rafael Carrera: Defender and Promoter of Peasant Interests in Guatemala, 1837–1848. *The Americas* 31:72–95.

MILES, SUZANNE W.

1983 *Los pokomames del siglo XVI*. Publication no. 43. Seminario de Integración Social Guatemalteca. (Translation by Flavio Rojas Lima.) Guatemala City: Editorial "Jose de Pineda Ibarra."

MOLINA, DIEGO

1983 *Las confesiones de Maximón*. Guatemala City: Artemis y Edinter.

MONDLOCH, JAMES L.

1980 K'e?s: Quiché Naming. *Journal of Mayan Linguistics* 2:9–25.

MONTEJO, VICTOR

1991 In the Name of the Pot, the Sun, the Broken Spear, the Rock, the Stick, the Idol, Ad Infinitum and Ad Nauseum: An Exposé of Anglo Anthropologists' Obsessions with and Invention of Mayan Gods. Paper presented at the 90th Annual Meeting of the American Anthropological Association, Chicago.

NADEL, S. F.

1953 Social Control and Self-Regulation. *Social Forces* 31:265–273.

NYROP, RICHARD F., ED.

1983 *Guatemala: A Country Study*. Washington, D.C.: U.S. Government Printing Office.

O'BRIEN, LINDA
1975 Songs of the Face of the Earth: Ancestor Songs of the Tzutuhil Maya of Santiago Atitlán, Guatemala. Ph.D. dissertation, University of California at Los Angeles.

O'NEALE, LILA M.
1945 *Textiles of Highland Guatemala*. Publication 567. Washington, D.C.: Carnegie Institute of Washington.

ORELLANA, SANDRA L.
1973 Ethnohistorical and Archaeological Boundaries of the Tzutujil Maya. *Ethnohistory* 20:125–142.

1975 La introducción del sistema de cofradía en la región del lago Atitlán en los altos de Guatemala. *América Indígena* 35:845–856.

1981 Idols and Idolatry in Highland Guatemala. *Ethnohistory* 28:157–177.

1984 *The Tzutujil Mayas: Continuity and Change, 1250–1630*. Norman: University of Oklahoma Press.

P.C.I. (PROJECT CONCERN INTERNATIONAL)
1987 *Informe final: Encuesta simplificada de salud y nutrición materno infantil*. Santiago Atitlán, Guatemala.

PAUL, BENJAMIN, AND LOIS PAUL
1952 The Life Cycle. In Sol Tax, ed., *Heritage of Conquest*. New York: The Macmillan Co.

1962 Ethnographic Materials on San Pedro Laguna, Solola, Guatemala. Microfilm Collection of Manuscripts on Cultural Anthropology. Chicago: University of Chicago Press.

PAUL, BENJAMIN D., AND WILLIAM J. DEMAREST
1988 The Operation of a Death Squad in San Pedro la Laguna. In Robert M. Carmack, ed., *Harvest of Violence: The Maya Indians and the Guatemalan Crisis*. Norman: University of Oklahoma Press.

PAUL, LOIS, AND BENJAMIN D. PAUL
1963 Changing Marriage Patterns in a Highland Guatemalan Community. *Southwestern Journal of Anthropology* 19:131–148.

1975 The Maya Midwife as Sacred Specialist: A Guatemalan Case. *American Ethnologist* 2:707–726.

PERERA, VICTOR
1993 *Unfinished Conquest: The Guatemalan Tragedy*. Berkeley: University of California Press.

PÉREZ, GLORIA, AND SCOTT ROBINSON
1983 *La misión detrás de la misión*. Mexico City: Claves Latinoamericanas.

PINTO SORIA, J. C.
1986 *Centroamérica, de la colonia al estado nacional (1800–1840)*. Guatemala City: Editorial Universitaria de Guatemala.

PRATT, MARY LOUISE
1992 *Imperial Eyes: Travel Writing and Transculturation*. New York: Routledge.

PRECHTEL, MARTÍN
1990 *Grandmother Sweat Bath*. Santa Fe: Weaselsleeves Press.

PRECHTEL, MARTÍN, AND ROBERT S. CARLSEN
1988 Weaving and Cosmos amongst the Tzutujil Maya. *Res* 15:122–132.

PRENSA LIBRE
2008 Escuadrones de la muerte actúan con libertad en el país. *Prensa Libre*, November 24.
PRICE, BARBARA J.
1982 Cultural Materialism: A Theoretical View. *American Antiquity* 47:709–741.
R.C.B. (*Resource Center Bulletin*)
1987 The Rise of the Religious Right in Central America. *Resource Center Bulletin* No. 10.
1988 Evangelicals Target Latin America. *Resource Center Bulletin* No. 15.
RECINOS, ADRIAN
1950 *Popol Vuh: The Sacred Book of the Ancient Quiché Maya.* Translated by Delia Goetz and Sylvanus G. Morley. Norman: University of Oklahoma Press.
1957 *Crónicas indígenas de Guatemala.* Publication no. 20. Universidad de San Carlos de Guatemala. Guatemala City: Editorial Universitaria.
RECINOS, ADRIAN, AND DELIA GOETZ
1953 *The Annals of the Cakchiquels.* Norman: University of Oklahoma Press.
REINA, RUBEN E.
1966 *The Law of the Saints: A Pokomam Pueblo and Its Community Culture.* Indianapolis and New York: Bobbs-Merrill Co.
RELACIÓN DE LOS CACIQUES Y PRINCIPALES DEL PUEBLO DE ATITLÁN.
[1571] 1952 *Anales de la Sociedad de Geografía e Historia de Guatemala* 26:435–438.
RICARD, ROBERT
1933 *Conquête spirituelle du Mexique.* Paris: Institut d'Ethnologie.
RODRÍGUEZ, MARIO
1972 The Livingston Codes in the Guatemalan Crisis of 1837–1838. In Rodríguez et al., *Applied Enlightenment: 19th Century Liberalism.* Publication no. 19. Middle American Research Institute. New Orleans: Tulane University.
1978 *The Cádiz Experiment in Central America, 1808–1826.* Berkeley: University of California Press.
RODRÍGUEZ, MARIO, RALPH LEE WOODWARD, JR., MIRIAM WILLIFORD, AND WILLIAM J. GRIFFITH
1972 *Applied Enlightenment: 19th Century Liberalism.* Publication no. 19. Middle American Research Institute. New Orleans: Tulane University.
ROJAS LIMA, FLAVIO
1984 *La simbología del lenguaje en la cofradía indígena.* Cuadernos del Seminario de Integración Social Guatemalteca, no. 29. Guatemala City: Seminario de Integración Social Guatemalteca.
1988 *La cofradía: Reducto cultural indígena.* Guatemala City: Seminario de Integración Social Guatemalteca.
ROSALDO, RENATO
1993 *Culture and Truth: The Remaking of Social Analysis.* Boston: Beacon Press.
RUS, JAN, AND ROBERT WASSERSTROM
1980 Civil-Religious Hierarchies in Central Chiapas: A Critical Perspective. *American Ethnologist* 7:466–478.
RUZ LLUILLIER, A.
1973 El Templo de las Inscripciones, Palenque. *Colección Científica no. 7, Arqueología.* Mexico City: Instituto Nacional de Antropología e Historia, Universidad Autónoma de México.

SAHLINS, MARSHALL

1985 *How "Natives" Think: About Captain Cook, For Example.* Chicago: University of Chicago Press.

SCHELE, LINDA

1976 Accession Iconography of Chan-Bahlum in the Group of the Cross at Palenque. In Merle Greene Robertson, ed., *The Art, Iconography and Dynastic History of Palenque, Part III.* Pebble Beach: Robert Louis Stevenson School.

SCHELE, LINDA, AND JEFFREY H. MILLER

1983 *The Mirror, the Rabbit, and the Bundle: "Accession" Expressions from the Classic Maya Inscriptions.* Washington, D.C.: Dumbarton Oaks Research Library and Collection.

SCHELE, LINDA, AND MARY ELLEN MILLER

1986 *The Blood of Kings: Dynasty and Ritual in Maya Art.* Fort Worth: Kimbell Art Museum.

SCHEVILL, MARGOT BLUM

1989 Living Cloth: 19th-Century Highland Mayan Huipiles. *Latin American Art* 1: 71–75.

SCHLESINGER, STEPHEN, AND STEPHEN KINZER

1982 *Bitter Fruit: The Untold Story of the American Coup in Guatemala.* Garden City, N.Y.: Doubleday.

SCOTT, DAVID CLARK

1991a Guatemalan Town Insists It's Still Off Limits to Army. *Christian Science Monitor,* 30 May.

1991b In Guatemalan Town, Life Revives after Army Exodus. *Christian Science Monitor,* 23 May.

SCOTT, JAMES C.

1985 *Weapons of the Weak: Everyday Forms of Peasant Resistance.* New Haven: Yale University Press.

SEXTON, JAMES D.

1978 Protestantism and Modernization in Two Guatemalan Towns. *American Ethnologist* 5:280–302.

1981 *Son of Tecun Uman: A Mayan Indian Tells His Life Story.* Tucson: University of Arizona Press.

1985 *Campesino: The Diary of a Guatemalan Indian.* Tucson: University of Arizona Press.

SEXTON, JAMES D., AND CLYDE M. WOODS

1982 Demography, Development, and Modernization in Fourteen Highland Guatemalan Towns. In Robert M. Carmack, John Early, and Christopher Lutz, eds., *The Historical Demography of Highland Guatemala.* Institute for Mesoamerican Studies, No. 6. Albany: State University of New York.

SHERMAN, WILLIAM

1969 A Conqueror's Wealth: Notes on the Estate of Don Pedro de Alvarado. *The Americas* 6:124–139.

SIMON, JEAN-MARIE

1987 *Guatemala: Eternal Spring, Eternal Tyranny.* New York: W. W. Norton.

SMITH, CAROL A.

1984 Local History in a Global Context: Social and Economic Transitions in Western Guatemala. *Comparative Studies in Society and History* 26:193–228.

SMITH, CAROL A., ED.
1990 *Guatemalan Indians and the State: 1540 to 1988*. Austin: University of Texas Press.
SMITH, M. ESTELLE
1982 The Process of Sociocultural Continuity. *Current Anthropology* 23:127–142.
SMITH, ROBERT
1959 Indigo Production and Trade in Colonial Guatemala. *Hispanic American Historical Review* 39:181–211.
SMITH, WALDEMAR RICHARD
1975 Beyond the Plural Society: Economics and Ethnicity in Middle American Towns. *Ethnology* 14:225–243.
1977 *The Fiesta System and Economic Change*. New York: Columbia University Press.
STANZIONE, VINCENT
2003 *Rituals of Sacrifice: Walking the Face of the Earth on the Sacred Path of the Sun*. Albuquerque: University of New Mexico Press.
STAVENHAGEN, RODOLFO
1968 Seven Fallacies about Latin America. In James Petras and Maurice Zeitlin, eds., *Latin America: Reform or Revolution*. Greenwich, Conn.: Fawcett.
STEPHENS, JOHN L.
[1841] 1969 *Incidents of Travel in Central America, Chiapas and Yucatan*. 2 vols. New York: Dover Publications.
STOLL, DAVID
1982 *Fishers of Men or Founders of Empire: The Wycliff Bible Translators in Latin America*. London: Ziff Press.
1988 Evangelicals, Guerillas, and the Army: The Ixil Triangle under Ríos Montt. In Robert M. Carmack, ed., *Harvest of Violence: The Maya Indians and the Guatemalan Crisis*. Norman: University of Oklahoma Press.
1990 *Is Latin America Turning Protestant: The Politics of Evangelical Growth*. Berkeley: University of California Press.
1993 *Between Two Armies in the Ixil Towns of Guatemala*. New York: Columbia University Press.
n.d. (forthcoming) Jesus Is Lord of Guatemala: The Prospects for Evangelical Reform in a Death Squad State. In Emmanuel Sivan and Gabrielle Almond, eds., *Accounting for Fundamentalism*. Chicago: University of Chicago Press.
TARN, NATHANIEL
1998 *Scandals in the House of Birds: Shamans and Priests on Lake Atitlán*. New York: Marsilio.
TARN, NATHANIEL, AND MARTÍN PRECHTEL
1981 Metaphors of Relative Elevation, Position and Ranking in *Popol Vuh*. *Estudios de Cultura Maya* 13:105–123.
1986 Constant Inconstancy: The Feminine Principle in Atiteco Mythology. In Gary Gossen, ed., *Symbol and Meaning beyond the Closed Community: Essays in Mesoamerican Ideas*. Studies on Culture and Society, vol.1. Albany: Institute for Mesoamerican Studies.
1990 "Comiéndose la fruta": Metáforos sexuales e iniciaciones en Santiago Atitlán. *Mesomérica* 19:73–82.
TAUBE, KARL
1985 The Classic Maya Maize God: A Reappraisal. In Merle Greene Robertson and

Virginia Fields, eds., *Fifth Palenque Roundtable, 1983*, vol. 7. San Francisco: Pre-Columbian Art Research Institute.

1994 The Birth Vase: Natal Imagery in Ancient Maya Myth and Ritual. In Justin Kerr, ed., *The Maya Vase Book: A Corpus of Rollout Photographs of Maya Vases*, vol. 4. New York: Kerr Associates.

TAUSSIG, MICHAEL

1992 *The Nervous System*. New York: Routledge.

TAX, SOL

1937 The Municipios of Midwestern Guatemala. *American Anthropologist* 39:423–444.

1941 World-View and Social Relations in Guatemala. *American Anthropologist* 43:27–42.

1953 *Penny Capitalism: A Guatemalan Indian Economy*. Publication no. 16. Smithsonian Institution, Institute of Social Anthropology. Washington, D.C.: Smithsonian Institution.

1990 Can World Views Mix. *Human Organization* 49:280–286.

TEDLOCK, BARBARA

1982 *Time and the Highland Maya*. Albuquerque: University of New Mexico Press.

TEDLOCK, DENNIS

1985 *Popol Vuh: The Definitive Edition of the Mayan Book of the Dawn of Life and the Glories of Gods and Kings*. New York: Simon and Schuster.

1993 *Breath on the Mirror: Mythic Voices and Visions of the Living Maya*. New York: Harper.

THOMPSON, GINGER, AND DAN ALDER

2004 Tattooed Warriors: The Next Generation—Shuttling Between Nations, Latino Gangs Confound the Law. *New York Times*, September 26.

THOMPSON, J. ERIC.

1970 *Maya History and Religion*. Norman: University of Oklahoma Press.

TOBAR CRUZ, PEDRO

1958 *Los montañeses*. Guatemala City: Ministerio de Educación Pública.

TODOROV, TZVETAN

1982 *The Conquest of America: The Question of the Other*. New York: Harper and Row.

U.S. BUREAU OF THE CENSUS AND U.S. DEPARTMENT OF COMMERCE

2001 Profile of the Foreign-Born Population in the United States.

VAN OSS, ADRIAAN C.

1986 *Catholic Colonialism: A Parish History of Guatemala, 1524–1821*. Cambridge: Cambridge University Press.

VOGT, EVON Z.

1969 *Zinacantan: A Maya Community in the Highlands of Chiapas*. Cambridge: Harvard University Press.

WALLERSTEIN, IMMANUEL

1974 *The Modern World System I: Capitalist Agriculture and the Origins of the European World-Economy in the Sixteenth Century*. San Diego: Academic Press.

WARREN, KAY B.

[1978] 1989 *The Symbolism of Subordination: Indian Identity in a Guatemalan Town*. 2d ed. Austin: University of Texas Press.

WASSERSTROM, ROBERT

1983 *Class and Society in Central Chiapas*. Berkeley: University of California Press.

WATANABE, JOHN M.
1992 *Maya Saints and Souls in a Changing World.* Austin: University of Texas Press.

WILLIAMS, FRANCIS EDGAR
1977 *"The Vailala Madness" and Other Essays.* Edited by Erik Schwimmer. Honolulu: University of Hawaii Press.

WILLIAMS, H.
1960 Volcanic Collapse Basins of Lake Atitlán. *International Geographical Congress* 21:110–116.

WILLIFORD, MIRIAM
1972 Las Luces y la Civilización: The Social Reforms of Mariano Galvez. In Mario Rodríguez, Ralph Lee Woodward, Jr., Miriam Williford, and William J. Griffith, *Applied Enlightenment: 19th Century Liberalism.* Publication no. 19. Middle American Research Institute. New Orleans: Tulane University.

WILSON, RICHARD
1991 Machine Guns and Mountain Spirits. *Critique of Anthropology* 11:33–61.
1995 *Maya Resurgence in Guatemala: Q'eqchí Experiences.* Norman: University of Oklahoma Press.

WINTER, NEVIN O.
1909 *Guatemala and Her People To-Day.* Boston: L.C. Page and Co.

WOLF, ERIC R.
1957 Closed Corporate Peasant Communities in Mesoamerica and Central Java. *Southwestern Journal of Anthropology* 13:1–18.

WOODWARD, RALPH LEE, JR.
1972 Social Revolution in Guatemala: The Carrera Revolt. In Mario Rodríguez, Ralph Lee Woodward, Jr., Miriam Williford, and William J. Griffith, *Applied Enlightenment: 19th Century Liberalism.* Publication no. 19. Middle American Research Institute. New Orleans: Tulane University.
1990 Changes in the Nineteenth Century Guatemalan State and Its Indian Policies. In Carol A. Smith, ed., *Guatemalan Indians and the State: 1540 to 1988.* Austin: University of Texas Press.
1993 *Rafael Carrera and the Emergence of the Republic of Guatemala, 1821–1871.* Athens: University of Georgia Press.

WORTMAN, MILES
1975 Government Revenue and Economic Trends in Central America, 1787–1819. *Hispanic American Historical Review* 55:251–286.

XIMÉNEZ, FRAY FRANCISCO
[c. 1730] 1977 *Historia de la provincia de San Vicente de Chiapa y Guatemala de la orden de Predicadores.* Vols. 1 and 2. Guatemala City: Sociedad de Geografía e Historia de Guatemala.
1985 *Primera parte del tesoro de las lenguas Cakchiquel, Quiché y Zutuhil, en que las dichas lenguas se traducen a la nuestra española.* Special Publication no. 30. Guatemala City: Academia de Geografía e Historia.

YOWELL, SHARON KAY
1986 An Exposition and Analysis of the Scientific Contributions of Gregory Bateson. Ph.D. dissertation, University of Colorado at Boulder.

ZAPATA ARCEYUZ, VIRGILIO
1982 *Historia de la iglesia evangélica en Guatemala.* Guatemala City: Génesis Publicidad.

Index

Adams, Richard N., 195n3
agricultural metaphor, 49, 52–57, 59, 62, 104, 119–120, 192nn3,4
Aguirre Beltrán, Gonzalo, 193n6
aj'kun. See shamanism
Ajtz'iquinajay, 42, 75–76, 79, 84, 90, 91, 192n1; defined, 42. See also amak
alcohol consumption, 93; and cofradías, 82, 95, 97, 153–155, 168; Pre-Columbian, 82
Alvarado, Pedro de, 84, 89
amak, 74–78
Amak Tz'utujil, 75–76, 91
Amnesty International, 144, 188n7
ancestors, 50, 54–56, 57, 61–62, 119–120. See also Jaloj-K'exoj
Andrade, M. J., 191n6
Annals of the Caqchiquels, 76
Annis, Sheldon, 48, 190n7, 197n10, 200n14
Arboleda, Fray Pedro de, 32, 78, 82
Archdiocese of Oklahoma City, 37, 93
architecture, 35, 40–41
Assemblies of God, 16–17, 36, 123, 167, 189n4, 190n10
Association of Protestant Pastors, 129, 196n7
Atiteco Cofradías: Ch'eep San Juan, 97, 193n8; Concepción, 64; decline of, 127–128, 164, 196n6, 200n15; San Antonio, 32, 193n8; San Gregorio, 193n8; San Juan, 7, 32, 64, 80, 98, 193n8; San Martín, 96, 193n8; San Nicolás, 64,

193n8; Santa Cruz, 125, 128, 152–157, 178–180; Santiago, 9, 64, 128, 168. See also cofradías
axis mundi. See World Tree
Aztecs, 79, 84, 193n6; Nahua, 51

Barrios, Justo Rufino, 107, 114–118. See also Liberal Party
Bateson, Gregory, 20, 48, 49
Berryman, Phillip, 21
Betancor, Alonso Paez, 32, 78, 82
birth control, 135–136. See also population: growth
Bitter Fruit, 107
Brintnall, Douglas E., 120
bundles, 52, 80–81, 103, 193n8. See also Old Ways
Burgess, Paul, 117
Butler, James H., 191n6
Butler, Judy Garland, 191n6

cacao, 79, 85; as currency, 194n11; and proselytization, 92
calpul. See chinamit
Cambranes, Julio Castellanos, 71, 101, 102, 112, 114–118
Campesino Unity Committee (CUC), 18, 189n5
Canby, Peter, 191n12
cantones, 39, 126
Carlin, Ramon A., 191n6
Carlsen, Robert S., 7, 18, 31, 32, 43, 56, 113, 144, 146–148, 157, 163, 189n5, 192nn1,8, 197n10